European Convention on Human Rights

Sixty Years and Beyond

European Convention on Human Rights

Sixty Years and Beyond

Editors

B. Krishnamurthy
Geetha Ganapathy-Doré

New Century Publications
New Delhi, India

NEW CENTURY PUBLICATIONS
4800/24, Bharat Ram Road,
Ansari Road, Daryaganj,
New Delhi – 110 002 (India)

Tel.: 011-2324 7798, 4358 7398, 6539 6605
Fax: 011-4101 7798
E-mail: indiatax@vsnl.com • info@newcenturypublications.com
www.newcenturypublications.com

Editorial office:
LG–7, Aakarshan Bhawan,
4754-57/23, Ansari Road, Daryaganj,
New Delhi – 110 002

Tel.: 011-4356 0919

First Published: **2012**

ISBN: **978-81-7708-296-8**

Published by New Century Publications and printed at Salasar Imaging Systems, New Delhi.

Designs: Patch Creative Unit, New Delhi.

PRINTED IN INDIA

About the Book

The Europeans always claim that they have historically and traditionally developed a human rights culture and adherence to liberalism. On the human rights front, they believe that they are leading by their sterling example. Several European jurist scholars have attempted to contest, criticise and challenge fundamental rights and the system perpetuated to promote and protect them with the sole aim of strengthening and reinforcing them.

The present volume examines and evaluates the contribution of the European human rights regime, established 60 years ago under the auspices of Council of Europe. It dwells on lessons which Europe and other countries can learn from this experience—at once rich and rewarding—in protecting and promoting human rights. The contributions from scholars, both Indian and European, cover different aspects of this experience and its outcome.

About the Editors

B. Krishnamurthy is a faculty member in the Department of Politics and International Studies, Pondicherry University, Pondicherry. He is the author of *Indo-French Relations: Problems and Perspectives (2005)* and *Jawaharlal Nehru and the Freedom Movement in French India* (2007). He has co-edited with Geetha Ganapathy-Doré a volume on *Changing World Order: India, EU and the US–A Trialogue* (2009). He is specialising in European Studies and human rights.

Geetha Ganapathy-Doré is a research accredited Associate Professor of English at the Faculty of Law, Political and Social Sciences of the University of Paris 13, Paris. She is the author of *The Post-colonial Indian Novel in English* (2011) and co-author of a textbook *English for EU Law* (2002). She has edited a volume of essays on Anita Desai's *In Custody* (2009) and co-edited 4 other books in English and French dealing with either Post-colonial literature on European and international relations.

Contents

SECTION V: EPILOGUE

Contributors

Pierre-Yves Monjal Professor of Public Law in the University of Paris 13 and at Sciences po., Paris. A specialist in European Union Law, he has published many books and a great number of Articles in relation to this field of study. He is currently Head of the CERAP (Centre for Studies and Research on Administration and Politics). He has formerly been legal adviser to the Ministry of Economy and Budget on questions involving Community law. He is an elected member of the Montrichard Municipal Council and its deputy mayor.

Charles Reiplinger Teaches public law, legal and political theory in Paris (Université Paris Nord). He is an elected member of the faculty council. He is a member of the Institut Michel Villey pour la culture juridique et la philosophie du droit (Université Paris II) and of the Centre de recherches administratives et politiques (Université Paris Nord). He has worked on the influence of British Calvinist theology on modern Constitutional Law during the American colonial period (seventeenth century), and has precisely studied the Fundamental Orders of Connecticut (1639) and the Articles of Confederation of United Colonies of New England (1643), to show the foundations of modern public law have been first drawn and applied by the English in America since 1620's. He also works on contemporary public law, mostly constitutionnal, and takes interest in administrative and private (criminal) law. He believes legal concepts cannot be usefully understood without a philosophical and political point of view.

Dominique Hiebel Teaches public law, history of law and fundamental Rights in Paris (Université Paris 13). She is a member of the Centre d'études et de recherches sur l'action locale–CERAL (Université Paris 13) and a member of the Scientific Committee of the Institute of Roman Law (Université Paris 2). She is an elected member of the faculty council and a Vice-Dean of the Faculty of Law of the University Paris 13. She has a specialization in Roman Law, and has worked on the contio, a Roman republican popular assembly. Her works focus on popular political participation, law making and the characteristics of deliberations.

S.A.M. Pasha — Currently affiliated with the Department of Political Science, Jamia Millia Islamia, New Delhi, India. Prior to this, he had worked at Aligarh Muslim University, Aligarh, North-Eastern Hill University, Shillong, Meghalaya, and University of Jammu, Jammu Tawi. His areas of academic research pertain to Islam-Politics interplay, Human Rights Theory, and India's Foreign Policy. He had already authored a book titled Islam in Pakistan's Foreign Policy. His Articles were published in reputed journals such as, World Affairs, Journal of Institute of Muslim Minority Affairs, International Studies, and others. Besides, he attended and presented papers in International Seminars both in India and abroad. Of late, he also presented two papers in Turkey.

Robert Etien — Dean of the Faculty of Law, Political and Social Sciences of the University of Paris 13 which hosts four thousand students in the disciplines of Law, Economic and Social Administration, and Political Science, three research centres, more than hundred and fifty teachers and twenty-five members of administrative staff. He is Director of the Master's Degree in Business and International Trade with Emerging Nations. He heads the CERAL (Centre for Research on Local Action) research centre. He had previously served as Vice-President of the administrative board of the University of Paris 13 and is currently President of the University Statutes

Commission. Formerly an elected member of the University's administrative board, he now sits in the Faculty Council as an elected member. His award-winning thesis focuses on "The Institutionalization of Opposition in Western Democracies". His research interests revolve around political institutions, local institutions, emerging nations and state intervention. He is particularly interested in new concepts such as sustainable development, participative democracy, new governance, emerging nations, territorial rights, tourismatic. He has numerous publications to his credit. He has frequently lectured in various countries: Belem (Brazil), Pondicherry (India), Fez (Morocco) , Lecce, Trento (Italy), Athens (Grèce), Vermont (USA). He is a recipient of the civil honours : "Chevalier dans l'Ordre de la Légion d'Honneur" and "Chevalier de l'Ordre du Mérite et des Palmes académiques".

Pawan Kumar

Passed his LL.B. and LL.M. from Faculty of law, Maharishi Dayanand University, Rohtak. After qualifying UGC NET in December 2003, his commenced his teaching career from National Institute of Law, Faridabad in July 2004 as Lecture in law and thereafter in January 2005 joined Vivekananda Institute of Professional Studies, New Delhi. In March 2007 his was selected as faculty member in Institute of Law, Kurukshetra University, Kurukshetra and thereafter in July 2007, he joined B.P.S. Women University, Khanpur Kalan, Sonepat, one of the founding faculty members. He has presented more than twenty research papers in national and International conference and published more than a dozen Articles in various journals of national repute. He completed his thesis on the topic "Establishment and Administration of Minority Educational Institutions under the Indian Constitution: A

Socio-Legal Critique".

B. Krishnamurthy Faculty member in the Department of Politics and International Studies, Pondicherry University. He is the author of Indo-French Relations: Problems and Perspectives (2005) and Jawaharlal Nehru and the Freedom Movement in French India (2007).He has co-edited with Geetha Ganapathy-Doré a volume on Changing World Order:India, EU and the US–A Trialogue (2009). He is specialising in European Studies and human rights.

S. Jeeva Research scholar in the Department of Politics and International Studies, Pondicherry University. His field of research is European Development Cooperation Policy.

S. Mohammed Azaad Law Student, presently in his fourth year of study from Dr. Ambedkar Government Law College, Chennai, a renowned legal institution in the nation. He has Participated in the International Moot Court Competition held at Vienna during April 2011. He has got a flair for Public Speaking which has earned him grand titles in many Inter Collegiate Competitions including the coveted Mylapore Academy Trophy. At the National level also he has actively associated himself with selective Moot Court competitions held at Kolkatta, Mumbai, Bangalore and other centres.

P. Marudanayagam Former Professor and Head of the Department of English, Pondicherry University, Puducherry. At present, he is serving as Senior Fellow in the Centre for Classical Tamil, Chennai.

Geetha Ganapathy-Doré Research accredited Associate Professor of English at the Faculty of Law, Social and Political Sciences at the University of Paris 13. She is currently Vice-Dean in charge of Public Relations and an elected Member of the Faculty Council and the Academic Council of the University. She is the author of The Postcolonial Indian Novel in English

(Cambridge Scholars Publishing, 2011) and the co-author of a text book on English for EU law (Ellipses 2002). She has coordinated four research seminars for the European Society for the Study of English conferences in Helsinki, Strasbourg, London and Turin. She has edited a book on Anita Desai (2009) and co-edited four more books. She is also a book reviews editor for Postcolonial Text. She has written a wide range of Articles on postcolonial literature and culture in English and French and translated some Indian short stories from Tamil and English into French.

Himanshu Damle — Graduate student in the Department of Philosophy, Pondicherry University. Doctoral thesis deals with the potential reading of Complexities using French Theory, a way to get over the analytical paradigm of stringency via notional learning modules of neural networks. A physicist by basic training, core interests lie in 'Accelerationism', philosophical theorizing on 'dromos' inherent in capitalism to dislodge the system from within, rather than reliance on the agent/agency without. At present, based in Pune, and working for the media unit of an NGO involved in issues pertinent to People Living With HIV/AIDS.

Amruth G. Kumar — Assistant Professor, School of Education of Pondicherry University. He did his Ph.D in Education from School of Pedagogical Sciences, MG University. He is a Post-Doctoral award winner of University grants Commission (UGC) of India and had several papers in National and international journals.

Introduction

B. Krishnamurthy
and
Geetha Ganapathy-Doré

I

The Europeans, especially the French, consider themselves to be the 'originators' and 'champions' of human rights. The *Magna Carta* of 1215; the Petition of Rights of 1628; the *Habeas Corpus* Act of 1679; the English Bill of Rights of 1689; the Declaration of the Rights of Man and Citizen of 1789 and the Declaration of Rights of Woman (drafted by the French play-writer and pamphleteer Olympe de Gouges and addressed to the Queen Marie-Antoinette) of 1790 are referred to as mile stones in the history of mankind in its quest for claiming and achieving rights. The European imprint is also discernible in the American Declaration of Independence of 1776 and the American Bill of Rights of 1791.

However, instances of the severe violations of human rights committed by the Europeans, either within the continent or elsewhere, were abound in history, which reached the height of infamy during the course of the two World Wars. [1] The European introspection and repentance on whatever had happened during the course of war resulted in the establishment of the United Nations (UN), which aimed at abolition of war once and for ever.

UN Charter

Though the UN Charter is the first document in history to recognise universal human rights and to link it with peace and security (Article 55), the Charter contradicted itself with its reaffirmation of State sovereignty over domestic social issues. delegates of the founding conferences in San Francisco, who were having more concern for the State authority than to the individual human rights and welfare, rejected a proposed Charter provision that would have given the UN the mandate to protect, not simply to promote, human rights. [2]

Moreover, Article 2, Para 7 of the Charter, which provided that "nothing contained in the present Charter shall authorize the UN to intervene in matters which are essentially within the domestic jurisdiction of any state" was being used to question the competence of the UN to entertain allegations of breach of human rights by individual states. Again, it was read as imposing restrictions on the power of the UN from acting on matters of enforcement and protection of human rights. The Communist regimes were entertaining their own reservations on the stand on human rights of the Western democracies and were not ready to cooperate with the latter in erecting a human rights regime under the auspices of the UN. As a result, the UN system failed to create under its auspices a durable and practicable human rights enforcement mechanism at the global level.

Universal Declaration of Human Rights

The Universal Declaration of Human Rights (December 10, 1948), through which the comity of nations dedicated themselves to the cause of protection, promotion and defence of human rights, though remains the central normative document in the international human rights regime, turned out to be merely aspirational, since the UN lacked the unity to agree upon a practical, enforceable treaty. The United States, among others, vetoed the creation of a right to individual petition. [3]

Council of Europe

Meanwhile, the Europeans entertained the idea of organizing at the regional level an institution to put an end to war and to maintain peace. [4] The vision for a Council of Europe (CoE) was laid out by Winston Churchill in a couple of wartime speeches. With such a Council's work, Churchill hoped to see the war end with "the enthronement of human rights." The Congress of Europe convened by the International Committee of Movements for European Unity was held at The Hague from May 8 to 10, 1948. In the "Message to Europeans" adopted at the final plenary session the delegates proclaimed among others:

"We desire a Charter of Human Rights guaranteeing liberty of thought, assembly and expression as well as the right to form a political opposition"; and

"We desire a Court of Justice with adequate sanctions for the implementation of this Charter".

This desire for a Charter of Human Rights and for a Court of Justice with adequate sanctions for its implementation resulted in the establishment of the International Juridical Section of the European Movement under the chairmanship of Pierre-Henri Teitgen, former French Minister of Justice. In his opening speech at the Convention that created the CoE, Teitgen maintained that the "sovereignty of justice" is worth dying for. Further, he proclaimed that the court would become the 'conscience of Europe'.

Statute of the CoE

The Statute of the CoE, a regional intergovernmental organisation, aiming to achieve greater unity among the Member States, was signed at St. James's Palace, London on May 5, 1949, by the Foreign Ministers of ten European States and it came into effect from August 3 of the same year. In the Preamble, the Contracting Parties declared that they are "reaffirming their devotion to the spiritual and moral values which are the common heritage of their peoples and the true source of individual freedom, political liberty and the rule of law principles which form the basis of all genuine democracy". The first Article of the Statute sets out the aim of the organization as 'to achieve a greater unity between its Members'. It was believed that 'the maintenance and further realisation of human rights and fundamental freedoms' would be a mean to achieve this aim.

Article 3 of the Statute maintains: "Every Member of the Council of Europe must accept the principles of the rule of law and of the enjoyment by all persons within its jurisdiction of human rights and fundamental freedoms, and collaborate sincerely and effectively in the realization of the aim of the Council as specified in Chapter 1".Thus, maintenance of human rights and respect for the rule of law are not only included among the objectives of the CoE, they are actually made a condition of membership. Moreover, the violation of this condition is a reason for the suspension or expulsion of a member, in accordance with Article 8 of the Statute, so that the obligation is evidently meant to be taken seriously. Thus, the CoE proved to be the broadest grouping with the political will needed to create a practical regime of supranational law. [5]

European Convention on Human Rights (ECHR)

The European Convention for the Promotion of Human Rights and Fundamental Freedoms (better known as European Convention on Human Rights-ECHR), one of the legal sources of the CoE's human rights system, was signed at the sixth session of the Committee of Ministers in Rome on November 4, 1950 by the Member States of the Council, with the aim to protect and promote some of the rights enumerated in the Universal Declaration of Human Rights. [6]

All the member states of the European Union except France ratified the ECHR before they joined the Union and France did so only in 1974. The Convention had been ratified by all Member States of the CoE by the time Cold War was over. In 1990s, when some Central and East European countries applied for membership, the Council decided to condition all subsequent admissions on the ratification of the Convention. As a result, one of the conditions put forth to the Central and East European States who sought membership to the CoE in the 1990s had been the restoration of democracy and the Polish accession was delayed until full elections had been held. [7] Consequently, all the forty seven Western, Central and East European Member States of the CoE, with a total population of more than 800 million, adhere to the European Convention and the resultant human rights system. [8]

The Convention deals mainly with civil and political rights. Article 1 of the Convention maintains: "The High Contracting Parties shall secure to everyone within their jurisdiction the rights and freedoms defined in Section I of this Convention". The first thing to be noted about this Article is that it contains an immediate obligation on the Contracting Parties to secure the rights and freedoms guaranteed and not merely an undertaking to do so at some future date. The second important principle announced in Article 1 is one of universality in the application of the Convention, which secures the rights and freedoms set out therein 'to every one within the jurisdiction'. [9] Thus, the beneficiary of the rights and freedoms which the Convention guarantees is "every one", within the "jurisdiction" of the States Parties to it, that is, it matters not what a person's nationality may be.

The fact that the benefit of the Convention is not limited to nationals of the Contracting Parties has considerable practical importance. The Commission's statistics show forty-nine applications were filed by nationals of non-member states or stateless and fifty-six in 1971 and 72, respectively. [10] This may very well be taken as an illustration where the states as well as their citizens share the same duties and obligations towards non-citizens as they do towards their own or fellow citizens.

Section 1 of the Convention sets out in Articles 2 to 13, twelve rights and freedoms [11] like right to life, liberty and security of person and due process of law; entitlement to a fair and public hearing within a reasonable time by an independent and impartial tribunal established by law (on the face of any criminal charges against individual); freedom from *ex post facto* laws and punishment (No one shall be held guilty of any criminal offence on account of any act of or omission, which did not constitute a criminal offence under national or international law at the time when it was committed. Nor shall heavier penalty be imposed than the one that was applicable at the time the criminal offence was committed); right to respect for the individual's private and family life, his home and correspondence; right to freedom of thought, conscience and religion; right to freedom of expression; right to freedom of peaceful assembly and association with others; and right to marry (at marriageable age) and to found a family. Right against torture or inhuman or degrading treatment or punishment, slavery or servitude and against performing forced or compulsory labour too were confirmed by the Convention.

Article 13 maintains that an "effective remedy before a national authority" be provided to anyone whose rights have been violated, while Article 14 provides for enjoyment of rights to all without discrimination on any ground such as sex, race, colour, language, religion, political or other opinion, national or social origin, association with a national minority, property, birth or other status...Articles 15 to 18 deal, respectively, with derogation in time of emergency, restrictions on political activity of aliens, prohibition of abuse of rights and limitations on use of restrictions on rights.

The European Convention imposes obligations upon States Parties to respect a variety of provisions. Unlike international treaties of the classical kind, the Convention comprises more than mere reciprocal engagements between the Contracting Parties. It creates over and above a network of mutual and bilateral understandings and objective obligations, which in the words of the Preamble, benefit from a 'collective enfocement'. It is always emphasised that the Convention constitutes a "constitutional instrument of European Public Order."

Enforcement Mechanism

While the UN had failed in creating proper and workable

enforcement mechanism or international control system to protect and promote human rights, the CoE had succeeded in creating such an organisational set up. When it became clear that it would take the UN a long time to reach agreements in the instruments designed to transform the Universal Declaration into binding treaty obligations and to introduce practical enforcement mechanism, the signatories of the European Convention have come forward "to take the first steps for the collective enforcement of certain of the Rights stated in the Universal Declaration" (Preamble). This progressive step was possible, since the governments of European Countries were like-minded and have had a common heritage of political traditions, ideals, freedom and the rule of law.

Article 19 of the Convention provides for the setting up of machinery for the examination of complaints of any violation of human rights and fundamental freedoms on the part of the signatories. It has provided for two institutions to ensure the observance of the engagements undertaken by the High Contracting Parties: the European Commission for Human Rights and the European Court of Human Rights (ECtHR).

European Commission for Human Rights

The Commission consists of a number of members equal to that of the High Contracting Parties to the Convention (Art. 20), elected for a six-year term by the Committee of Ministers and serve in their personal capacities. Initially the Convention did not provide strict requirements on persons to be elected as members of the Commission (Art. 21). By ratifying the Convention a state is deemed to have accepted the jurisdiction of the Commission to receive complaints from other States Parties alleging a violation of the Convention. The Applicant State does not have to demonstrate any special interest in or relationship to the victim of the violation or in its subject matter. However, a number of inter-state complaints were politically motivated while quite a few were routed on humanitarian grounds. As a general rule, states are reluctant to file cases against other states, fearing that it will be interpreted as an unfriendly act and adversely affect their diplomatic relations.

Right of Individual Petition

The right of an individual to file complaint against a state charging it with a violation of the Convention, conditioned on that state's prior recognition of the right of private petition. That recognition is not deemed to be automatic when the state ratifies the Convention; it requires a special declaration (Art. 25.1). It was decided that the Commission's competence to receive individual petitions had to be recognised by a minimum of six signatory countries. Sweden was the first country to accept the right of individual petition on February 4, 1952, followed by Ireland and Denmark in the next year. Iceland, Federal Republic of Germany and Belgium accepted the right of individual petition in 1955, thus making the Commission competent to receive individual applications directed against these six states. The Commission began to exercise its powers in this regard since July 5, 1955. Gradually an overwhelming majority of States Parties have accepted the Commission's jurisdiction to deal with private petitions. As such, the Commission continued to entertain both inter-state complaints and private petitions which may be filed by any person, non-governmental organisation or group of individuals claiming to be the victims of violation of the rights set forth by the Convention committed by the States Parties.

Condition of Admission

Article 26 provides that before international remedies may be invoked, available domestic remedies must be exhausted (in case of violation of rights guaranteed by the Convention). This is actually derived from the principle of subsidiarity, which insists that any thing should be handled at the lowest possible level, where it could be accomplished perfectly. "The

Commission may only deal with the matter after all domestic remedies have been exhausted, according to the generally recognized rules of international law, and within a period of six months from the date on which the final decision was taken." This provision is applicable to both private petition and inter-state application. The rule of exhaustion of domestic remedies dispenses States from answering before an international body for their acts, even before they have had an opportunity to correct matters through their own legal system.

As per Article 27, there are some additional conditions for individual cases. They should not be anonymous; not substantially the same as a matter already examined by the Commission or through another international procedure; not incompatible with the provisions of the European Convention and not manifestly ill-founded.

After asserting the facts (Art. 28), the Commission tries to achieve a friendly settlement between the parties and if no solution could be arrived at, a detailed report is sent to the Committee of Ministers. If the case was not referred to the Court, the Committee of Ministers was expected to decide whether a violation had occurred (Art. 32). As such the Committee used to perform a quasi-judicial function. Generally, it used to prescribe a period for correction of violence and review. The original provisions of the Convention dealing with the Commission had been amended by the third protocol, which came into effect on November 21, 1970, accelerated and simplified the procedure before the Commission.

European Court of Human Rights (ECtHR) [12]

Under Article 56 of the Convention, the Court could come into existence only when eight of the High Contracting Parties had declared acceptance of its compulsory jurisdiction. Ireland led the way in February 1953, followed by Denmark and Netherlands in the next year. By September 1958 required acceptances were obtained and then the Court was constituted in January 1959. The Court composed of a number of judges equal to that of the Members of the CoE (Art. 38). Judges were elected for nine-year term by the Parliamentary Assembly, composed of national parliamentarians from Member States of the CoE, from a list of three nominees submitted by each Member State. They serve in their individual capacities and must be persons of "high moral character", who "possess the qualifications required for appointment to high judicial office or be jurisconsuls of recognised competence." (Art. 38.3) The Convention does not require the judges and Commission members to be nationals of the Member States of the Council. This explains the presence on the Court of a Canadian national, Prof. R. St. J. Macdonald, who was elected on the nomination of Liechtenstein.

The Court functioned through a Chamber of seven judges. The Commission of Human Rights and the Governments of the High Contracting Parties to the Convention alone may bring a case before the Court and then only after the Commission had acknowledged the failure of efforts to reach a friendly settlement. The judgment of the Court is final and legally binding on the States Parties, which are obliged to comply with its findings.

Just Satisfaction

Article 50 of the Convention provides that when the Court finds a State responsible for violation of the Convention, it may "afford just satisfaction to the injured party". However, it lacks the power to reverse domestic judicial decisions or to annul national laws and does not have the power to grant any remedies other than 'just satisfaction", which may consist of monetary damages where no other relief is available. In recovering such damages, an injured party is not limited to compensation for specific monetary damages suffered, but may also receive compensation for non-pecuniary damages. Sometimes the mere finding of a violation of the Convention together with an award to cover actual costs and expenses will be deemed to amount to "just satisfaction". The Court also often requires States to pay compensation to the person or persons whose rights have been violated.

Since the Convention is a formulation adopted within the framework and under the auspices of the CoE, its executive and legislative arms-the Committee of Ministers and the Parliamentary Assembly-play important role in facilitating the application and implementation of the Convention [Arts. 15(3), 21(1), 39(1) and 57]. Articles 32 and 54 confer some supervisory functions relating to the enforcement of the rights it guarantees on the Committee of Ministers, consisting of Foreign Ministers of the Member States, the governing body of the CoE. Until it is deemed in compliance, a state in violation must report on its progress to the Committee of Ministers. [13]

Protocols to the Convention

The catalogue of rights guaranteed by the Convention has been amplified, amended and expanded by means of fourteen additional protocols. While some of them added specific rights to the Convention, others amended the supervisory mechanism. The Protocol 1 added right to property, to education and the undertaking by the States Parties to hold free and secret elections at reasonable intervals. The Protocol 4 to the Convention, which came into force on May 2, 1968, provides for freedom from imprisonment for inability to fulfil a contractual obligation, freedom of movement and residence, freedom from exile and a guarantee against the collective expulsion of exiles.

While Protocol 6 to the European Convention adopted by the CoE in 1983 (which entered into force in 1985) abolished death penalty during peace times, Protocol 13 of 2002 abolished it under all circumstances. Protocol 7 requires States to accord aliens various due process safeguards before they may be expelled from a country where they reside. That instrument also provides for a right to appeal in criminal proceedings, for compensation in cases of miscarriage of justice, for the right not to be subjected to double jeopardy, as well as for equality of rights and responsibility between spouses.

The control system/enforcement mechanism has undergone several structural and procedural reforms over the past sixty years. Protocol 2, which came into force on November 21, 1970, had amended the earlier provisions of the Convention regarding the Court and gave it advisory powers in legal matters concerning the interpretation of the Convention and its protocols to the Committee of Ministers on request. [14] Protocol 8 of 1985 allowed the Commission to streamline its procedures and increase its efficiency by setting up chambers for straightforward cases and committees for applications that could be easily ruled inadmissible or struck from the list. Art. 2 of Protocol 8 amended Article 21 of the Convention and provided that similar requirements were applicable to the judges of the Court and the members of the Commission. While Protocol 9 of 1990 extended to individual applicants the right to request the Court to deal with the case, Protocol 10 of 1992 reduced the majority required for the Committee of Ministers to find a violation in cases not referred to the Court from two-thirds to a simple majority.

Need for Reforms

However, when the procedures of the enforcement mechanism have become better known and it proved to be quite successful, there was a flood of applications before the Commission. While in 1981, the Commission had recorded 400 applications, by early 90s, number of applications increased manifold. In 1997, the number of application rose to 4,750. In fact, the Commission was expected to entertain applications submitted by nationals of forty seven member states, a potential pool of more than 800 million people. On the other hand, the cumbersome nature of the control machinery of the Convention resulted in a heavy workload on the Commission and the Court. As for the Court, having dealt with only twenty six cases between its creation in 1958 and 1976, in 1997 alone it gave some 200 judgments. This factor as well as the expanding membership of the CoE led to reform of the system.

Protocol 11

As amended by Protocol 11, which was concluded on May 11, 1994, and came into force on November 1, 1998, the two-tier system of the Commission and the Court had been replaced by a single-tier and permanent Court. For a transitional period of one year (until October 31, 1999), the Commission continued to deal with the cases that it had previously declared admissible. The aim of this Protocol was to simplify the structure, shorten the length of proceedings and strengthen the judicial character of the system by making it fully compulsory. The Committee of Ministers supervised the execution of judgments but was not dealing with cases not referred to the Court. The jurisdiction of the Court with respect to individual and inter-state cases had become mandatory. Any national of any States Party to the Convention was allowed to petition to the Court, as acceptance of the right of individual petition has become an obligation for the States. Applications by individuals were to be examined by the Court's judges (it was earlier done by Committee of Ministers) and the procedure had become strictly judicial.

The possibility of a friendly settlement of cases as well as the principle of possible re-examination of a case was retained. The judges' term of office was reduced to a maximum of six (instead of nine) years, and an age limit had been introduced and set at seventy years. The terms of office of one half of the judges elected at the first election, expired after three years, so as to ensure that the terms of office of one half of the judges are renewed every three years. Matters brought before the Court were first submitted to a Committee of three judges who can immediately declare them inadmissible without further examination. On admission, the case was submitted to a

Chamber of seven judges who decide on both its admissibility and substance [Arts. 27(1) and 29].

The parties may in exceptional cases ask for a case to be re-examined by a Grand Chamber of seventeen judges, subject to the agreement of a Filtering Committee. The Chamber may also relinquish a case to the Grand Chamber before it had rendered its judgment where it raises a serious question affecting the interpretation of the Convention or its Protocols or where the resolution of a question might have a result inconsistent with a judgment previously delivered by the Court. The Chamber or Grand Chamber's judgments are conveyed to the Committee of Ministers, which is expected to monitor their execution, as was the case in the former system. Thus, Protocol 11 made the Court a single, full-time institution, whilst bringing to a close the remarkable contribution of the European Commission of Human Rights and adapting the role of the Committee of Ministers. It simplified the supervision system and even radically transformed it. The system, being purely judicial, undoubtedly represents an improvement on the previous mechanism. The right of individual petition and the Court's compulsory jurisdiction no longer depend on decisions by States: they have been automatic since the entry into force of Protocol 11 or, for those States that have subsequently ratified the Convention, since the date of their respective ratification.

Victim of its Own Success

Unfortunately, the system has become, to a certain extent, a victim of its own success. While 4,200 petitions were received in 1988, 18,000 were received in 1998; 35,000 in 2002 and more than 39,000 in 2003. Against this, some 844 and 703 cases were decided in 2002 and 2003 respectively. With regard to inter-state complaints, just 18 state complaints have been submitted since 1945. While majority of the complaints have been received from individuals in countries newly parties to the Convention, such as Poland, the Ukraine and Russia, older members were subjected to lesser number of complaints. Because of the ever-raising number of complaints and cases, proceedings took several years before being decided by the Court.

Protocol 14

This situation led to the reform of the supervisory system initiated in May 2004 by Protocol 14, which is designed to allow the Court to process submitted cases more efficiently and help eliminate its massive backlog of cases and consequent delays. Protocol 14 offered new action possibilities to the Committee of Ministers-the possibility to request an interpretation from the Court if the Committee of Ministers considers that the supervision of the execution of a final judgment is hindered by a problem of interpretation of the judgment, and to engage "infringement" proceedings before a Grand Chamber of the Court if the Committee of Ministers considers that a state persists in its refusal to abide by a final judgment in a case to which it is a party. [15]

In extreme situations, non-complying members can be booted from the CoE by a two-thirds vote of the Committee of Ministers. The threat of suspension is Strasbourg's most powerful lever, because membership in the CoE is generally being considered as a prerequisite to membership in the European Union, a 'privileged club' of peace and prosperity. In the 1990s, after the fall of the Berlin Wall, the ex-Communist states rapidly joined this European club that was ready to admit them without much fuss. Even today, for much of the former Communist world, Strasbourg remains the public face of Europe and the CoE, the EU's antechamber, a prelude to EU full-fledged membership.

Overloading of the Court

Pending ratification by Russia which was a must for the coming into force of Protocol 14, the Court continued to reel under the phenomenal increase in the number of cases. While

2007 saw 41,650 new applications in 2008 the figure exceeded 49,850. Whereas the now extinct European Commission of Human Rights had to deal with 45,000 cases to a judicial formation over a period exceeding forty years, the new Court allocated almost 50,000 cases in the year 2008 alone. Throughout its lifetime the Commission declared as inadmissible or struck out some 32,000 applications. The figure for the Court in this regard for 2008 alone went beyond a whopping 30,000. By the time Protocol 11 came into force on November 1, 1998 establishing a full-time Court and thus, opening up direct access for 800 million Europeans, the Court had delivered fewer than 1,000 judgments.

By 2005, the Court had delivered almost 6,000 judgments and less than three years later in September 2008 the Court delivered its 10,000th judgment. During the course of 2008 alone it handed down 1,543 judgments. [16] The Court's caseload continued to increase in 2009. By the end of the year, over 57,000 new applications had been allocated to a judicial formation. Although the Court disposed of over 35,000 applications, the backlog continued to grow, with almost 120,000 applications pending at the end of 2009. [17] Situation has not relented and by the end of 2010 it had reached approximately 140,000 applications, which is an increase of 17 per cent, thus bringing the deficit amounting to more than 1,600 applications per month. [18]

Causes of Overloading

Primary cause of overloading of the Court is the fact that it has to deal with a growing number of repetitive cases, admittedly well-founded, but which should have been disposed of at national level once the relevant principles have become well-established in Strasbourg case-law. Yet another cause of this saturation is that some of the new member States have a high case-count with three of them-Russian Federation [19], Romania and Ukraine and Turkey. For instance, by the end of 2008, 97,300 allocated applications were pending before the

Court. These four laggards accounted for over half (57 per cent) of its docket. [20] This situation continued in 2009 as well and at the end of 2009, 119,300 allocated applications were pending before the Court. These States once again accounted for over half (55.7 per cent) of its docket in more or less same proportion. [21] As in previous years, by the end of 2010, these four States accounted for over half (55.9 percent) and adding Italy (7.3 percent) and Poland (4.6 percent), about two-thirds of the case-load (67.8 percent) was being shared by these six States. Consequently, the highest number of judgments offered in 2010 concerned Turkey (278), Russia (216), Romania (143) and Ukraine (109). Adding Poland (107) and Italy (98), almost two-thirds (63.4 percent) of the judgments delivered during the year were concerned with these six States. [22]

Russian Intransigence

Obviously, Russia was the only country in the forty seven member CoE that had refused to endorse the reform of the Court by ratifying Protocol 14. By way of expediting the reforms in spite of the Russian intransigence, at its 119th Ministerial Session in Madrid on May 12, 2009, the Committee of Ministers opted to go ahead by concluding an agreement, which provided for the immediate application of the single-judge procedure and the new powers of three-judge Committees solely to those countries which have acquiesced to them, either by ratifying Protocol 14 bis (which was adopted in Madrid and came into force on October 1, 2009) or by declaring that they accept their provisional application. As such, Protocol 14 came to be applied provisionally in respect of eighteen countries with tangible results.

In early 2010, the Russians consented to ratify the Protocol after the CoE agreed to address their complaints, including a demand that Russian judges be involved in reviewing complaints against Russia. The Duma gave its approval to Protocol 14 on January 15, 2010, clearing way for its ratification by Russia on February 18, 2010. Consequently, Protocol 14 came into force on June 1, 2010, in all the forty-seven States Parties to the Convention. [23]

Comparable Jurisdiction

In substantial number of States Parties, the Convention enjoys the status of domestic law, and so it may be invoked as law in the national courts. For instance, by the Human Rights Act of 1998, Britain volunteered to incorporate European Convention on Human Rights into domestic law. Likewise, the enactment of the European Convention on Human Rights Act, 2003 by Ireland made rights under the Convention enforceable in Irish courts in certain circumstances. [24] With the coming into force of the United Kingdom's Human Rights Act in 2000 and the Irish ECHR Act in 2004, the law of European human rights is operative in the domestic courts of every member state. That makes domestic courts a driver of enforcement and uniformity in their own right. [25] In other cases, implementing legislation may be required to enforce the rights it guarantees unless existing national law already ensures the protection of comparable rights. Besides, it is to be noted that the accession of the European Union (EU) to the European Convention on Human Rights (ECHR) became a legal obligation under the Treaty of Lisbon. The Council of Europe's Steering Committee for Human Rights and the European Commission are currently elaborating the legal instrument for accession.

Some Scandinavian countries have thus far not accorded the Convention the status of domestic law. Still, even in these countries, national courts frequently look to the Convention when interpreting and applying domestic law in order to avoid its violation. Only when domestic law does not provide relief capable of remedying a violation of the Convention may recourse be had to the international institutions. This commonly leads to States making legislative or other changes of a general character (usually to prevent the repetition of the violation) in response to the Court's judgments on specific cases. Austria and Germany have amended their laws on detention before trial; the United Kingdom has changed prison rules in order to comply with a judgment regarding the right to access to a court; and the Netherlands has introduced amendments to the law of military discipline.

Again, the Court's judgments against particular states may contain statements of general principle concerning interpretation of the Convention, with possible consequences for the legal orders of other states. The Netherlands, for example, has responded to judgments against other states, such as *Marckx v. Belgium* and *Goodwin v. the United Kingdom* [26], by adapting its own domestic law or practice. Unfortunately, this practice is not as widespread as it should be. Philippe Boillat, Director General of Human Rights and Legal Affairs of the Council of Europe, believes that the fact that judgments are only issued in the official languages of CoE –English and/or French, prevents its wider use. [27] This shortcoming needs to be corrected and the judgments are to be issued in other European languages also, so as to ensure their wide circulation and follow up action.

Responsibility of the Member States

As mentioned earlier, though a given judgment only applies to the respondent state, it often has implications for law throughout Europe. The Parliamentary Assembly, which includes delegations from each state's legislature, prods states to bring their laws into conformity with the case law of the Court. [28] However, there are certain shortcomings on the part of the member states in this regard. As noticed earlier, failure on their part in disposing of a large number of repetitive cases at the national level once the relevant principles have become well-established in Strasbourg case-law remains the primary cause of overloading of the Court. The States must bear responsibility to formulate and implement the necessary internal reforms without any delay. Inordinately lengthy proceedings and the failure to enforce domestic judgments cause further concern.

While arguing that the Court needs to be off-loaded of undue pressure of enormous avoidable cases so that it can concentrate on meritorious and significant ones, *Jean-Paul Costa,* President of the European Court of Human Rights, insists on the need to encourage subsidiarity and solidarity between domestic systems and the European mechanism, and points out that it is an indispensable means of reducing the flow of incoming applications, especially not that much meritorious ones. He also maintains that constant increase in the number of domestic remedies, provided effectively and resulted in fair and complete redress, is the need of the hour. Moreover, the President insists that the Convention case-law should be declared binding *erga omnes* and all the member states would have to amend their legislation accordingly. Domestic courts would have to develop their own case law, in the light of a verdict of the ECtHR against another State. Such a positive and constructive step alone can solve the problem of overloading of cases and quicken the process of getting timely justice and redress. [29]

Again, the President of the ECtHR emphasises on the importance of providing information to applicants about the Convention and the case-law of the Court and insists that such information is indispensable for the implementation of the Convention at domestic level. The Court has to improve the HUDOC database and that should be facilitated by voluntary contributions from the member States. Factsheets needs to be launched and to be regularly updated and supplemented by other information sheets. The admissibility criteria of the Court should be popularized among the professionals, such as NGOs and bar associations. Jean-Paul Costa believes that these measures, if taken seriously by the member states shall solve the problem of overloading of cases and ensure speedy trial and timely justice. [30]

Achievement of CoE's Human Rights Regime

The Strasbourg court is a civil court, where individual Europeans sue their own states for violating their human rights. So far, the ECtHR has delivered several landmark judgments, upholding the rights enumerated in the Convention and challenging the authority of the states. It routinely confronts member states over their most culturally sensitive, hot-button issues. Strasbourg has, for instance, stared down France on the issue of Muslim immigration; Ireland on abortion; Greece on Greek Orthodoxy; Turkey on Kurdish separatism; Austria on Nazism; Britain on gay rights and corporal punishment. When the Turkish Court convicted Abdullah Ocalan and sentenced him death penalty, the ECtHR ordered the Turkish Government to defer the punishment till its consideration of the case.

In "Soering case", the Court unanimously held that the extradition of a German national from the UK to the USA (where the applicant feared he would be sentenced to death on a charge of capital murder and be subjected to 'death row' phenomenon), would constitute a breach of Article 3 of the Convention which prohibits torture and inhuman and degrading treatment and punishment. In the Marckx case, the Court emphasised that Belgian legislation discriminating against illegitimate children violated the Convention. In the Brogan case, the Court felt that periods of detention under anti-terrorist legislation in the UK prior to appearance before the Judge or other Judicial Officer of at least four days violated the Convention, which prompted a notice of derogation under Article 15 by the UK Government. [31] On the whole, it is an impressive record of political courage and singular achievement.

All these achievements strengthen the image of the Court and quite naturally it has become for all practical purposes the Constitutional Court for civil and political rights of Europe. It has adopted a more teleological and flexible approach to the interpretation of the Convention and has emphasized that the

Convention is a living instrument to be interpreted in the light of present-day conditions and this approach applies not only to the substantive rights protected under the Convention, but also to those provisions such as Arts. 25 and 46 which govern the operation of the Convention's enforcement machinery.

The Court had an opportunity to interpret most rights guaranteed by the Convention. Large number of cases has raised due process issues, i.e. they have dealt with the interpretation and application of Articles 5 (right to liberty and security of person) and 6 (right to a fair hearing). It has rendered important decisions on questions of freedom of expression (Art. 10); freedom of association (Art. 11) and right to privacy and interference with the right to a family life (Art. 8). Leading jurists have "hailed the Strasbourg court as an embryonic constitutional chamber, or a supreme court in utero". Scholars invariably describe it with superlatives. Among the world's systems of human rights, it has been dubbed "the most advanced and effective"; "pre-eminent"; the "most successful"; "certainly the most fully developed and the best observed"; "no doubt the most developed and successful." [32] It is also dubbed as "a sort of world court of human rights."

The achievements of the ECtHR was a miracle of sort and that, fifty years after its establishment, the application of the Convention and its review by the Court have made an indisputable contribution to improving human rights in Europe, in particular by raising the standards of protection required and gradually harmonising legislation and practices. [33] The establishment of a Court to protect individuals from human rights violations is an innovative feature for an international convention on human rights, as it gives the individual an active role on the international arena (traditionally, only states are considered actors in international law). The European Convention is still the only international human rights agreement providing such a high degree of individual protection.

Commissioner for Human Rights

Besides, the CoE established the position of the Commissioner for Human Rights in October 1999, who is expected to promote the effective observance and full enjoyment of human rights, to identify possible shortcomings in the law and practice of Member States and to assist them with their agreement, in their efforts to remedy such shortcomings. The Commissioner pays special attention to the protection of human rights in times of crisis, undertakes regular visits to Member States to focus *inter alia,* the situation of vulnerable persons. He also organizes seminars on thematic issues such as the rights of the elderly, and the rights of the aliens arriving at the border of Member States and publishes annual report. Further, he maintains close contact with the NGOs and professional groups involved in monitoring situations that lead or may lead to human rights violations.

To sum up, the human rights enforcement system under the CoE has proved to be the most fully developed and observed human rights instrument and the first comprehensive and reasonably successful step in collective enforcement of Universal Declaration. The European Convention is the major contributor to human rights law not only regionally but also at the global level and maintains a standard of achievement in its own right of a unifying Europe. It has brought into being a complicated machinery of judicial adjudication, and elevates European States to rank high in the international "league table". [34] It is a remarkable fact that this single text can thus be applicable in all forty seven States Parties, with their very different legal systems.

Thankfully, contemporary Europe bears no comparison to that of 1940s, and the Convention, a unique and living instrument, has played a key role in achieving this. There is no wonder that the diplomat and scholar Antonio Cassese proclaims, "[N]o other human rights treaty can claim the level of influence of the European Convention." The claim that the Convention remains "the single most important legal and political common denominator of the States of the continent of Europe" by Justice Rolv Ryssdal of Norway, the then President of the Court, in his piece titled "The Coming of Age of the European Convention on Human Rights," published in the inaugural issue of the *European Human Rights Law Review* (1996), proves true till date.

II

The central theme of the present volume is to examine and evaluate the contribution of the European human rights regime, established sixty years ago under the auspices of the CoE, in protecting and promoting human rights in Europe and what lessons Europeans as well as others can learn from this experience, at once rich and rewarding. The contributions from scholars, both Indian and European, cover different aspects of this experience and its outcome.

The Europeans always claim that they have historically and traditionally inherited and developed a human rights culture and adherence to liberalism. In the human rights front, there is a belief that they are leading by their sterling example. Several European jurist scholars attempted to contest, criticise and challenge fundamental rights and the system perpetuated to promote and protect them, with the sole aim of strengthening and reinforcing them.

The present volume comprises five sections. Section I deals with the 'European Convention on Human Rights Reassessed in the Contemporary Context'. It opens with a thought provoking Article by Pierre-Yves Monjal, entitled "Can European Fundamental Rights be Contested?" where he critically reviews the European Convention and particularly the role of the ECtHR, by systematizing the historical, legalist and organizational criticisms. He emphasises that fundamental rights are contestable and they have to be "severely criticized, called into question, hurtled" so as to continue to further reinforce them.

Charles Reiplinger, in his article titled "Towards a

European Law of Representative Democracy", concentrates on the Article 3 of the additional Protocol 1 to the European Convention, which was concluded on March 20, 1952 and provides for free elections at reasonable intervals by secret ballot, under conditions which will "ensure the free expression of the opinion of the people in the choice of the legislature". He maintains that in Europe, legislative powers are being transferred from the national parliaments to local as well as international institutions, specifically to the European Union and terms this phenomenon as 'globalisation of law'. He surmises that Article 3 of the Protocol 1 appears to be a fundamental provision of a European law of political liberties.

One of the most serious casualties of the post-September 11 environment is the erosion of civil and political rights in the region and the human rights standards, which were painstakingly developed since World War II, were being violated with impunity. [35] On the face of criticism that its anti-terrorism laws are incompatible with the letter and spirit of the European Convention, Britain opted for derogation from the obligation of implementing the European Convention on the basis of Article 15 of the ECHR. Dominique Hiebel, in her paper on "Security and Anti-terrorism Laws: What Future for Individual Rights and Liberties in the European Union?" laments that the future for individual rights and liberties in the EU is bleak in such an environment.

In his paper titled "Rights of Multiculturalism, Muslims and Europe", S.A.M. Pasha maintains that contemporary Europe has been grappling with the intricacies involved in the phenomenon of multiculturalism and the presence of minority Muslim communities in the European countries like France, United Kingdom, Germany and Netherlands have been a subject of concern to policy, epistemic and citizen communities. Rise of international terrorism, involving Muslim youth of European citizenship, has posed a new dilemma to these governments and this factor has further vitiated and complicated the issue. Their effort to tackle this problem either in policy terms of integration or assimilation has failed to bear fruit so far. In this context, Pasha argues that the phenomena of multiculturalism has not only posed a policy dilemma to the European governments but also brought to the fore the chinks in the political philosophy of liberalism and maintains that it is going to be a litmus test not only to the political skills of the European statesmen but also to the capabilities and acumen of the intelligentsia.

Section II deals with the dialogue between the National Constitutions of the Member States of the CoE on the one hand and the European Convention on the other. Though the ECHR is not designed to provide a general protection of the environment as such and does not expressly guarantee a right to a clean, green and healthy environment, it indirectly offers certain degree of protection with regard to environmental matters, as the ECtHR has established that public authorities must provide such information to persons when their rights to life (Art. 2) and to respect for private and family life and the home (Art. 8) are threatened. In the particular context of the environment, the Court has also found that there exists a strong public interest in enabling individuals and groups to contribute to the public debate by disseminating information and ideas on matters of general public interest. [36]

Robert Etien, in his paper titled "The Principle of Sustainable Development in France: The Charter of Environment in the French Constitution", draws from this experience, concentrates on the French Constitutional Charter of 2003 dealing with environmental rights and contends that though it is a remarkable text, its application is not yet effective. He also maintains that it is necessary to add new rights pertaining to political regimes, exercise of power and regime of democracy to this compilation of declarations of liberties. He concludes that the French Charter represents a veritable reconstruction which is set in a new and universal perspective that takes into account the impact of emerging nations, such as China and India.

Both the European Convention and the Indian Constitution have drawn from the UDHR. Pawan Kumar in his Article on "European Convention for the Protection of Human Rights vis-à-vis Fundamental Rights under Indian Constitutional Law" compares provisions contained in the Convention with the provisions of the Indian Constitutional law, especially Fundamental Freedoms. He claims that the framers of Indian Constitution took cognizance of the Convention. However, in establishing an enforcement mechanism, the Europeans have taken the lead. On the other hand, the Supreme Court of India has evolved a remedy in the form of Public Interest Litigation to secure fundamental rights to the people, who have no means to get their rights protected otherwise.

Though the EU's adherence to the ECHR was debated upon for a quite long time and the recent entry into force of Lisbon Treaty actually put an end to this dilemma by resolving in favour of such a move, propagation of democracy, respect for human rights, rule of law and good governance remained one of the primary objectives of the European Common Foreign and Security Policy and the Union always linked its development cooperation policy with the human rights record of the recipient country. Accordingly, a good human rights record attracted substantial and uninterrupted economic assistance, while an adverse record invited its reduction, suspension and even abrogation. As such, the EU projected itself as a normative power and Rosa Balfour quite rightly maintains that the Union's source of legitimacy for resorting to lofty principles like protection and promotion of human rights in its external policy and global action stems from ECHR. [37]

In Section III an earnest attempt is made to see the Convention through the prism of international relations. B. Krishnamurthy and S. Jeeva in their paper titled "Human Rights Dimensions of European Foreign and Development Cooperation Policies: A Case Study of India-EU Relations" examine the European human rights policy and its linkage with the European Development Cooperation Policy, taking India-

EU relations as a case study. They argue that this linkage policy fails to achieve its goal in the case of India, whose economy is not solely dependent on the EU. Instead, the member states of the Union, individually as well as collectively, are ready to sacrifice their high-sounding principles for the sake of political and economic considerations.

The traditional Westphalian principles of state sovereignty and non-interference as the normative basis of international law is being displaced by growing popular support for rights-based democracy as a universally valid public philosophy. The movement for making the human rights a reality has played an interesting and important role in this direction. Now, it is argued that human rights do not fall under the category of matters essentially within the domestic jurisdiction of the states. It is also argued that by ratifying the Charter the members have surrendered their reserve domain in this respect and have provided the subject to the category of matters which are essentially of the international concern. International law prohibits intervention. It does, however, leave considerable room for action bordering on interference towards protection and promotion of human rights. The debate on "Sovereignty versus Humanitarian Intervention" forms the subject of study of S. Mohammad Azaad's paper, in which the author emphasises on the need to establish coherent policies and procedures that facilitate rapid responses to man-made catastrophes.

Literature and philosophical writings in any language, belonging to any particular region and time, reflect the ideas and ideals of the writer as well as the political, socio-economic and cultural life of the people concerned. As such, it depicts the concept of human rights and at times, even the humanity's struggle to protect and to get restored its rights. Certain well-known literary figures like Milton are known for championing the cause of human rights in their life and work.

Some literary, philosophical and pedagogical approaches

to the Convention forms the subject of study of Section IV. P. Marudanayagam in his Article "The Jewish Question and the Lessons to Learn" draws from several Jewish authors who have reflected over the predicament faced by their community in their writings. While he accepts that those twentieth century Jewish writers may not be considered by some others as sincere and serious–minded champions of human rights and their works of art may not be objective and dispassionate accounts of what happened to the Jews, before and after Hitler, Marudanayagam still maintains that in any kind of stock-taking undertaken to find out if the European Convention has served the objective of protecting human rights, the "Jewish witness" of this type has to be taken into account.

Another Article that has roots in literature is Geetha Ganapathy-Doré's "Forced Marriages in the European Court of Human Rights and the European Court of Justice". It is based on the observation that marriage in a modern and patriarchal set-up is less of a sacrament than a socio-economic institution. Referring to Article 8 of the European Convention which insists on respect for private and family life and the home and the right to marry (at marriageable age) and to found a family as provided by Article 12, Geetha analyses the legal complications arising out of inter-religious and interracial marriages in Europe and the impact of jurisprudence, in her effort to see what lessons could be learnt for the protection of the individual faced with the collective weight of society and culture, and how women's rights form the foil to human rights in some aspects.

Himanshu Damle's "Human Rights as Glimpsed from the Lens of Post-1968 French Philosophy" focuses on new philosophers and Arendt/Agamben. While the former view human rights as a universal ideal, the latter are critical of it as intervening of the political life into the private sphere. His paper attempts to offer openings and limitations in their discourse on human rights. Damle maintains that "the only universal human right that Badiou and Rancière envision is the right to intervene in the name of infinite universality, and they remain far from any institutionalization of universal human rights. Instead their theories are geared towards a critical evaluation of the underlying presuppositions of doing politics, and providing rights. This critical evaluation is done in preparation of 'truthful' politics, which entails for both Rancière and Badiou a radical break with notions of politics that are defined in terms such as citizenship, freedom of speech or a return to ideal enlightenment values—"Politics aims at a constant possibility", in their view.

Human rights education has been stressed in all human rights documents and viewed as 'an essential contribution to the development of a global human rights culture'. For instance, the policy document, "Leading by Example: A Human Rights Agenda for the European Union for the year 2000" adopted by the *Comité des Sages* and launched at a Conference held in Vienna in October 1998 maintains: "Human Rights education should be given a high priority within the Union as a whole. Building a culture of mutual respect, understanding, and harmony represents a long-term challenge. Since it is a process that may take decades and even generations, the earlier it begins the better."

Amruth G. Kumar, in his paper on "Critical Pedagogy in Human Rights Education" maintains that the major aim of human rights education is to provide pupils and students with the ability to accompany and produce societal changes. He argues that education is to be seen as a way to empower people, improve their quality of life and increase their capacity to participate in the decision-making processes leading to social, cultural and economic policies and concludes that Critical pedagogy, a dialectic un-restful pedagogy, is the pedagogy of human rights since it promotes critical social thinking and a challenge to automatic obedience and submission and as such, critical thinking and social awareness must be part of teachers' preparation to compliment the wonderful initiative of endorsing Human Rights in schools.

The Epilogue attempts to explore the possible lessons to be learnt by both Europeans and South Asians from the experience of the Convention. It elaborates the environment in contemporary Europe, where human rights are continued to be violated in spite of the human rights regime that has been established under the frame work of the Convention. South Asian condition is also analysed, juxtaposing it with the European situation. The fact that South Asia lacks even a regional convention then stares at our face. The Epilogue examines what the Europeans have to do for improving the situation and what initiatives the South Asians have to take to establish a regional system to protect and promote human rights.

Notes

1. Klaus Günther, "The Legacies of Injustice and Fear: A European Approach to Human Rights and their Effects on Political Culture", in Philip Alston et al., *The EU and Human Rights*, New York: Oxford University Press, 1999, p. 124. Günther is forthright in maintaining that Europe's history is a history of suppression, violence, war, and of the annihilation of human beings and groups of human beings.
2. Seyom Brown, *International Relations in a Changing Global System: Toward a Theory of the World Polity*, Boulder: Westview Press, 1992, pp. 101-114.
3. Michael D. Goldhaber, *A People's History of the European Court of Human Rights,* New Brunswick, New Jersey, and London: Rutgers University Press, 2007, pp. 171-172.
4. Such an organization eventually came into existence and has rightly chosen Strasbourg as its head-quarters. A plaque in that city square claims that it is a city which had suffered more than any other city in Europe because of the folly of the men who thought that they could solve their problems through war.
5. Goldhaber, n. 3, pp. 171-172
6. The first ratification of the Convention was that of the United Kingdom, which was deposited on March 8, 1951; further ratifications were received in the course of 1952 from Norway, Sweden and the Federal Republic of Germany and the Convention entered into force on September 3, 1953, when the

necessary ten instruments of ratification had been deposited. By the end of 1974, the Convention had been ratified by all eighteen member states of the then CoE.

7. Ralph Beddard, *Human Rights and Europe*, Cambridge: Grotius Publications Ltd., 1993, III edition, p. 2.
8. Dean Spielmann, "Human Rights Case Law in the Strasbourg and Luxembourg Courts: Conflicts, Inconsistencies, and Complementarities", Philip Alston *et al.,* n. 1, p. 757.
9. Article 14 makes this even more explicit when it states: "The enjoyment of the rights and freedoms set forth in this Convention shall be secured without discrimination on any ground such as sex, race, colour, language, religion, political or other opinion, national or social origin, association with a national minority, property, birth, or other status".
10. The fifty-six of 1972 included six Hungarians, five Israelis, eight Moroccans and three each from Czechoslovakia, Nigeria, Poland and Tunisia.
11. While three more were added by the First Protocol, Fourth Protocol increased the number by four. Thus, nineteen rights and freedoms are the object of the European Convention System of protection.
12. Goldhaber, n. 3, p. 176. The *Palais des Droits de l'Homme*, where the ECtHR is housed, was designed in the early 1990s by the modernist architect Sir Richard Rogers, best known for Paris's Pompidou Centre and London's Millennium Dome. The two cylinders housing the courtrooms are clad in steel and unified by a glass atrium, symbolizing the Court's accessibility to the common man.
13. *Ibid.*, p. 6.
14. However, the Court gave its first advisory opinion only in 2008. On the basis of Article 47 of the Convention, the ECtHR had been asked by the Committee of Ministers of the CoE to give its opinion on certain legal questions concerning the gender balance in the lists of candidates submitted with a view to the election of judges to the ECtHR. The Court found that, in not allowing any exceptions to the rule that the under-represented sex must be represented, the current practice of the Parliamentary Assembly was not compatible with the Convention: where a Contracting Party had taken all the necessary and appropriate steps with a view to ensuring that the list contained a candidate of the under-

represented sex, but without success, and especially where it had followed the Assembly's recommendations advocating an open and transparent procedure involving a call for candidatures, the Assembly could not reject the list in question on the sole ground that no such candidate featured on it.

15. *Supervision of the Execution of Judgments of the European Court of Human Rights–Annual Report, 2010*, Strasbourg: Council of Europe, Directorate General of Human Rights and Legal Affairs, April 2011, p. 13.
16. European Court of Human Rights, *ANNUAL REPORT 2008*, Strasbourg: Registry of the European Court of Human Rights, 2009, p. 11.
17. European Court of Human Rights, *Annual Report 2009*, Registry of the European Court of Human Rights, Strasbourg, 2010, pp. 5-6 (Foreword by *Jean-Paul Costa,* President of the European Court of Human Rights).
18. European Court of Human Rights–Annual Report 2010 (provisional version), Strasbourg: Registry of the European Court of Human Rights, January 2011) Foreword, p. 6
19. The ECtHR has grown increasingly popular with Russians as their last hope for justice and Russian applications account for almost a third of approximately 120,000 cases pending in the Court, which has passed hundreds of rulings against the Russian Government, finding officials guilty of corruption, torture and other misconduct.
20. *Annual Report 2008*, p.11. 28 per cent of the cases are directed against Russia, 11.4 per cent of the cases concern Turkey, 9.1 per cent Romania and 8.5 per cent Ukraine.
21. *Annual Report 2009*, p. 11
22. *Annual Report 2010*, pp. 10-11.
23. *Annual Report 2009*, p. 12.
24. The Human Rights Act of 2003 was signed into law on June 30, 2003 and its provisions came into effect on December 31, 2003. The Act does not incorporate the substance of the Convention into Irish law. The Act gives further effect (subject to constitutional provisions) to the European Convention on Human Rights and Fundamental Freedoms together with its associated protocols. The Act adopted what is known as the 'interpretative model' of incorporation. It seeks to ensure that the courts in interpreting and applying any statutory provision or

rule of law shall, as so far as possible, do so in a manner which is compatible with the obligations of the State under the Convention and its protocols. The Act imposes on all Government and State agencies a requirement to perform functions in a manner compatible with obligations under the Convention.

25. Goldhaber, n. 3, p. 6.
26. App. no. 17488/90, Grand Chamber judgment of March 27, 1996; a case concerning protection of journalistic sources.
27. Philippe Boillat, "The European Convention on Human Rights at 60: Building on the Past, Looking to the Future", http://human-rights-convention.org/Articles-interviews-2/.
28. Goldhaber, n. 3, p. 6.
29. Annual Report 2008, pp. 5-6: Foreword. The Stockholm symposium held in June 2008 under the auspices of the Swedish chairmanship of the Committee of Ministers of the CoE, under the title "Towards Stronger Implementation of the European Convention on Human Rights at National Level", helped to lay down markers for the future in this regard.
30. Annual Report 2010, p. 6: Foreword.
31. Article 15 provides for derogation from the Convention in case of emergencies.
32. Goldhaber, n. 3, pp. 1-2.
33. European Court of Human Rights, *Annual Report 2009*, Strasbourg: Registry of the European Court of Human Rights, 2010, pp.5-6 (Forward by *Jean-Paul Costa)*.
34. Beddard, n. 7, p. 1.
35. Report by the International Helsinki Federation for Human Rights Anti-terrorism Measures, Security and Human Rights, Developments in Europe, Central Asia and North America in the Aftermath of September 11, April 2003, p.11-13. Incidentally, the ECtHR had delivered its first judgments concerning detention without trial under anti-terrorism legislation in 1960/61 in the case of *Lawles v. Ireland,* an issue still relevant today.
36. Virginie Flores, "Is the Environment Protected under the ECHR", http://portal.unesco.org/ci/en/files/26685/12095497593 presentation_virginie_flores.pdf.
37. Rosa Balfour, "Principles of Democracy and Human Rights: A review of the European Union's strategies towards its

neighbours" in Sonia Lucarelli and Ian Manners (eds.), *Values and Principles in European Union Foreign Policy,* London and New York: Routledge, 2006, p. 117.

Section I

European Convention on Human Rights Reassessed in the Contemporary Context

1

Can European Fundamental Rights be Contested?

Pierre-Yves Monjal

There is certainly something provocative, not to say, shocking, in wanting to examine the contestable or questionable nature of fundamental liberties (human rights). This calling into question sounds all the more shocking when it is the Europeans themselves, and the French in particular, who venture into this area for at least two reasons.

- It comes down to reconsidering all the efforts that have been accomplished in the political and legal terrain by the very same Europeans since 1950 (date of adoption of the European Convention on Human Rights) and which have enabled them to build a European constitutional order based on the safeguarding of the fundamental rights of individuals.
- It also comes down to behaving like a spoiled and capricious child, who would want to have everything (Declaration of the Rights of Man, The European Convention on Human Rights (ECHR), the Charter of Fundamental Rights) and who, while it is protected in every aspect, would indulge in refusing to have anything to do with and criticize these rights, whereas many other countries have not yet got down to the stage of formulating these rights.

Nevertheless it might be said that acts of criticising, expressing doubts on the real scope of fundamental liberties and their function in the legal order of the States parties to the Convention, come under the freedom of expression guaranteed by its Article 10 and defined in the case law of the Strasbourg

Court on January 21, 1999, in Fressoz and Roire v France: "it is applicable not only to "information" or "ideas" that are favourably received or regarded as inoffensive or as a matter of indifference, but also to those that offend, shock or disturb. Such are the demands of pluralism, tolerance and broadmindedness without which there is no "democratic society". [1] This right includes the freedom to hold opinions and to receive and impart information and ideas without interference by public authorities and regardless of frontiers.

One could certainly argue that such a degree of freedom of expression should not be used to call into question the texts that grant us such a right. However, coming to such a conclusion, which consists in abstaining from criticizing fundamental liberties on the basis that it is admitted as a valid hypothesis that the freedom of expression should not be used to go against those that accord it to us (the ECHR and its judges), carries an unforeseen risk. Indeed it signifies that fundamental rights, by virtue of their function and their nature, are not contestable, that they fall outside the ambit of critical examination because it is objectively indecent to contest them.

It is clear that these guilt-provoking procedures are used by totalitarian or at least authoritarian regimes to try to consolidate and justify their legitimacy. Strange paradox indeed! All the more curious because criticizing a system that confers rights on you and grants legal guarantees does not in itself seem contestable *à priori*. Let us note that one of the fundamental rules of administrative litigation and of the European Union is that the acts which do not cause grievances are not contestable under proceedings for annulment. No interest to act can, in fact, be admitted.

For all that, the legitimacy of a system as sophisticated as the rights of man, in a democratic perspective could not be consolidated or admitted but at the cost of a confrontation, a debate and an opposing of points of view: to put it simply, a critical review. It is on the premise that I want to go ahead, even if the path to follow looks perilous. Indeed in France objections made to human rights are considered politically incorrect, not to say scandalous, and in addition, defended by the tenants of extremist doctrines of the right wing or the left wing.

Am I then politically incorrect? No!. Just academically and intellectually curious. In order to fully flourish, research and reflection must be able to freely and without any taboo, set down the terms of subjects of their investigation.

Am I then extremist? It would be the case, if I held for inalienable truth what follows and affirmed the same without demonstrating. I am going to precisely construct arguments that I hope will be rigorous and which will call for either support or rebuttal. My intention is not to convince at the ideological level. I aim at exploring paths that have not been treaded hitherto or are not any longer treaded, academically speaking. There is no ambiguity here. My academic or intellectual activity does not get mixed up with my political convictions; does not constitute a technical or smart alibi which would hypocritically dissimulate a form of partisan proselytism.

At the bottom of it, the criticism of fundamental liberties, from what I have been able to read and understand, is not in itself a recent phenomenon. This criticism has been systematic from the time that Rights of Man appeared in 1789: Jeremy Bentham, Gracchus Babeuf, Edmond Burke, Karl Marx, Joseph de Maistre, Auguste Comte, Georg Wilhelm Friedrich Hegel...are some of the critics we know. The reproaches made to the ECHR—the topic of my study—are not formulated by such brilliant minds. The current criticisms are, in fact, made by detractors whose origin and motivations are very different. I shall try and systematize these criticisms. There are three types: Historicist Criticism, Legalist Criticism and Organizational Criticism.

I. Historicist Criticism

This current of thought appeared in the 18th and 19th

centuries and was incarnated by Marx, Christophe de Savigny and Hegel in its organizational dimension and by Nicolas de Condorcet, Benjamain Constant and Comte in its rationalist dimension. Two tendencies could be found in current historicist criticism which try to demonstrate that the system of fundamental liberties is historically regrettable for the European states themselves first (A) and the States that are partners of Europe next (B).

A. European Nationalist Barbarity as Regrettable Source of Fundamental Liberties: This criticism is known and consists in wanting to contextualize the ECHR in order to reveal all its original ambiguity. Indeed, the Convention and the European system of safeguarding human rights were born out of the debris of the Second World War, European nationalisms, Nazism and Fascism. The most barbarous and unspeakable treatment which had been meted out to the Jewish, Gipsy populations and civilians have definitely shown that during these darkest hours of our history, Europeans have perpetrated an irreparable assault on humanity and the dignity of Man.

Some French historians have surprisingly dubbed these as "European civil wars" or "fratricidal wars" as if they were mere family quarrels. Very rare are works of public law, of law and especially constitutional history which have dwelt on the collaborationist period of the Vichy regime. Still rarer are those who tried to study the characteristics of the Pétainist regime. For most of the time, either the period is not dealt with or it is treated as a parenthesis in history: the anti-Republican parenthesis. The greatest historian of this famous "parenthesis" which is a term that borders on revisionism, had long been and quite significantly, an American, Robert Paxton. In contrast to Germany, where the post-war generation feels a sentiment of shame with regard to their history in relation to the Jewish people, France continues to entertain a suspicious silence and is not certainly ashamed of its own national history.

Irrespective of these remarks, the Second World War had

largely demonstrated the triple failure of States: failure in their capacity to contain aggressive nationalist ideologies; failure in their capacity to protect people and property thanks to their parliamentary and judicial institutions; failure in their capacity to organize regional diplomatic relations around pacifist values. It is therefore the failure of the state that is at stake here. For the constitutionalists, the republican and parliamentary system has shown, as far as France is concerned, its total incapacity to defend human rights. The greatest institutions of the Republic—The State Council (*conseil d'état*), the Final Court of Appeal (*la Cour de cassation*), the police, the justice department and the army have not been able or did not want to stop the collaborationist ignominy and Nazi barbarity.

Based on the foregoing, the historicist current of thought explains that the ECHR, which is not criticized as such, carries an inherent vice, a profound ambivalence of origin: it is the telltale sign of the triple failure of the States mentioned earlier, the current stigma of the States' powerlessness in a chaotic background. The birth certificate of the Convention bears the stamp of Nazism, Fascism, totalitarianisms, anti-Semitism, nationalism and republican powerlessness. Worse still, it is the redemptory act of an irreparable barbarity. This very Catholic idea of redemption has produced a consequence about which it is possible to reason further.

In fact, this redemptory system which the Human Rights have become has lead to a state of affairs where governments have definitely renounced the idea of re-appropriating fundamental rights. It is the European Court of Human Rights (EctHR), which, as ultimate arbiter, dictates the values of the Convention to the member states. This relinquishment, which is undoubtedly justified by the wish of the states to redeem themselves by depriving themselves (through a kind of self-punishment) forever of the national control of fundamental rights, gives the judges of the Court more power. The latter is thus an offspring of the historic errors of Europeans and their redemptory yearnings to subject themselves to a mechanism that dominates them.

Such are the first sources of criticism addressed by the historicists to human rights. Human rights are to be deplored and regretted, not because they are without any basis, unjustified or useless in themselves, but because they are the consequences of irreparable errors committed in the course of European history. In conclusion, they say: "Human Rights, Alas!"

B. Fundamental Liberties as Foreseeable Source of "the Hatred of the West": The title for this second part has partly been borrowed from the Swiss sociologist Jean Ziegler, member of the United Nations High Commission for Human Rights and former rapporteur of the United Nations on Food. In 2008, he published a work called *The Hatred of the West*. I am not going to discuss in detail the contents of the book, which though not free from errors, constitutes a scathing indictment of the West.

After reviewing a part of European colonial history, French and English in particular, the author questions the mysterious state in which a portion of the people (Europeans and North Americans) who hardly make up 15 per cent of the world population detain 80 per cent of the riches of the world in addition to having dominated the planet for centuries and continue to do so. Among the several arguments that form the indictment, the author, after very objectively describing what was colonialism and what it provoked as disaster on the human and political level, takes up a classical argument of the third world which, according to him, is one of the reasons for the hatred of the West.

In his view, human rights, the ECHR, the political system that has been derived from it...have all become a new instrument for dominating the world. Post-colonialism accommodates this very subtle and self-justificatory form of domination. It is not so much the well-known human rights clause of the EU law that is included in commercial and cooperation agreements that is questioned here, but the manner in which Europeans use the Human rights argument in order to judge, according to their own yardstick, the political behaviour of third world partners (from Africa especially).

In other words, the concerned states ask this question: Who are you to teach a lesson? The Europeans surrounded by the unsoiled virginity that the ECHR and its new doctrine have bestowed on them, while one has to remember that sixty-five years ago the limits of abomination had outrageously been breached? Who is still teaching the Human Rights to the States of the third world?

The former colonizers from whom these States snatched their independence, in other words, the very same Europeans who have maintained strong economic interests and powerful political allies there to the detriment of democracy? So, whether it be Rwanda, Darfour, Ivory Coast, to confine ourselves only to these three African countries, the Europeans could legitimately speak about Human rights being flouted and violated because they are indeed flouted and violated. However, Europeans do not have the legitimacy to want to give lessons, covered with shame as they are and uppish, particularly with regard to their own history.

What is basically denounced by the third world countries, it is not so much the sacred nature of human rights, their usefulness, the tragic evidence of their negligence as the manner in which they are brandished, put up by the Europeans themselves who have barely come out of barbarity. There is no doubt, and this is the point of view I am trying to defend at this stage, that the Europeans are sincere in their discourse and their wish to make Human rights a universal standard. This is without doubt. But the political arrogance that characterizes some of them hardly hides the truc intention of this discourse: show that the Europeans, the Westerners, are superior in their moral, political, democratic and legal evolution to the rest of the world. It is this sense of superiority, this blind belief which accounts largely for the confusion and hatred.

These are fundamental liberties for the tenants of historicist critical thesis: moral and guilt-provoking proceedings of an arrogant and Western post-colonialism which does not enough look back at its own history and the lessons which it has to learn from it.

II. Legalist Criticism

This criticism comes from normativist jurists (or positivists) who, ill at ease with the *jus naturaliste* approach of law, prefer to take shelter under the intellectually comfortable and technically reassuring arsenal of the Kelsenian School. The Viennese paradigms are reassuring in the sense that they reduce the validity of the norm to a process of subsomption and a coherent hierarchy between judicially controllable norms. All French, German and EU public law bears the imprint of this principle which is based on the idea that the legality that is found by a norm is anchored only in the notion of validity. The ECtHR by its contestable interpretations (A) and its will to keep enlarging the field of individual rights (B) calls into question the very validity of the Convention.

A. A Contestable Technique of Interpretation of Fundamental Liberties: The rules governing the interpretation of treaties are essentially derived from international custom. Articles 31 to 33 of the Vienna Convention of 1969 (CV69) give the guidelines for the official interpreters of the treaties who are the States, their jurisdictions and international jurisdictions. Thus, treaties have to be interpreted in "good faith" following the ordinary meaning attributed to treaties in their context in the light of their subject and purpose. Even if the notion of interpretation in good faith remains difficult to grasp, it is nonetheless true that the fundamental idea that should govern the interpreter is that the interpretation he/she wants to arrive at should construe the intention of the authors of the treaty—that is to say the will of the States parties—as it was manifest at the time of adoption of the Convention.

The legal basis of this instruction is that the validity of the international norm pertains to the will of the States and to the *pacta sunt servanda* principle. An interpretation that does not respect the initial will of the States would incontestably call into question their sovereignty and indirectly the validity of the treaty itself.

We may not agree with this analysis. That is my case, besides. Jurists specialized in EU, the Europe with twenty-seven member states know sufficiently well the case law of the Court of Justice of European Communities to realize that its interpretative work has far superseded the initial will of the member states. However, if one looks at it closely, the Court of Justice has based its interpretation on the stipulations of original treaties in a highly demonstrative and pedagogical fashion. It has drawn some solutions which are certainly original, but without never acting above the law. Moreover, the States have the full control over these treaties. They happen to either validate the case law of the Court of Justice or restrict some others.

When we look at the European Convention and the ECtHR, we have witnessed a surprising development on the part of the latter which seemed to make a mockery of the sovereignty of States parties. This is how in 1975, in order to discover in the famous Article no 6, the principle of the judge's right that the Court explained: "that it was ready to consider that there was space for it to draw inspiration from Articles 31 to 33 of CV69". In this case, a dissenting opinion of a judge specified that "this decision of 1975 constituted a typical example of the aspirations of the law maker through the ages".

Since then and particularly the end of the eighties, the Court regularly has declared that "the Convention and its protocols must be interpreted in the light of today's conditions. It follows that their provisions could not be uniquely interpreted in conformity with the intention of their authors as they were expressed in 1950". In the name of the theory according to which the Convention is a living instrument, the n Court has freed itself thoroughly from the conventional techniques of interpretation and initial will of the authors of the ECHR.

As a result, the value of the ECHR is no longer conventional but Praetorian henceforth. The Court has absorbed the Convention to give it a legal value totally defined by the Court. Therefore, it is no longer the States which are masters of the content and scope of Human Rights, but, the European judge through an interpretative artifice that some will deem as a legal "*coup de force*".

To continue in this register, the Court has not hesitated to give legal force to its rules of procedure which I find legally contestable. Its legal basis is certainly the Convention itself. But these regulations have been drafted by the Court itself and not ratified by the States parties. As we know one of the noted principles of international law is the formal manifestation of the will of the States in the process of standardization of acts. In other words, an act according to international law does not become the norm and get mandatory unless the States have manifested their will to be bound by it (especially through ratification).

In 2003, the Court declared that the rules have the same value as the Convention! Thus, some simple recommendations that figured in the provisional measures to be adopted while escorting illegal aliens to the frontier have become binding on the States parties. The States, if they did not abide by them (recommendations which, by essence, are not mandatory), would see their responsibility involved, whereas the ECHR does not at all regulate the question of provisional measures. Three dissenting opinions of judges have strongly criticized this manner of proceeding which consisted in the ECtHR drawing inspiration from what was done by the International Court of justice at The Hague in this area, which, contrary to ECHR, did have a legal basis to do so (pronounce provisional measures). The dissenting judges concluded that the

Strasbourg Court went ahead with an extension of competence which must stem from "a legislative but not judiciary act".

B. A Questionable Will to Extend Subjective Rights: The ECtHR, thanks to its singular method of interpretation of the ECHR had literally discovered an impressive number of subjective rights. This vision of law is not abstract and impersonal contrary to what the objective law posits. In this sense, the law corresponds to individual prerogatives that the people could draw from the body of rules that constitutes objective law. However, the existence of this notion is criticized "in the name of logic". In fact, law is a social discipline which is constructed from general considerations and not from individual claims that one puts together. The primacy of the subjective on the objective law would go against public good, if not against general interest. Individual prerogatives are but the result of the rule of objective law and would not in any case stem from individual will. The collective, the common interests must prevail over the individual.

In order to illustrate my point, the famous Article 1 of Protocol 1 of 1955 pertaining to the goods and which are hereafter applicable to the payment of social benefits, to loans that one could reasonably expect to see materialized, to copyright for brands, and to royalties. Article 6§1 of the Convention relating to the entitlement for an equitable access to a trial, which makes it possible for the cause to be heard regarding any contestation of its rights and obligations of a civil nature, allows one to react to procedures falling within administrative, criminal and fiscal law. It is not sure that the notion of civil obligations subsumes questions that come under fiscal law especially.

The most known decisions are those that have been handed down by virtue of Article 8 of the ECHR which affirms that "Everyone has the right to respect for his private and family life, his home and his correspondence". But certain decisions of the Court, in the name of an open and assumed subjectivism, tend to call into question very profound principles of the social organization of States: the right of the homosexuals to marry, the right to adoption of such couples, the succession regime of natural children, the possibility for a woman to have recourse to abortion.

When examined closely, this Praetorian creation seems to henceforth constitute the true meaning of the Convention. This meaning is indeed and more often found in the case law of the Strasbourg Court than in the text itself of the Convention. Some judges have even argued that the Court had transformed the treaty by replacing the written norm by a set of precedents. Thus, we would get closer to Common Law in the sense that its own precedents have force of law.

However, and it is where the tenants of legalist criticism undoubtedly find the most disturbing aspect, the Court itself decided that it was not bound by its earlier decisions. It nevertheless holds that for reasons of legal security, foreseeability and equality before law that it can depart from its previous decisions only for a valid reason. Closer analysis, however, reveals that the Court's decisions are drafted in such a way as to absolutely avoid shutting the perspective for the future. It is not necessary for the Court to justify its overruling. The whole art consists in not enouncing norms—constraining by nature—in order to have full freedom. The Court's decisions inherently carry the seeds of its overruling. We reach this paradoxical situation in which the Court produces a law that is non-normative and therefore archaic.

III. Organizational Criticism

Organizational criticism consists in examining the institutional logic and the organization of the process of safeguarding fundamental rights. A closer look enables the partisans of this current of criticism to see that the producers of the standardized moral value underlying the decisions of the ECHR are the judges. The basic question that has to be asked is: Could the framing of these moral norms that are valid for

800 million Europeans and forty seven States result from the forty seven judges sitting in Grand Chambers consist of 17 judges while taking important decisions?

Are the European societies, philosophers, intellectuals, sociologists, politicians no longer capable of fostering these values, these norms? Do fundamental rights not play the role of restraining instruments of minds and national institutions for the great benefit of some hard core moralists whose alibi would be legal protection and the standardized safe-guarding of human rights? Under the pretext of conferring inalienable rights, and in order to avoid any contestation, an ideology is spread whose name remains to be identified: liberal individualism or sectarian communitarianism...Two points must be remembered: The implicitly moralizing scope of the decisions of the ECtHR (A) and the limits of the judges' legitimacy (B).

A. The Implicitly Moralizing Scope of ECHR Decisions: Is the ECHR a convention, a normative text—which holds a meaning for a jurist—or on the contrary, a set of moralizing principles? It is both at the same time. The alternative approach which consists in saying that it is either a norm or a catalogue of values is not a good one. It automatically closes a debate whose complexity is immense and which obliges us to make a clear-cut choice between this simplistic and Manichean alternative.

Legally speaking the ECHR is a convention. That is to say a legal text that will be binding on the States members, as much by virtue of international law and the *pacta sunt servanda* rule as by virtue of the internal law of each member State. For France, it is Article 55 of the Constitution that specifies, in accordance with the monist theory of international public law that the treaties have a value superior to law. The organizational outcome of this solution is that practically all the institutions of the State, its legislative, executive and judiciary bodies are obliged to draw lessons from the scope of the Court's decisions. Organizational criticism thus sustains that it is an exogenous law that makes the legislators, and sometimes the constitutional authorities and the judiciary submit to a standard (the Court's jurisprudence) which the States do not control.

Indeed on a strictly legal level, the argument can hold water. As long as the States are able to control the international standards which are binding on them, thanks especially to their power of revising the treaties, there is no dissymmetry. They are, in this case, bound by a Convention they control. This is notably the case with the Treaty on the European Union where it is stipulated that the states (ordinary procedure) or the Council of the European Union (simplified procedure) can amend the text. But within the framework of the ECHR and in particular the case law of the Court, the States have totally lost this power to control the standards.

They are thus subject to a system which, on the one hand, gets totally out of hand and on the other, constitutes an attack on their sovereignty. This change indeed aims at protecting human rights thanks to a system that is external to the States—the strasbourg Court. But this idea is maintained as a kind of eternal repentance, as if taking for granted the notion that these very same States are not in a position to safeguard human rights. It is unfortunately and undoubtedly true.

This pessimistic observation thus maintains the idea that fundamental rights fall under a universal or at least regional scrutiny. But we ought to be wary of this Universalist temptation. Let us not forget that it is on this presupposition France had built and especially justified the unjustifiable: colonialism.

At another level, but which is, nevertheless, linked to the preceding one, organizational critics sustain that the submission of States (I would say their compliance with the commitments taken) to a system they do not control cannot further be denounced by them and by whosoever, for that matter. In fact, this is a topic that has been touched upon in my introduction. It has become institutionally untenable for the

State and unthinkable, while communicating with the media, to criticize the solutions brought by the European judge as well as fundamental rights.

Very often the solutions of the judges pertain to two sensitive subjects : homosexual marriages (in the name of right to marriage) and the adoption of children by homosexual couples (in the name of non-discrimination, and of the right to found a family), ban or not of the Islamic veil (or the minarets) in the secular States (in the name of freedom of religion and equality between men and women) or ban on body scan while embarking on a flight (in the name of human dignity and protection of private life).

In all these cases, the solutions adopted by the Court based on the ECHR are not questionable or can be questioned only with great difficulty, because it will boil down to indirectly but surely holding a homophobic, reactionary or conservative discourse (heterosexual marriage), a traditionalist and homophobic discourse (adoption of children by homosexual couples), or a Sarkozist discourse (it is a typical French joke, meaning, tight control at airports).

The slide towards moralism is very obvious here. Under the pretext of legal decision, the ECtHR gives rise to a post-modern ethics which cannot any more be questioned. Indeed approving the marriage between a man and a woman would be at once backward, conservative, reactionary and homophobic attitude. Questioning the right to privacy or the principle of dignity during checks at the airport will boil down to yielding to security instincts. Admitting as founded the ban on the Islamic veil could be analysed as an Islamophobia that does not dare speak its name...These are some examples among others.

B. Limits of Legitimacy of European Judges Dealing with Fundamental Rights: Organizational critics assert that the fundamental rights have paradoxically become tyrannical. We will be constrained and the States too in the first place to recognize the judgments of the Strasbourg Court as periodical truths. It is the judges who have the last word by virtue of the principle of "*res judicata*". Thus, the manufacturing of moral values in Western societies would not any longer belong to the States, intellectuals or societies themselves, but to the forty seven judges of Strasbourg. One could always sustain that the judges do nothing but validate by law the profound aspirations of the society, that they just give account of what actually is: the end of marriage as institution, individualistic aspirations, secularization of societies etc.

Whatever the case, the question of the legitimacy of the Strasbourg judges could be raised. In the name of who or what do they pronounce their decisions? The question is perhaps badly put. In Europe, contrary to the US, judges are not elected by the people. In fact, how could an institution whose members have not received any popular mandate judge the law of the States which has been adopted by the elected representatives of these nations? The question finally comes down to that. A judgment of the ECtHR does not simply lay down the new norm protecting individual rights. It determines at the same time the conventionality of the law of the State. Let us not forget that it ascertains the failure of the states to fulfil treaty obligations, whether it be the State as legislator, as public power or as judge. In other words, European judges become the arbiters of the laws of the States and what they represent on the sociological, ideological and societal levels.

The question of the legitimacy of the judges is therefore not superfluous. For organizational critics, the legitimacy is much less in so far as the Strasbourg judges do not have a full mastery of the working languages (English and French), have limited knowledge of law and their individual itineraries show that they seem to be more politicians than judges. The average duration for a case is six years (this goes against the grain of effective appeal). Besides the dominant ideology of the institution is liberal individualism that is largely shared and promoted by its members (the judges). But the judges in exercise know pretty well that they hold the supreme political power in Europe over the States (forty seven) and the people (800 million).

This power consists in subordinating national legislation adopted by parliaments and thereby subjugating the supreme courts of these States. Furthermore, and in this regard the Swiss litigation on minarets is going to be fascinating to watch. For the first time the judges will have to sit on judgment over the conventionality of the constituting referendum (which forbids the construction of new minarets). I am not talking about the substance of the case. I am just discussing the functional aspect. This is how the judges, in their role, while they are not subject to any kind of political control, are going to judge the sovereign people? That is the question. For a part of French constitutionalists, there cannot exist supraconstitutional norms, norms that are binding on the people except by admitting that the people are not or are no longer sovereign. The discussion is endless.

This question of the legitimacy of the judges is not new. The founders of European constitutionalism, among whom is the famous Austrian born Hans Keslen, had dealt with it earlier. Thus, in his organic model of constitutionality of laws, the famous jurist saw the logical necessity of having the elected representatives and parliamentarians as judges of law (of the constitutional court). Once elected, certain judges among them could thus legitimately aspire to be the guardians of the Constitution at the heart of their assembly.

It is this model that should be the norm in the European system of safeguarding human rights. On this particular point, it could be said that we are reaching it. In fact, Article 22 of the Convention stipulates that "The members of the Commission shall be elected by the Committee of Ministers by an absolute majority of votes, from a list of names drawn up by the Bureau of the Consultative Assembly; each group of the Representatives of the High Contracting Parties". The next Article specifies that the members of the Commission shall be elected for a period of six years.

This link with the consultative assembly is decisive in the Kelsenian and European democratic diagram. It shows us that the members of this consultative assembly (318) who had been designated in and by their national parliaments are, first of all, representatives of their people. Their legitimacy is there. They could therefore behave as arbiters of law. The control of conventionality they exercise is not only justified from a purely legal point of view, but also from the political or democratic points of view.

Nonetheless, the limits of this organizational analysis are very quickly reached. Once elected the judges are above scrutiny, out of the reach of the States and the people. The question of democracy cannot be reduced to popular representation (highly symbolic in this particular case). It includes and requires control mechanisms. If these do not exist (as is the case), the notion of democracy itself is apparently called into question. We know that the notion of appearance constitutes for the Court a very important parameter of perception that the people must have of their institutions.

Conclusion

Are fundamental rights contestable? Yes, they are. They have to be severely criticized, called into question, hurtled. What is at stake here is a civilizational choice. What is at stake here is human dignity. For all these reasons, the struggle for their betterment should not cease. We have to contest them, contradict them and consider the weaknesses of the system with one single purpose: to continue to further reinforce these fundamental rights.

-Translated from French by Geetha Ganapathy-Doré

Note

1. http://www.iidh.ed.cr/comunidades/libertadexpresion/docs/le_europeo/fressoz percent20and percent20roire.htm , retrieved on April 9, 2010.

2

Towards a European Law of Representative Democracy

Charles Reiplinger

The third Article of the additional protocol to the European Convention of Human Rights (ECHR), concluded on March 20, 1952, provides that "The High Contracting Parties undertake to hold free elections at reasonable intervals by secret ballot, under conditions which will ensure the free expression of the opinion of the people in the choice of the legislature". [1] This rule, that we affectionately call "P1-3", is legally binding, effective, and, of course, subject to the jurisdiction of the European Court of Human Rights (EctHR) [2], for all the members of the Council of Europe (CoE), apart from Switzerland and the Principality of Monaco. My initial motive for commenting on it was its peculiar wording, remarkable in the body of European law: it seems to recognize, implicitly at least, what we could call a collective right, a right that would directly be granted to people, in our case, the right of the people to the free expression of its opinion in the choice of the legislature. It is the one and only occurrence of the word "people" in the whole Convention, as it now exists, modified by Protocol n°11, and extended by Protocols n°4, 6, 7, 12, and 13. It is formally remarkable. The aim of my paper is to provide some background details on P1-3 and to look at how it constitutes a collective right, which is just a question among other not less interesting issues.

P1-3 is a very substantial provision, even if it is not directly part of the Convention. We are all likely to think protocols are most often lesser, minor, palliative measures which are unimportant compared to the original convention.

This said, the additional protocol was passed even before the convention came into effect, and fills in wide gaps, as, for instance, protection of private property, another liberal fundamental value. In our case, it is nothing less than the consecration of a human right to representative democracy. To this extent, it is a structural provision of a European law of liberties, precisely political liberties, as important as freedom of speech, as the Court itself had said, in its first decision concerning P1-3: “According to the Preamble to the Convention, fundamental human rights and freedoms are best maintained by "an effective political democracy". Since it enshrines a characteristic principle of democracy, Article 3 of Protocol No. 1 (P1-3) is accordingly of prime importance in the Convention system”. [3]

Interpreting and applying P1-3 thus implies dealing with important questions, legally and politically speaking. There are sometimes unexpected questions. I suppose it is a distinctive feature of mechanisms that protect liberties to face unexpected situations. Let me first deal with minor problems, before I tackle the most important ones.

A first curiosity, this Article, which establishes a human right, and correlatively a state obligation, to representative democracy, has lead to the condemning, by the Strasbourg Court, of the United Kingdom, which I believe is the mother of modern representative democracy. I can’t help smiling at the thought that the ECtHR is now in a position of giving lessons of liberal democracy to the country where liberal democracy was undoubtedly conceived and born, and which has not, contrarily to its neighbours, known any authoritarian regime since the late seventeenth century, apart from what it did in its former colonies, of course. Although, with only three violations of P1-3 on its account, the UK is far behind Italy, condemned fifteen times, because of its restrictions on the right to vote, as measures conceived to fight against the mafia, that were considered excessive by the Court; behind Turkey, condemned five times, and Latvia, condemned three times.

France is quite a good student, as it has been put on trial just once for an alleged violation of P1-3, and has been cleared by the Court in 2005. To end these modest statistics, issued by the Court, we can notice that out of the 10573 decisions that state a violation of the convention, only thirty seven concerns P1-3. By way of comparison, it could be noted that the right to a fair trial has been violated 3559 times.

The Court's jurisprudence has increased, slowly but steadily, in quantity and quality, since the founding decision of Mathieu-Mohin and Clerfayt of 1987. And put together, these decisions now form part of a growing body of European law on representative democracy. The Court on this matter has the same influence that it had and still has on European judicial systems: convergence. Not only by establishing common rules applicable to the contracting parties, but also, as it does for all liberties, by grounding its interpretations on the common elements it can find in the internal law of the members. It does not hesitate to compare internal rules to finally decide if, for example, the right to vote has been legally restricted or not.

Not only does the Court create, by interpreting P1-3, a growing common body of rules on representative democracy, but it also operates, by doing so, a synthesis of the different European democratic traditions. First, we will see that knowing what "the choice of the legislature" is, according to P1-3, is not obvious. Then, we will see that P1-3 is written as an obligation for the states, to actively do something, and to this extent, it is formally remarkable. But the Court classically believes it to be the source of three basic individual rights, the right to vote, the right of eligibility, and the right to equal treatment in the voting process. And we will finally see that this provision includes, explicitly but not directly, a collective dimension, in "the free opinion of the people in the choice of the legislature". Such a collective concept is not recognized by the Court as a collective right, but used as a standard to limit the acceptable restrictions to the individual rights guaranteed by P1-3.

1. What is a Legislature?

As this provision is meant to apply to the choice of the legislature, it is first important to understand what is, or not, a legislature, according to P1-3 and as interpreted by the Court. European law is conceptually independent from national law, even if, for a Frenchman, and others, the word "legislature" is instinctively considered to be a synonym for national parliament. But, apart from the Convention's conceptual autonomy, the Court's interpretation has to take into account, for the sole reason they exist, the very different normative approaches that can be found among the European countries. And that is why, since 1987, the Court has regularly stated that "The word "legislature" does not necessarily mean only the national parliament; it has to be interpreted in the light of the constitutional structure of the State in question". [4] In this light, it seems that the Court's approach is mostly, but not only, material and centered on the powers effectively detained by national institutions. And of course, it is not limited to what each state considers to be its legislature. The Court's approach is obviously extensive, and P1-3 does apply to other institutions than national parliaments. It also applies to some local authorities (a), as well as international authorities (b).

a. P1-3 Applied to Local Authorities

In the case of a strongly decentralized state, all the more so in a federal state, important normative powers are detained by local authorities. Principally for that reason, the Court believes the designation of such authorities enters the range of P1-3.Thus, in the Mathieu-Mohin and Clerfayt case of 1987, it has decided that the Flemish Council in Belgium was a part of the Belgian "legislature", construed according to the words in P1-3 : "The Court notes at the outset that the 1980 reform vested the Flemish Council with competence and powers wide enough to make it, alongside the French Community Council and the Walloon Regional Council, a constituent part of the Belgian "legislature" in addition to the House of Representatives and the Senate (see paragraphs 24-25, 27 and

37 above); those appearing before the Court were agreed on this point". [5] We can understand why even the Belgian state as a defendant did not want to hold the contrary. In the case of a federal state, pretending that state legislatures are not really legislatures, because they are somehow submitted to a federal parliament, would legally and politically be unreasonable. It is commonly admitted in a federal state, the legislative power is somehow distributed between the states and the federal institutions.

So, such a solution which consists in applying P1-3 to a state legislature in a federal state is not a big deal. It becomes more interesting when the state involved is not supposed to be a federal one. This is what happened to France, when, in a case opposing one of our colleagues, working in the University of New Caledonia, and the French State, the Court decided, on January 11, 2005 that P1-3 had not been violated by French law. There is, in New Caledonia, an ongoing constitutional process to freely determine whether the Caledonians become independent. A French law, passed in 1999, provides that the people who had settled in the Island after 1989 cannot participate in the elections of the local normative institution, called the Congress.

Well, the New Caledonian Congress, because of the context, detains normative attributions that are normally held in France by the national parliament. And this delegation of powers is directly authorized by the French Constitution. In this case also, the Court has considered that such a local authority had to be considered as a part of the legislature, according to P1-3. The Court's approach is essentially material, once again: "The Court must ensure that "effective political democracy" is properly served in the territories to which the Convention applies, and in this context, it must have regard not solely to the strictly legislative powers which a body has, but also to that body's role in the overall legislative process. Having regard to the powers conferred on Congress in the 1999 Institutional Act, the Court considers that it is no longer a purely consultative body but has become an institution with a decisive role to play, depending on the issues being dealt with, in the legislative process in New Caledonia.

It therefore finds that the Congress is sufficiently involved in this specific legislative process to be regarded as part of the "legislature" of New Caledonia for the purposes of Article 3 of Protocol No. 1". [6] But the Court also considers other aspects, and it is finally a body of elements that is used to decide if an institution is or not a legislature. In the French case, it stated that the acts passed by the New Caledonian Congress "are systematically submitted to the *Conseil d'Etat* for its opinion and, once enacted, have statutory force. They may also be reviewed by the Constitutional Council, prior to enactment". As an American professor Alfred Amman, from Bloomington in Indiana, once said to me, "if it looks like a duck, walks and talks like a duck, well, it's a duck". This approach, focused on the real consequences a legal act may have on the people, has logically brought the Court to apply P1-3 to some local authorities. Subsequently, it also leads the Court to apply P1-3 to international authorities.

b. P1-3 Applied to International Authorities

In the important case of Matthews v. UK, judged in 1999, the Court has been asked to consider the European Parliament as being part of the "legislature", according to P1-3, and more precisely, the British legislature. The inhabitants of Gibraltar, a British overseas territory in Africa, had not been given the right to vote in 1994 for the European Parliament. Although it is called a Parliament, for a long time, the European Parliament has been a symbolic institution with very few normative powers. But, since 1993 and the Maastricht treaty, it has gained normative powers, though it still shares most of them with another institution, the Council of the European Union. Nevertheless the Court "thus finds that the European Parliament is sufficiently involved in the specific legislative processes leading to the passage of legislation under Articles 189b and 189c of the EC Treaty, and is sufficiently involved in the general democratic supervision of the activities of the European Community, to constitute part of the "legislature" of Gibraltar for the purposes of Article 3 of Protocol No. 1". [7]

It is clear that participation in the normative activity is a major criterion, but we can see it is not the only one, and that democratic supervision is also taken into account. The Court's approach is global, and it specifies that: "In determining whether the European Parliament falls to be considered as the "legislature", or part of it, in Gibraltar for the purposes of Article 3 of Protocol No. 1, the Court must bear in mind the *sui generis* nature of the European Community, which does not follow in every respect the pattern common in many States of a more or less strict division of powers between the executive and the legislature. Rather, the legislative process in the EC involves the participation of the European Parliament, the Council and the European Commission". [8]

In the Mathieu-Mohin and Clerfayt case, the Court had already said it would take into account the states' constitutional structure, and in Matthews v. UK, it widened its global approach to international organizations, focusing on the powers, or part of the power, that institutions effectively have, to know if they have to be elected according to the provisions of the Convention. Behind this, we can find a major principle used in protecting liberties, these last years, in Europe, for what I know. Judges now take into account mostly and above all, the effects a decision can have in order to decide what rules must be applied. In this case, a sort of principle of proportionality, applied to the mechanisms that protect liberties. The more potential damage an institution can make, the more it is likely to be controlled by judges. It is because European law today has a great influence on people's lives that the European Parliament must be subject to a democratic election and come under an effective control of the ECtHR. I must underline the fact that in France, this realistic approach is nowadays more and more shared by the Constitutional Council, the administrative and judicial judges, and I believe the main impulse still comes from the ECHR.

Nevertheless this decision was not easy. Two members of the Court had a dissenting opinion [9] published in which it is clearly said that in their opinion, the European Parliament should not be considered as a legislature, or a part of the legislature, for various reasons. First, they hold that the *travaux préparatoires* clearly show that no one intended P1-3, when it got drafted, to apply to international institutions. It was conceived as limited to the national parliaments. But, they admit it is not a real problem, the Convention must be adapted with time. A new context can justify a new interpretation. Then, the two dissenting judges dispute the amount of powers granted to the European Parliament in 1994, believing that they are not enough of them to consider the institution as a legislature. And finally, they hold that the European Parliament cannot furthermore be considered as *the* legislature of Gibraltar, precisely because it appears that Gibraltar is often exonerated from European law, that very few European rules do have a direct effect on the territory. In other words, in Gibraltar, the European Parliament appears to be a minor normative authority. In fine, they did not convince the Court.

There are other problems that can come from such an extension of P1-3 to international institutions. The Court itself states that there are other institutions involved in the European legislative process. We know the Council of the European Union, composed of members of European governments, is still the most important European normative authority. Why should it not be elected, considering its normative powers? Well, this is precisely why the Court does not only take into account normative powers, but also other criteria, such as democratic supervision. Obviously, the Council of the European Union has no legal power of supervision over the European Commission, for instance. So, including the European Parliament in the concept of legislature with the intention of making sure that every European citizen votes for it, is a logical decision, considering the Court's approach. The

European Parliament is becoming increasingly important in the European legislative process, and the European legislative process is becoming increasingly important in our European lives. And I think the Court may have taken into account the fact that this importance would be growing with time.

2. Which Rights, Whose Rights?

Drafted formally as an active obligation for the states (a), P1-3 is not clear about who has granted rights, and what precisely these rights are (b). It is also notable because it uses a remarkable standard to protect these rights, a collective concept, “the free expression of the people in the choice of the legislature” (c).

a. A Truly Liberal Debt

Within the framework of political theory, the European Convention is undoubtedly exclusively liberal, materially and formally, although it has been concluded at a time when the second generation human rights was asserting itself, to use the words of Professor Karel Vasak. [10] This second generation human rights, influenced by socialist political thought, grounded on equality as main value, mostly affirms new rights in the form of an obligation made to political authorities to actively do something. For example, the right to education, the right to a health system, when they exist, are considered more than classical liberties.

The European Convention does not contain any right of this second generation, and formally all the rights it declares are rights granted to individuals, using the words “everyone has the right to...”. This is what is called a positive right, something that we possess. It also uses often the words “no one shall be, deprived of, forced to, held prisoner…”. This is what is called a negative right, which supposes that other people, and of course the authorities, refrain from doing something. In other words, the Convention is a classical liberal declaration of human rights. In our case, it seems like P1-3 creates a legal claim for individuals, an obligation for the states to actively do something. And obviously the Court has noticed it.

However, it refuses to consider that this specific form should have specific consequences: “The inter-State colouring of the wording of Article 3 (P1-3) does not reflect any difference of substance from the other substantive clauses in the Convention and Protocols. The reason for it would seem to lie rather in the desire to give greater solemnity to the commitment undertaken and in the fact that the primary obligation in the field concerned is not one of abstention or non-interference, as with the majority of the civil and political rights, but one of adoption by the State of positive measures to "hold" democratic elections”. [11]

The thing is, even within a strictly liberal scope, effectively maintaining liberties already supposes a few active obligations for political authority. We can see here that legislative elections are one of them, as is also the obligation to build a decent judicial system, complying with the requirements of the Convention. Besides, even the famous liberal economist Adam Smith and his followers, do admit that the State has active obligations, as enacting legal rules in certain matters, maintaining a police force, a judicial system, and building roads. These activities are known as the regalian activities.

From the Court’s point of view, it is important to decide what precisely can be brought before it, and who can bring such action; in other words, to what extent one or more individuals can ask the Court to protect some of their rights, based on P1-3. Considering the Court’s powers, such a protection can only be obtained by an individual action before the Court, under Article 25 of the Convention. Nothing in the Convention can allow the Court to hear the complaints of a people, nor is it authorized to ask the states, at its own initiative, to do something. So the Court had to grant, for it to be effective, that P1-3 creates, like the rest of the Convention, individual rights-three or five, depending on the way we count.

These rights are also protected by a standard, a collective limit, the due respect of "the free opinion of the people in the choice of the legislature".

b. Five Individual Rights and a Collective Limit

Let's deal first with a minor problem: the Court has never been asked to condemn the total lack of election, in other words, the violation of the obligation to organize two elections with a reasonable interval. Hopefully, our problems are not that bad, we have not reached such a situation where a European State would not at all organize a legislative election. Such a failure can happen, in an extreme situation, in case of a war, as it happened in former Yugoslavia in the 1990s, or more recently, between Russia and Georgia. But, hopefully, Europe is globally peaceful now, and this has not been a real legal problem.

In practice, the Court has decided that P1-3 directly protects three individual rights: The right to vote, the right of eligibility, and the right to an equal treatment before the election process. Since 1987, the Court has always, in all its decisions concerning P1-3, recalled "that Article 3 of Protocol No. 1 implies subjective rights to vote and to stand for election". [12] These two rights are the strongest and clearest consequences of P1-3, to which can be added a principle of equal treatment, which is not always, but often, recalled by the Court, specifically when it has to deal with a particular electoral system: "The phrase "conditions which will ensure the free expression of the opinion of the people in the choice of the legislature" implies essentially-apart from freedom of expression (already protected under Article 10 of the Convention)-the principle of equality of treatment of all citizens in the exercise of their right to vote and their right to stand for election". [13] It is a right to a relative equality, and the Court specifies: It does not follow, however, that all votes must necessarily have equal weight as regards the outcome of the election or that all candidates must have equal chances of victory. Thus no electoral system can eliminate "wasted votes". [14] The Court considers that equal treatment may not be perfect because it would be impossible to arrive at a perfect system.

Affirming these three rights is a reasonable interpretation of P1-3. It is neither restrictive, nor wide. It is not restrictive, because P1-3 has become an effective source of individual rights, and at start it was not that obvious it would be. It is not a wide interpretation either in the sense it could be held that the P1-3 includes more rights such as freedom of speech and freedom of association. The point is freedom of speech and liberty of association are already protected by two specific Articles in the Convention, Articles 10 and 11. So it is useless for the Court to ground them on P1-3, and it is a fact that when a violation of these liberties is alleged, it is mainly on the basis of Articles 10 or 11.

The Court sometimes states that a violation of Article 10 or 11 implies the violation of P1-3. But, when a main Article of the Convention is infringed, the Court does not need to specify to what degree P1-3 also protects it. Ye t, although in practice it is of no use, it can be held, imagining Articles 10 and 11 to be non-existent, that the P1-3 protects overall five individual rights: right to vote; right of eligibility; right to an equal treatment before the election process; freedom of speech; and liberty of political association.

Finally, in spite of its remarkable formulation, P1-3 is not that original. It declares, implicitly, and protects the conventional political individual rights. But, it has a remarkable aspect, which lies in the obligation made to the states to respect, in any case, "the free expression of the opinion of the people".

c. A Collective Limit: the Free Expression of the Opinion of the People

Let us say it is not a collective right, because technically it is not a right. "The free expression of the opinion of the people" is not directly protected by P1-3, and cannot directly be used, by no-one, by itself, as the basis for an action before the Court. Therefore it is not a right, individual nor collective, and appears to be a judicial standard, a concept used by the judge to set the final frontier of what the states can do to restrict the rights guaranteed by P1-3.

As a result the mechanism of P1-3 is as follows: the Court considers that five individual rights are stated and to be protected ; the Court admits these rights may be restricted by the states, as all other liberties, specifying that these restrictions must be judged in relation to the situation, legal and historical, of each state. But, ultimately, the Court specifies that no restriction will be allowed, if it goes against the free expression of the choice of the people. It is strongly underlined by the Court, for example in the case of Hirst vs. UK, judged on October 6, 2005. The Court asserts that "it has to satisfy itself that the conditions do not curtail the rights in question to such an extent as to impair their very essence and deprive them of their effectiveness; that they are imposed in pursuit of a legitimate aim; and that the means employed are not disproportionate. In particular, any condition imposed must not thwart the free expression of the people in the choice of the legislature–in other words, they must reflect, or not run counter to, the concern to maintain the integrity and effectiveness of an electoral procedure aimed at identifying the will of the people through universal suffrage". [15]

The free expression of the people is seen as a goal, as a purpose, as a concern, says the Court, which will reveal whether a restriction adopted for another purpose is or not tolerable. It appears to be very close to another neighbouring concept, underlying Article 11, and which; in France, is protected by the Constitutional Council, the active protection of pluralism, equally seen as a collective goal. The Court also clearly states such a link, in a 2008 decision, Yumak and Sadak vs. Turkey: "The "free expression of the opinion of the people in the choice of the legislature" is a matter on which Article 11 of the Convention also has a bearing, guaranteeing as it does the freedom of association, and thus indirectly the freedom of political parties, which represent a form of association essential to the proper functioning of democracy. The expression of the opinion of the people is inconceivable without the assistance of a plurality of political parties representing the several currents of opinion flowing through a country's population. By reflecting those currents, not only within political institutions but also, thanks to the media, at all levels of life in society, they make an irreplaceable contribution to the political debate which is at the very core of the concept of a democratic society". [16]

To get back to P1-3, in practice, knowing what restrictions are likely to damage the free expression of the people, is the problem. There are mostly three problems: legal restrictions on the right to vote; legal restrictions on the right of eligibility; and last, but not the least, the use of different voting systems. I must again underscore the fact that the right to vote and the right of eligibility are individual rights. In our case, the Court explicitly aims at protecting a collective value, and not directly these individual rights. In other words, the main goal is not to preserve each individual right to vote, but to ensure that the electoral process does effectively reflect the opinion of the people. Thus, the individual right to vote is protected first because "Any departure from the principle of universal suffrage risks undermining the democratic validity of the legislature thus elected and the laws it promulgates. Exclusion of any groups or categories of the general population must accordingly be reconcilable with the underlying purposes of Article 3 of Protocol No. 1". [17]

The Court applies the same logical argument to restrictions on the right of eligibility. Restrictions must not lead to depriving the legislative body of its representativeness. The elected person is not really the one protected, and again the aim is to protect the collective will of the people as it has been expressed. For example, in the case of an incompatibility between a profession and a parliamentary mandate, the Court has judged that "the Special Supreme Court had caused him to forfeit his seat and had deprived his constituents of the candidate whom they had chosen freely and democratically to represent them for four years in Parliament, in breach of the principle of legitimate expectation. In this connection, the Court notes that the Government have not advanced any ground of pressing significance to the democratic order that could have justified the immediate application of the absolute disqualification. This situation is therefore in breach of the very substance of the rights guaranteed by Article 3 of Protocol No. 1". [18]

We must finally examine the difficult question of voting systems. For example, between the British first past the post system and proportional representation, there is a big difference. The aims are not the same, and the results will not be the same either. We all know that the choice of a voting system has a huge impact on the result of elections. It has even been shown by mathematicians, Nicolas de Condorcet, and later Kenneth Arrow [19], that there is no perfect voting system, and that it is not always possible to make unquestionable collective choices.

The Court is obviously careful when it comes to deal with a claim in relation with the use of a particular voting system: "As regards the method of appointing the "legislature", Article 3 (P1-3) provides only for "free" elections "at reasonable intervals", "by secret ballot" and "under conditions which will ensure the free expression of the opinion of the people". Subject to that, it does not create any "obligation to introduce a specific system" such as proportional representation or majority voting with one or two ballots. Here too the Court recognizes that the Contracting States have a wide margin of appreciation, given that their legislation on the matter varies from place to place and from time to time. Electoral systems seek to fulfil objectives which are sometimes scarcely compatible with each other: on the one hand, to reflect fairly and faithfully the opinion of the people, and on the other, to channel currents of thought so as to promote the emergence of a sufficiently clear and coherent political will". [20]

In practice, the Court has already refused to consider that a threshold of 10 per cent of the votes, required for a list to be elected in Parliament, was an excessive restriction, in the case of Yumak and Sadak Vs. Turkey, judged on July 8, 2008. I must specify that four judges [21] had their dissenting opinion published on that specific point, considering P1-3 had been violated, because the 10 per cent threshold was, in their opinion, an excessive restriction, in contradiction with the free expression of the people. But they did not convince the Court in this very sensitive matter, and we can understand the Court is careful.

Conclusion

The Court's jurisprudence under the P1-3 is not famous enough, as it is relative to the most important principles of liberal democracy. It also reveals how difficult the conciliation of different constitutional traditions could be. But, by nature, this case law is growing into a European common law, fundamental law, of representative democracy. I believe the most important aspect for the moment is organic, with this simple question: in a democracy, who, exactly, must be elected, and by whom? I assume that the Court's answer is reasonable: it depends on the powers effectively held by the public institutions. It is realistic, but then it leads to an extensive definition of legislature, including local and international authorities. It is precisely because in Europe there now is a double movement: legislative powers are being transferred from the national parliaments to local as well as international institutions, specifically the European Union. I believe it is a good example of what can be called globalization of law. I myself find interesting to share these thoughts in India, today the world's biggest democracy. By doing so, I take my little share in this globalization of law, of representative democracy, in the convergence of our fundamental values. This convergence in Europe is now a fact, with regard to the right to vote, the right of eligibility, and essentially the growing submission of normative authorities to the principle of election.

Notes

1. The European Convention on Human Rights, Protocol 1. http://www.hri.org/docs/ECHR50.html#P1 retrieved on July 17, 2010.
2. Cf. Art. 5 of the protocol: "As between the High Contracting Parties the provisions of Articles 1, 2, 3 and 4 of this Protocol shall be regarded as additional Articles to the Convention and all the provisions of the Convention shall apply accordingly".
3. ECHR, Mathieu-Mohin and Clerfayt v. Belgium, 03/02/1987, n°9267/81.
4. http://www.legislationline.org/documents/action/popup/id/7925 retrieved on July 17, 2010.
5. http://stari.iusinfo.si/EUII/EUCHR/dokumenti/1987/03/CASE_OF_MATHIEU-MOHIN_AND_CLERFAYT_v._BELGIUM_02_03_1987.html retrieved on July 17, 2010.
6. ECHR, Py v. France, 01/11/2005.
7. ECHR, Matthews v. UK, n°24833/94.
8. http://www.lapres.net/mathews.html retrieved on July 17, 2010.
9. The joint dissenting opinion of Judges John Freeland and Jungwiert could be consulted at http://www.webcitation.org/51Wx37qMR retrieved on July 19, 2010.
10. Karel Vasak, "Human Rights: A Thirty-Year Struggle: The Sustained Efforts to Give Force of Law to the Universal Declaration of Human Rights", *UNESCO Courier* 30:11, Paris: November 1977.
11. ECHR, Mathieu-Mohin and Clerfayt v. Belgium, 03/02/1987, n°9267/81.
12. http://portal.coe.ge/downloads/Judgments/Labita percent20v. percent20Italy percent20Eng.pdf retrieved on July 17, 2010.
13. http://www.legislationline.org/documents/action/popup/id/7925
14. *Ibid.*
15. ECHR, Hirst v. UK, 10/06/2005, n°74025/01.
16. ECHR, Yumak and Sadak v. Turkey, 07/08/2008, n°10226/03.
17. ECHR, Hirst v. UK, 10/06/2005, n°74025/01.

18. ECHR, Lykourezos v. Greece, 09/15/2005, n°33554/03.
19. Cf. Kenneth J. Arrow, *Social Choice and Individual Values*, 2nd edition, John Wiley and Sons, Inc., New York: 1963. Nicolas de Condorcet, *Essai sur l'application de l'analyse à la probabilité des décisions rendues à la pluralité des voix,* Paris, 1785.
20. http://www.legislationline.org/documents/action/popup/id/7925 retrieved on July 17, 2010.
21. http://cmiskp.echr.coe.int/tkp197/view.asp?action=html&documentId=837656&portal=hbkm&source=externalbydocnumber&table=F69A27FD8FB86142BF01C1166DEA398649 retrieved on July 17, 2010.

3

Security and Anti-Terrorism Laws: What Future for Individual Rights and Liberties in the European Union?

Dominique Hiebel

Human rights, democracy and rule of law constitute fundamental values for the European Union. Anchored in its founding Treaty (Art. 2, 3, 6 and 7 TEU), they have been strengthened by the adoption, on December 7, 2000, of a Charter of Fundamental Rights. The Lisbon treaty, which came into force on December 1, 2009, gives this Charter the same status as other treaties. [1] Thus, countries that wish to join the European Union (Art. 49 TUE), like those that want to negotiate a contract with it, are obliged to uphold liberties and fundamental rights. The Court of Justice of the European Union ensures the abidance of these values: [2] as such, it had decided to make an explicit reference to the Charter in a judgement dated June 27, 2006. [3] Moreover, an urgent preliminary procedure came into force in March 2008, which allows the Court to answer questions regarding these issues at short notice.

In this context, we might ponder upon the necessity of a paper entitled "Security and Anti-Terrorism Laws: What Future for Individual Rights and Liberties in the European Union?". The Treaty on the European Union consecrates the Charter of Fundamental Rights, recognizes rights and liberties as guaranteed by the European Convention for the Protection of Human Rights and Fundamental Freedoms as general principles governing EU law [4], and the Stockholm Programme recommends the ratification of that Convention.

The reply to that rhetorical question raised earlier is obvious.

In conformity with the Treaty, the The Hague Programme and its Action Plan, adopted for the period between 2004-2009, uphold the priorities of Liberty, Justice and Security and, among the ten priority areas of action, has accorded the first place to fundamental rights and citizenship. [5] More precisely, point 2 of the Action Plan mentions the Union's struggle against terrorism and takes care to base the strategy of Union on fundamental values of democracy, fundamental rights and the rule of law. [6]

If it was declared that a global struggle had to be conducted against terrorism, it was affirmed without ambiguity that this war had to be organized on the basis of the respect of human rights. A document of the Council of Ministers of November 30, 2005, relating to the European strategy against terrorism, is further entitled: "To combat terrorism globally while respecting human rights". Likewise, the Council Decision establishing the specific programme of "Prevention, Preparedness and Consequence Management of Terrorism and other Security related Risks" [7] for the period between 2007 and 2013, emphasizes the necessity to fight terrorism on a global level, but with due respect paid to individual rights and liberties.

Finally, the Stockholm Programme, adopted by the European council for the period between 2010 and 2014, shall continue to establish a space of liberty, security and justice. Its 26th point repeats the formulation of the first point of The Hague Programme, which it follows, in placing citizenship and fundamental rights at the heart of European preoccupations. These texts are in conformity with the founding Treaty and the Charter of Fundamental rights which consecrate human rights, democracy and the rule of law as essential values of the European Union.

The European Union seems to have thus come up with an adequate response for a controversial question: "How to protect liberty, through security, without denying its essence:

i.e., without violating fundamental rights and liberties?"

Nevertheless, some grey areas tarnish the picture: they are warning signs that our claim for vigilance needs to be reasonable, if the European Union wants to go by the objectives not only of respect but also of promotion of fundamental rights to which it is committed (point 1 of the Commission's Action Plan: The Union is bound to the respect of fundamental rights, but it is also engaged in actively promoting them). Moreover, the Council recognizes the paradox in its conclusions with reference to the adoption of the Stockholm Programme: "The challenge will be to ensure respect for fundamental rights and freedoms and integrity while guaranteeing security in Europe". [8]

This paper focuses on a particularly sensitive matter: that of collection and constitution of personal data bases. As the information report n°107 (2009-2010) established for the European Commission expresses it, the protection of personal data and private life is a major asset for the Union's citizens. Yet, as the European data protection Supervisor Peter Hustinx emphasizes it [9], if, on the one hand, the measures reinforcing the powers of repressive authorities and intrusive for citizens have witnessed a significant development in the past eight years, due to the pressure caused by terrorist acts, at the same time, the purviews of protection of personal data have witnessed very slow progress, on the other.

Because of the multiplication of databases, of evolutions in technology, increase in exchanges, many issues arise: Let us first look at the nature of agreements made between the European Union and the United States on this matter (I); then analyze the threat to individual liberties provoked by intrusions in private life, but also the threat of profiling, which leads to the risk of establishing "suspicion by category" (II).

1. Personal Data and Cooperation Treaties with the United States: A Necessary Collaboration, but at What Cost?: The international character of the terrorist threat calls undoubtedly for a cooperation between states and, in particular, a cooperation between the European Union and third countries. In order to fight efficiently against terrorism, inquiries must be exchanged and, for this purpose, conventions signed, which establish the framework according to which data will be collected, transferred and treated. In this paper, I have chosen to specifically focus on the nature of the agreement concluded in this matter by the European Union with the United States.

The question is to know to what extent the European Union can engage in such a cooperation, while making sure that United States will respect European citizens' fundamental rights. The scrutiny of the 2007 PNR Agreement, the Proposal for a Council Framework Decision of November 6, 2007 on the use of Passenger Name Record (PNR) for law enforcement purposes, and, last but not the least, the transitory agreement, Swift will help us answer this question.

A. 2007 PNR Agreement: After the September 11 attacks, [10] agreements have been signed in 2004 with the United States to organize the transfer of PNR data. [11] The purpose was to respond to requirements of an American law of November 19, 2001, which makes it incumbent on each airline company, including European companies ensuring flights at destination, departure or over United States territory, [12] to furnish American Customs an electronic access to data present in their reservations systems, any refusal being sanctioned by heavy financial sanctions, and by the interdiction to land in American airports.

Adopted under pressure put by United States [13], these agreements have generated fierce criticism, [14] until the Court of Justice of the European Union, to which the European Parliament referred the matter, [15] pronounced their annulment in a judgement of May 30, 2006. [16] However, this appeal of the Parliament had a paradoxical effect, as it had been remarked. [17] Apart from eliciting no response from the Court on the question of fundamental rights, which is a disgrace with regard to future agreements, it turned against its initiator, because the consultative role of the European Parliament was almost inexistent in the third pillar, in which the judgement of the Court had led to putting down the new agreement. Exit the Parliament, defeated in its claim of exercising an effective democratic role: it boiled down to a simple consultative one.

Following this ruling, a temporary agreement complying with the third pillar was signed. [18] It came into effect on July 31, 2007 and was replaced by a new agreement established for seven years on the decision of the Council of July 23, 2007. [19] And yet, if the agreement of 2004 gave rise to questions regarding fundamental rights, the 2007 Agreement generates as many doubts as well, even if the European Union, in its letter addressed to the US Department of Homeland Security, [20] ensures that the US presents an adequate level of protection for the PNR data.

These doubts, exactly, have been expressed by the European Parliament, [21] the European data protection Supervisor and Art.29 Data Protection Working Party. [22] These actors, far from sharing the enthusiasm of the Council and the Commission, insist on the lack of clear and proportioned provisions about data collection and processing, but also deplore that the implementation of a lot of provision is subject to the will of the US.

When we read the 2007 PNR Agreement, everything seems very acceptable, though; but the perspective changes, if we take a look at the letter written by the US to Luis Amado, President of the Council of the European Union. [23] This letter makes explicit the sense that the US gives to the Agreement and we are surprised by some of its provisions. Then, it can be noticed that the purposes of use of PNR Data can vary in the case of a unilateral modification of the American legislation; [24] that the possible decision to transfer European PNR data to other states may be unilaterally adopted by the US, without any prior consultation with the European authorities [25]; another worrying point is that the American authorities, in "case of necessity" can have an access to sensitive PNR data, that is able to reveal ethnic origin, philosophical, political or religious beliefs, trade union membership and the health and sex life of the individual, even if the DHS employs an automatic system to filter the sensitive codes and terms; [26]

American authorities have the possibility to decide, again unilaterally, whether a favourable response can be given to European passengers who want to consult and eventually rectify their data kept by the DHS. [27] Certainly, the agreement foresees that the DHS and European Union will periodically review, via a specially designated person, the implementation of guaranties [28]; however, this evaluation of the agreement's application–review–loses its annual and obligatory character. Further, only the Commissioner for Justice, Freedom and Security is in charge of that inspection, without the clear association of national data protection authorities. [29]

Lastly, the agreement lays down that data will be retained, not for three and a half years any longer, but for fifteen years, in the form of an "active conservation" in an analytical database for seven years, after which time the data are stored for a further period eight years, in a dormant, non-operational status, but without any assurance that files will be definitively be destroyed. [30]

Certainly, the 2007 Agreement has the merit to close years of uncertainty about the conditions in which American authorities reach PNR data of European passengers; small consolation if this uncertainty paves the way for an imbalanced text. To what extent can we be very pleased by the conclusion of such international agreements, if it results in bringing down European standards in the matter of protection of fundamental rights?

The course of measures taken in this matter does not necessarily incite optimism on our part.

B. The Council Decision Framework on the Use of

Passenger Name Record for Law Enforcement Purposes: Currently, the council decision framework on the use of Passenger Name Record (PNR) for law enforcement purposes is provoking, in its turn, many concerns. Once again, the European Parliament is ringing the alarm bell. If the Assembly, in its resolution of November 20, 2008, [31] admits the necessity for a stronger cooperation at a European rather than international level in the struggle against terrorism and organised crime, and accepts that data collection and processing can be appreciative tools for repressive objectives, it expresses serious reservations nevertheless. The formulation and the justification of the Commission's proposal but also the specifications brought by the Council leave aside too many juridical uncertainties about the question of compatibility with the ECHR and the Charter of Fundamental Rights. [32]

First, the question of proportionality: Article 8 of ECHR and Article 52 of the Charter of Fundamental Rights require that a massive interference in the right to protection of personal data should be "legitimate and justified by a pressing social need, provided for by law and proportionate to the end pursued, which must be necessary and legitimate in a democratic society"; [33] yet, if the fight against terrorism and organised crime may correspond to these exigencies, we can deplore, along with the Parliament, that the use of data, as it is envisaged by the decision framework, is not limited to these cases. [34]

Similarly, it is worrying that the proposition allows repressive authorities to obtain all data without any warrant, and without the obligation to prove why such an extension of competences was necessary. [35] Another stumbling block to which we will return later: such measures might result in an indiscriminate use of PNR data for profiling or for definition of risk assessment parameters; the Parliament emphasizes this danger, and recalls that "any kind of profiling based on ethnicity, nationality, religion, sexual orientation, gender, age or medical condition should be expressly banned as incompatible with the prohibition of any discrimination as defined in the Treaties and in the Charter of Fundamental Rights". [36]

Last, but very important argument: the European Parliament impugns the legitimacy of such tools, arguing that any information thus far provided by the US is anecdotal and that the Americans have never conclusively proved that the massive and systematic use of PNR data is necessary in the fight against terrorism and serious crime. [37] The recent and failed attack on the Amsterdam-Detroit flight, while PNR data of the terrorists were available for the US authorities allows us to question the reliability of a massive storage of such data. [38] Why store, if we are no longer able to treat this extensive flood of information effectively?

C. The Serialized Novel of SWIFT Agreement: At last, identical criticisms have been raised and continue to be expressed about the use made, in the name of war against terrorism, by the US of European personal data kept by the Belgian society, Society for Worldwide Interbank Financial Telecommunication (SWIFT). Having known in June 2006, via an American newspaper, that the administration of President Bush had obtained information possessed by SWIFT without informing European Union, on the occasion of a research programme relating to financial transactions linked to terrorism, European Parliament brought up the matter immediately. In a resolution of July 6, 2006, it expressed "its serious concern at the fact that a climate of deteriorating respect for privacy and data protection is being created;" [39] due to the American anti-terrorist politics. Art. 29 of the Data Protection Working Party, too, vigorously condemned the violation of fundamental rights in this affair. [40]

It became clear that the solution to put an end to such intrusions had to be made thanks to the conclusion of a bilateral agreement with the US, in order to define the conditions of communication of financial data. Guaranties were negotiated in spring 2007 by the Commission and the

Council of the European Union with the American Government. In particular, the creation of a storing centre on the European territory was a condition for suppressing the direct access of American authorities to European financial data collected by SWIFT. A European personality, recognized for its competences in the matter of personal data protection, had to be appointed in order to check the proper functioning of the supervision programme installed on the American territory. It all seemed well oiled and running smoothly...until new negotiations between the European Commission and the US established that the American authorities would finally have access to SWIFT's stored data on the server based in Swiss, initially planned for...avoiding such an access.

Since then, controversy has been rife against the temporary agreement relating to American access to data. Judge Bruguière, chosen to verify the functioning of the American supervision programme, was very reassuring in the report that he wrote. Unfortunately, to win over the adhesion of the most reserved, it would have been a good thing, if a great part of the report had not been declared confidential...on the request of the American authorities. [41]

Consequently, judging that it just being informed was not satisfactory, the European Parliament voted a new resolution on September 17, 2009, [42] in which it recalled some of the arguments developed about the PNR agreements previously mentioned.

Once again, European Parliament begins by reasserting its determination to fight against terrorism; however, once again, it insists on the fact that the struggle against terrorism must be inscribed in a framework worthy of European values and the rule of law, respectful of a "right balance between security measures and protection of civil liberties and fundamental rights", of private life and data protection, and "reaffirming that necessity and proportionality are key principles without which the fight against terrorism will never be effective". [43]

Things should have stayed at this level, but, after a new

and express request from the US, due to an internal modification of Swift, European ministers of internal affairs urgently signed on November 30, 2009 a temporary agreement on the renewal of American access to data. [44] That was just one day before the Lisbon Treaty, which places the European Parliament on an equal footing with the Council as a lawmaker in the area of data protection, [45] came into force.

This express signing provoked the anger of Euro-deputies, placed on the sidelines; anger expressed by their President, M. Buzek, in a letter dated January 15, 2010 addressed to José Luis Zapatero, President in Exercise of the Council of the European Union, in which he claims firmly that the question of the interim agreement must have been referred to the Parliament. The Parliament's discontent has been heard: the agreement came back before the Euro-deputies, who, on February 11, 2010, rejected the text with a large majority. [46] A new agreement has to be negotiated and the European Commission aims to have it signed before the end of June 2010. The agreement "will need to incorporate sufficient guarantees and safeguards," [47] applied without discrimination between the European and American citizens.

In view of these three cases, we can first regret that democratic control had been insufficient, while questions directly concerning European citizens' liberties were at stake. The reason was inherent to the pillar structure, and not to the apathy of Parliament, which never stopped expressing admonitions and recommendations. As matters relating to police and judiciary cooperation devolved to the third pillar, the Parliament was deprived of its co-decisional power. It was merely consulted.

The Lisbon Treaty assures a better democratic control and we can hope that Euro-deputies will claim with constant vigour and responsibility their interest in the protection of rights and liberties. In this view, it is necessary for the Parliament to have proper information and a complete knowledge of strategic documents in order to express a clear vote of the law. The foregoing seems a remark of common sense; but in the past, it was not always the case, as the Parliament expressed it, for example in its resolution of November 2009. [48]

In a second stage, without adopting an extremist discourse, we can legitimately be preoccupied, as is the European Parliament, by the fact that « international cooperation in the fight against terrorism has often served to diminish the level of protection of human rights and fundamental freedoms, notably the fundamental right to privacy, data protection and non-discrimination." [49] European Union, on the contrary, shall play a key role in the elaboration and promotion of international standards respectful of rights and freedoms in the matter of data protection; it would be regrettable, if only for the sake of its own discourse, that it supports requirements of third countries, even under the pressure of events.

The Council of the European Union, when it adopted the Stockholm Programme, took care to specify that it will be necessary for the next four years to "preserve the exercise of these freedoms and private life of citizens beyond national borders, specially via the personal data protection"; [50] we can just hope that Union authorities shall translate such declarations into reality. The European Commission, in its communication of June 10, 2009, asserts its determination to follow this way; but it is necessary to mitigate our optimism, because it specifies that what had been conducted with the US for data protection may be a reference for later agreements…

2. From Intrusion in Private Life to the Constitution of Terrorist Profiles

> For the confirmation of my identity,
> I depend entirely upon other people.
> —Hannah Arendt, The Origins of Totalitarianism, 476.

In response to terrorist threat, real "data warehouses" are established by interconnections of data bases, not only public, but also private.

A. The Wall of Private Life [51], from Now a Myth?: The utilisation for repressive purposes of data collected in private sector has witnessed a rapid expansion since the bomb attacks in Madrid and London. We can mention a directive of March 15, 2006 on electronic communications, [52] the collection of PNR data; this processing also concerns the financial sector: the Swift agreements have already been mentioned, but a directive of October 26, 2005 on the prevention of the use of the financial system for the purpose of money laundering and terrorist financing [53] also allows such collection.

Other worrying development, if it is not supervised with an extreme rigour: the collection and utilisation of biometric data. Resorting to such data interferes in the various juridical instruments of the EU with respect to the use of exchange of information. [54] The Prüm Decision of the Council [55] contains, from the point of view of protection of data, the most significant example of a system without centralised storage, since its foresees a massive exchange of biometric data among the authorities of member states. It expounds rules on the transmission of fingerprints and DNA data to other contracting parties, and their automatic comparison with pertinent data bases. [56]

In front of this growing recourse to biometric data [57], but worried too about the innovations to come, the European Court of Human Rights, in its judgment of December 4, 2008, S. and Marper against United-Kingdom, [58] recalled some important principles: in particular, this: "namely fingerprints, DNA profiles and cellular samples, constitute personal data within the meaning of the Data Protection Convention as they relate to identified or identifiable individuals." [59] The British Government had said that a DNA profile is nothing more than a sequence of numbers or a bar-code containing information of a purely objective and irrefutable character and that the identification of a subject only occurs in case of a match with another profile in the database.

An argument that did not convince the Court, which retorted that "profiles contain substantial amounts of unique personal data. While the information contained in the profiles may be considered objective and irrefutable in the sense submitted by the Government, their processing through automated means allows the authorities to go well beyond neutral identification." [60] As the Court has clarified, it is possible to arrive at conclusions about ethnic origin with the help of DNA profiles; that's why an increased protection is necessary with respect to Convention 108. But this judgment has gone too far, as the European court has reviewed its position about the question of fingerprints. Allowing a precise identification, these data are capable of affecting private life: also, their retention cannot be regarded as neutral or insignificant; on the contrary, it has important private-life concerns, needing serious sureties. [61]

For its part, the Court of Justice of the European Union, in a judgement of December 16, 2008, Heinz Huber vs. Deutschland, [62] recalled that processing of personal data is lawful only if it is necessary for the execution of a public interest mission or belonging to the exercise of public authority. Then, the Court declared that processing and storage of such data for statistical purposes are contrary to Community law.

These different ways of data collection, severely affecting private life, infringe upon domains that previously formed those of intimacy. [63] The processing of such personal data constitutes an interference with the right to respect for private life, under Article 8 of the ECHR and Article 7 of the Charter of Fundamental Rights of the European Union. [64] Such interference is only permitted under three cumulative conditions: the objective must be legitimate and meet objectives of general interest recognized by the Union or the need to protect the rights and freedoms of others according to Article 52 of the Charter of Fundamental Rights; the conditions under which the restriction is imposed must be provided for by law, in legislation or regulations which must be accessible to the individual concerned and protect that individual from arbitrariness through, inter alia, precision and foresee ability; [65] the means chosen must be proportionate to the end pursued so that they can be considered necessary and genuine.

There is an important case-law of the Strasbourg Court in this matter and we could think that the European Union as well as its member states are conscious of the importance of respecting rules relating to protection of private life of its citizens, even in the context of war against terrorism. Prevention, detection and investigation of terrorism are legitimate, core functions of the State.

Nevertheless, as the ECHR has established "contracting parties do not enjoy an unlimited power of appreciation. It is for the Court to rule on whether inter alia the States have gone beyond the "extent strictly required by the exigencies" of the crisis. The domestic margin of appreciation is thus accompanied by a European supervision". [66] We can regret with the European Parliament that "international cooperation in the fight against terrorism has often served to diminish the level of protection of human rights and fundamental freedoms, notably the fundamental right to privacy, data protection and non-discrimination, and take the view that the EU should act with greater resolve at international level to promote a genuine strategy based on full compliance with international standards and obligations in the area of human rights and the protection of personal data and privacy". [67]

However, the danger is not only present in these invasions of privacy, allowed in the name of the anti-terrorist struggle or against serious criminality.

B. The Worrying Faith in Profiling:

All are entitled to equal protection against any
discrimination in violation of this Declaration
and against any incitement to such discrimination.
—Universal Declaration of Human Rights, Article 7.

Over the past few years, resorting to profiling has witnessed an increasing development. [68] In this matter, practices of surveillance are not limited to watchfulness regarding some financial operations, but are extended to places and groups defined as presenting a risk. That opens the possibility of discrimination against some profiles of clients, like it was the case in 2004, when bank accounts of two British associations of help for Palestinian people were closed in an authoritarian manner and without any explanation. [69] In these conditions, the question of responsibility of private actors is raised, but also that of their competence to found some of their decisions, which may have heavy consequences, on the basis of more or less pertinent non probationary clues.

But how to reproach them for turning to such profiles based on personal data, when European authorities themselves utilize in broad day light these profiles? In this respect, we must recall the Council Recommendation of November 28, 2002 on terrorist profiles. According to this text, such updated profiles are a central element of the enhanced struggle against terrorism because they could reveal possible terrorist threats quite early. In practical terms, it means the reunion of physical, psychological or behavioural parameters that have been identified as being characteristics of people involved in terrorist activities.

In appendix A, it has to do, for example with: nationality, travel papers, means of transport, age, sex, distinguishing features, education, civil status...Nevertheless, the recommendation adds that such profiles must respect fundamental rights and freedoms. That is the reason why this profiling, based on the "collection of non-personal data", is often presented as technically acceptable one. Though, it can be easily understood, such practices of profiling lead inevitably to a mechanism of suspicion by categories, to strengthen social, economic and cultural divisions. The young Muslin man, Salafist, often travelling alone, will alert all intelligence services. As the Council of Europe Commissioner for Human Rights observed, "targeting people because they correspond to a stereotypic amounts to really making ethnic, racial and religious profiling". [70] It affects large numbers of people directly, and stigmatizes entire communities. [71]

The game is worth the candle, we could say, if such practices guarantee the security of citizens. But, once again, we must listen to the Commissioner for Human Rights who says that "technologies which enable "profiling" and "data mining", may seem to work up to a point, but inevitably lead to actions against large numbers of innocent people, on a scale that is both unacceptable in a democratic society and renders the "trawl" useless". [72]

The recent Omar Farouk Abdulmutallab affair seems confirm the Commissioner's rather severe words: "It is important to stress the inevitability in this: this is not something that can be fixed by better design. Attempts to identify very rare incidents or targets from a very large data set are mathematically certain to result in either an unacceptably high numbers of "false positives" (identifying innocent people as suspects) or an unacceptably low number of "false negatives" (not identifying real criminals or terrorists). As a very recent, authoritative study by the US National Research Council (the US National Academies) concluded: Automated identification of terrorists through data mining (or any other known methodology) is neither feasible as an objective nor desirable as a goal of technology development efforts."

We might think that the Commissioner for Human Rights is expressing here an isolated opinion. It seems to be far from the case. In its recommendation on the framework decision of the Council on the use of PNR for law enforcement purposes, the European Union Agency for Fundamental Rights is equally very critical about the use of profiling in the context of PNR.

The European Parliament joined itself with the Agency and solemnly recalled "that EU data protection rules place restrictions on the use of profiling on the basis of personal data (Article 8 of the Charter of Fundamental Rights and the

ECHR); concurs, therefore, with the FRA's opinion [73] that profiling based on PNR data should only be intelligence-led, based on individual cases and factual parameters" and asked for "that profiling based on PNR data should only be intelligence-led, based on individual cases and factual parameters". [74]

In 2003, the Committee on the Elimination of Racial Discrimination of the United Nations recommended that States and international organizations "ensure that measures taken in the struggle against terrorism do not discriminate in purpose or effect on grounds of race, colour, descent or national or ethnic origin" [75] and insisted on the fact that "the prohibition against racial discrimination is a peremptory norm". [76] The European Code of Police Ethics of the Council of Europe expressly recommends that "the police shall carry out their tasks in a fair manner, in particular, guided by the principles of impartiality and non-discrimination. [77]

These techniques of profiling have been denounced as having an anti-democratic character by the Commissioner for Human Rights; not only anti-democratic, but also lacking humanity, we might like to add. Computers are no longer limited to surveillance, but they make authorities focus on particular targets: this is called dataveillance; targets that correspond to stereotypes defined *a priori*, leading to a sort of reification of people, without taking into account one element which, however, constitutes all human richness: the personality. That is why it seems to us not totally inappropriate, in the face of this evolution of security tools, to recall Henry Troyat who expressed this idea in his book *Le bruit solitaire du coeur*: "What's important, it's not what is inscribed on identity papers of a person but in his heart".

Notes

1. With strong restrictions for Poland, United-Kingdom and Czech Republic which opted out. Lisbon Treaty, Article 6: "The Union recognizes the rights, freedoms and principles set out in the Charter of Fundamental Rights of the European Union of

December 7, 2000, as adapted at Strasbourg, on December 12, 2007, which shall have the same legal value as the Treaties.

"The provisions of the Charter shall not extend in any way the competences of the Union as defined in the Treaties. The rights, freedoms and principles in the Charter shall be interpreted in accordance with the general provisions in Title VII of the Charter governing its interpretation and application and with due regard to the explanations referred to in the Charter, that set out the sources of those provisions.".

Formally adopted in Nice in December 2000 by the Presidents of the European Parliament, the Council and the Commission, the Charter constitutes a political undertaking that has no binding legal effect. However, in the Lisbon Treaty, the Charter is given binding effect by the insertion of a phrase conferring on it the same legal value as the Treaties. To this end, the Charter was proclaimed a second time in December 2007.

2. The Charter applies to the European institutions, subject to the principle of subsidiarity, and may under no circumstances extend the powers and tasks conferred on them by the Treaties. The principles of the Charter also apply to the Member States when they are implementing Community law. The Court of Justice had already confirmed the duty of Member States to respect fundamental rights: for example, the judgment C-292/97 Karlsson and Others, April 13, 2000: "*In addition, it should be remembered that the requirements flowing from the protection of fundamental rights in the Community legal order are also binding on Member States when they implement Community rules. Consequently, Member States must, as far as possible, apply those rules in accordance with those requirements (Case C-2/92 Bostock [1994] ECR I-955, paragraph 16). Those fundamental rights include the general principle of equality and the obligation not to discriminate, and the Swedish Court asks whether the Swedish legislation at issue is compatible therewith.*"

3. Advocates-General Tizzano, Léger and Mischo have stated that "*the Charter has undeniably placed the rights which form its subject-matter at the highest level of values common to the Member States.*" For the first time, in its ruling of June 27, 2006 concerning the Directive on family reunification (Case C-540/03), the Court of Justice made explicit reference to the

Charter and stressed its importance. Ex: C-540/03, Parliament v. Council, June 27, 2006: "38. *The Charter was solemnly proclaimed by the Parliament, the Council and the Commission in Nice on December 7, 2000. While the Charter is not a legally binding instrument, the Community legislature did, however, acknowledge its importance by stating, in the second recital in the preamble to the Directive, that the Directive observes the principles recognized not only by Article 8 of the ECHR but also in the Charter. Furthermore, the principal aim of the Charter, as is apparent from its preamble, is to reaffirm 'rights as they result, in particular, from the constitutional traditions and international obligations common to the Member States, the Treaty on European Union, the Community Treaties, the [ECHR], the Social Charter adopted by the Community and by the Council of Europe and the case-law of the Court... and of the European Court of Human Rights'.*

4. Maastricht Treaty made the respect of the principles of the European Convention for the Protection of Human Rights and Fundamental Freedoms official; however, the European Court of Justice had already consecrated them as general community principles. The Lisbon Treaty, in its Article 6 expressly specifies that fundamental rights, as guaranteed by the European Convention, and as they stem from "*the constitutional traditions common to the Member States*" shall "*constitute general principles of the Union's law*". And the Charter of Fundamental Rights states that "*in so far as this Charter contains rights which correspond to rights guaranteed by the Convention for the Protection of Human Rights and Fundamental Freedoms, the meaning and scope of those rights shall be the same as those laid down by the said Convention. This provision shall not prevent Union law providing more extensive protection*".
5. Also, we can read: "*1. At the core of the Union's values: Fundamental rights and citizenship. Creating a fully-fledged policy. Fundamental rights are placed at the heart of the European project, as proven by the integration of the Charter of Fundamental Rights in the Constitution. Over the coming five years, the protection of personal data and the fight against discrimination in all its forms will be further promoted.*"
6. La Hague Program, point 2: "*2. A Union against terrorism: The fight against terrorism. Working toward a global response. The*

European Union can contribute decisively to the defeat of terrorism, by working together towards a global strategy to be established on the basis of its founding values: democracy, fundamental rights and the rule of law." S. Manacorda, "Les conceptions de l'Union européenne en matière de terrorisme" in *Terrorismes, Histoire et Droit,* H. Laurens et M. Delmas-Marty eds., Paris: CNRS Ed., 2010, pp.189-218; S. Peers, « EU responses to Terrorism » in *International and Comparative Law Quarterly*, 2003, 227s; J. Monar, "The EU's Approach post-September 11: Global Terrorism as a Multidimensional Law Enforcement Challenge" in *Cambridge Review of International Affairs*, Vol. 20, No. 2, June 2007, 267s.

7. Council Decision 2007/124/EC of February 12, 2007.
8. Council of the European Union, Presidency Conclusions on the Brussels European Council, December 10-11, 2009, title III, point 26: http://www.europa-eu-un.org/Articles/fr/Article_9310_fr.htm. Retrieved on July 21, 2010.
9. Automated individual decision of 13th July 2009 about the Commission's communication.
10. This is how A. Ceyhan, elaborated on it: "Contrary to a widely prevalent idea, terrorism has not triggered the technologization of security...Introduction of high technology in the field of security began well before 11th September, i.e., in the 1980s along with the fight against drugs and illegal immigration. The September 11 attacks only reinforced the globalization of this process. See A. Ceyhan, Technologie et sécurité: une gouvernance libérale dans un contexte d'incertitudes in *Cultures & Conflicts*, no. 64, Winter 2006, pp.11-32, 12. Ph. Guillot «Espace transatlantique..., *Sécurité et libertés à l'épreuve de la lutte contre le terrorisme,* Journée d'études Université de Rouen 25th February 2008 ; A. Weyermbergh, L'impact du 11 septembre sur l'équilibre sécurité/liberté dans l'espace pénal européen in *Lutte contre le terrorisme et droits fondamentaux,* Brussels: Bruylant 2002, pp.153 sq; R. Bellanova and P. De Hert, Protection des données personnelles et mesures de sécurité : vers une perspective transatlantique in *Cultures & Conflicts*, No. 74, Summer 2009, pp.63-80; **S.** Preuss-Laussinotte, « L'élargissement problématique de l'accès aux bases de données européennes en matière de sécurité ? in

Cultures & Conflicts, no. 74, Summer 2009, 81-90; V. Mitsilegas, Contrôle des étrangers, des passagers, des citoyens : surveillance et antiterrorisme, *Cultures & Conflicts*, no. 60, Winter 2005, 185-197 ; D.R. Rasmussen, "Is International Travel Per Se Suspicion of Terrorism ? The Dispute between the United States and European Union Over Passenger Name Record Data Transfers" in *Wisconsin International Law Journal* 26, no. 2, pp. 551-590.

11. Commission Decision: March 14, 2004: OJ L 235/11, 6.7.2004. The Agreement was signed on May 28, 2004. PNR Data are information relating to air passengers which are collected at the moment of commercial reservation. They furnish indications about the itinerary, flights concerned, personal contacts (home phone number, professional phone number etc.), prices allowed, credit card number, and special requests on board like specific dietary requests (vegetarian, Asiatic, casher...) or services relating to the health of the passenger.
12. Such a law risked coming into conflict with the European Union or national legislations on data protection. Then, the Commission engaged negotiations. The United States suspended the application of their law till March 2003 in order to try to reconcile American requirements with European legislation.
13. A. Ceyhan, Sécurité, frontières et surveillance aux Etats-Unis après le 11 septembre 2001 in *Cultures & Conflicts*, no. 53, Spring 2004, pp.113-145.
14. Before the conclusion of the agreement, the European Parliament had adopted resolutions in order to advise the Commission not to forget respect of European rules: resolution P5_TA(2003)0097 and P5_TA(2003)0429. Article 29 of Data Protection Working Party had expressed also an opinion: 4/2003 on the adequacy of the level of protection guaranteed by the United States for transfer of PNR: doc. 11070/03, WP 78. After the conclusion of the agreement, the Parliament has adopted another resolution in order to ask the Commission to annul its decision certifying that protection guaranteed by the US was adequate: P5_TA-PROV (2004)0245.
15. The Parliament invoked procedural irregularity as well as violation of rules of protection of personal data and proportionality principle.
16. CJCE, *European Parliament/ European Council and*

Commission, Joint affairs, 30th March 2006. C-317/04 and C-318/04.

17. See D. Lyon, Le 11 septembre, la « guerre au terrorisme et la surveillance généralisée » in *Au nom du 11 septembre...: les démocraties à l'épreuve de l'antiterrorisme,* Didier Bigo, Laurent Bonelli et Thomas Deltombe eds., Paris: La Découverte, 2008, 124s.
18. Decision 2006/729/PESC/JAI of the Council of the European Union dated October 16, 2006 relative to the conclusion of an agreement between the European Union and the United States on the processing and transfer of PNR data. OJ L 298, 27.10.2006. Concluded on October 19, 2006, it expired on July 31, 2007, except prolongation decided by written consent of the parties.
19. OJ L 204/18, 4.8.2007.
20. OJ L 204/25, 4.8.2007.
21. P6_TA (2006)0370.
22. Opinion 5/2007 on the follow-up agreement between the European Union and the United States of America on the processing and transfer of passenger name record (PNR) data by air carriers to the United States Department of Homeland Security concluded in July 2007, WP 138 adopted on August 17, 2007: "*The Working Party is not convinced the agreement succeeds in striking this right balance.*" (2)
23. OJ L 204/21, 4.8.2007. The G29, in its opinion, takes care of that letter: "*This opinion will, therefore, also thoroughly compare the safeguards of the DHS letter with the undertakings of 2004 and draw conclusions as to their privacy standard*".
24. OJ L 204/21, 4.8.2007: "*PNR may be used where necessary for the protection of the vital interests of the data subject or other persons, or in any criminal judicial proceedings, or as otherwise required by law. DHS will advise the EU regarding the passage of any U.S. legislation which materially affects the statements made in this letter*".
25. OJ L 204/21, 4.8.2007: "*EU PNR data is only exchanged with other government authorities in third countries after consideration of the recipient's intended use(s) and ability to protect the information. Apart from emergency circumstances, any such exchange of data occurs pursuant to express understandings between the parties that incorporate data*

privacy protections comparable to those applied to EU PNR by DHS, as described in the second paragraph of this Article".

26. OJ L 204/22, 4.8.2007: "*To the extent that sensitive EU PNR data (i.e. personal data revealing racial or ethnic origin, political opinions, religious or philosophical beliefs, trade union membership, and data concerning the health or sex life of the individual), as specified by the PNR codes and terms which DHS has identified in consultation with the European Commission, are included in the above types of EU PNR data, DHS employs an automated system which filters those sensitive PNR codes and terms and does not use this information. Unless the data is accessed for an exceptional case, as described in the next paragraph, DHS promptly deletes the sensitive EU PNR data. If necessary, in an exceptional case where the life of a data subject or of others could be imperiled or seriously impaired, DHS officials may require and use information in EU PNR other than those listed above, including sensitive data. In that event, DHS will maintain a log of access to any sensitive data in EU PNR and will delete the data within 30 days once the purpose for which it has been accessed is accomplished and its retention is not required by law. DHS will provide notice normally within forty eight hours to the European Commission (DG JLS) that such data, including sensitive data, has been accessed.*"
27. See OJ L 204/23, 4.8.2007; title IV, *Access and Redress.*
28. OJ L 204/24, 4.8.2007: "*DHS and the EU will periodically review the implementation of the agreement, this letter, U.S. and EU PNR policies and practices and any instances in which sensitive data was accessed, for the purpose of contributing to the effective operation and privacy protection of our practices for processing PNR*".
29. OJ L 204/24, 4.8.2007: "*In the review, the EU will be represented by the Commissioner for Justice, Freedom and Security, and DHS will be represented by the Secretary of Homeland Security, or by such mutually acceptable official as each may agree to designate*".
30. OJ L 204/23, 4.8.2007: "*DHS retains EU PNR data in an active analytical database for seven years, after which time the data will be moved to dormant, non-operational status. Data in dormant status will be retained for eight years and may be accessed only with approval of a senior DHS official designated*

by the Secretary of Homeland Security and only in response to an identifiable case, threat, or risk. We expect that EU PNR data shall be deleted at the end of this period; questions of whether and when to destroy PNR data collected in accordance with this letter will be addressed by DHS and the EU as part of future discussions. Data that is related to a specific case or investigation may be retained in an active database until the case or investigation is archived".

31. P6_TA (2008)0561.
32. The rules of protection of personal data that European institutions and member states have to respect are recorded in Article 8 of the ECHR, Articles 7 and 52 of the Charter of Fundamental Rights of the European Union, Article 286 of TUE and Article 5 of the Convention no. 108 of the Council of Europe for the Protection of Individuals with regard to Automatic Processing of Personal Data; at level of secondary law, the European Parliament and Council Directive 95/46/EC of October 24, 1995 on the protection of individuals with regard to the processing of personal data and on the free movement of such data; the framework decision of the Council 2008/977/JAI of November 27, 2008 entitled "Fight against terrorism: processing and protection of personal data in the framework of police and judicial cooperation in criminal matters".
33. Point 16 of the Parliament's resolution.
34. Point 16 of the resolution: "*...in this connection, deplores the fact that the purpose of this envisaged police cooperation measure is not limited to issues such as combating terrorism and organized crime*".
35. Point 17 of the resolution: "*...the proposal gives law enforcement authorities access to all data without a warrant; points out that the Commission has not demonstrated the need for new law enforcement powers, or that this goal cannot be achieved with less far- reaching measures*".
36. Point 23 of the resolution.
37. Point 18 of the resolution: "*...any information so far provided by the US is anecdotal and the US has never conclusively proven that the massive and systematic use of PNR data is necessary in the fight against terrorism and serious crime*".
38. S. Preuss-Laussinotte, Bases de données personnelles et politiques de sécurité : une protection illusoire ? in *Cultures &*

Conflicts, no. 64, Winter 2006, pp. 77-95.

39. P6_TA (2006)0317. http://www.europarl.europa.eu/document/activities/cont/201004/20100427ATT73594/20100427ATT73594EN.pdf retrieved on July 21, 2010.
40. Opinion 10/2006 on the processing of personal data by the Society for Worldwide Interbank Financial Telecommunication (SWIFT), WP128, November 22, 2006. In its conclusion, it recalls that "*any measures taken in the fight against crime and terrorism should not and must not reduce standards of protection of fundamental rights which characterize democratic societies. A key element of the fight against terrorism involves ensuring the preservation of the fundamental rights which are the basis of democratic societies and the very values that those advocating the use of violence seek to destroy*".
41. For example, M. Alex Türk, President of the Commission nationale de l'informatique et des libertés (CNIL–National Commission on Computing and Liberty) expressed his surprise to the French National Assembly when he was heard by the Commission of European Affairs on September 29, 2009: "*We thought at the end that an on-site check was necessary to verify, on behalf of the European Union, that the checks and investigations carried out by American authorities of fight against terrorism are strictly limited to the needs of this fight. Our demand with respect to this point was satisfied and the European Union let us know that it would designate « an eminent personality » having competence in the matter of protection of personal data. I was personally very satisfied with what I then considered to be the victory of the European Commissions on Computing and Liberty, but I had been too optimistic...Heard after his return before the Article 29 group gathering 29 National Commissions on Computing and Liberty, he declared that everything was fine, that the American authorities were very efficient in their fight against terrorism and that nothing went against the system for it not to be maintained as it was. He, declared, however, that he could not submit his report because the American authorities had decided to consider it confidential. For the first time and to the great surprise of European National Commissions on Computing and Liberty, a control rendered confidential the report of a*

controlling authority! Then on, we had no guarantee from the European controlling authority that all would go in accordance with the agreement signed between the EU and the US. However, it is on the basis of this unknown report of Mr. Brugière that the European Commission considered that there was no longer any reason to forbid the US from having access to data on intra-European transactions from this new centre." For the full text of the hearing: http://www.assemblee-nationale.fr/13/pdf/europe/c-rendus/c0117.pdf. Retrieved on July 21, 2010.

42. European Parliament resolution of September 17, 2009 on the envisaged international agreement to make available to the US Treasury Department financial payment messaging data to prevent and combat terrorism and terrorist financing: P7_TA(2009)0016.
43. http://www.europarl.europa.eu/sides/getDoc.do?type=MOTION &reference=B7-2010-0244&language=EN retrieved on July 21, 2010.
44. OJ L 8/11, 13.01.2010: Agreement between the European Union and the United States of America on the processing and transfer of Financial Messaging Data from the European Union to the United States for purposes of the Terrorist Finance Tracking Program.
45. Art. 9A TEU.
46. The resolution rejecting the agreement was passed by 378 votes to 196, with 31 abstentions. The link to read the response of SWIFT: http://www.swift.com/about_swift/press_room/swift_news_archive/2010/data_privacy/SWIFT_statement_EU_Parliament_Rejection.page?lang=en. Retrieved on July 21, 2010.
47. Specification given by Diego López Garrido, Spanish Presidency representative.
48. P7_TA (2009)0016:"*13. Requests the Commission and the Presidency to ensure that the European Parliament and all national parliaments will be given full access to the negotiation documents and directives*". Euro-deputies, during the debate of September 16, 2009, have pointed this lack of information: for example, Jan Philipp Albrecht, on behalf of the Verts/ALE Group: "*In fact, however, fundamental rights are being eroded and proper public debate on them frustrated. Every effort is*

being made to exclude parliaments and hold back information. This sort of untransparent approach is unacceptable for a democratic Europe."; Sophia in 't Veld, on behalf of the ALDE Group "*The fight against terror has practically become a kind of runaway train, with the Council showing utter contempt for European citizens and parliamentary democracy*". To read the whole debate,
http://www.europarl.europa.eu/sides/getDoc.do?pubRef=-//EP//TEXT+CRE+20090916+ITEM-005+DOC+XML+V0//EN. Retrieved on July 21, 2010.

49. P6_TA (2009)0019, resolution of January 14, 2009 on the situation of fundamental rights in the European Union 2004-2008, point 23.
50. Council of the European Union, Presidency Conclusions on the Brussels European Council, December 10-11, 2009, title III, point 27.
51. The expression "Wall of Private Life", in French "mur de la vie privée" was first used by the French MP Royer-Collard, during the discussion of the Law on the Press of 1819.
52. Directive 2006/24/EC of the European Parliament and of the Council of March 15, 2006 on the retention of data generated or processed in connection with the provision of publicly available electronic communications services or of public communications networks and amending Directive 2002/58/EC of July 12, 2002 concerning the processing of personal data and the protection of privacy in the electronic communications sector (Directive on privacy and electronic communications).
53. Directive 2005/60/EC.
54. Europol: see the Council decision of April 6, 2009 (2009/371/JHA), OJ L 121/37, 15.5.2009. SIS II : see the Council decision N° 2007/533/JHA of June 12, 2007 on the establishment, operation and use of the second generation Schengen Information System (SIS II), OJ L 205/63, 7.8.2007 (PJCCM); VIS : Visa Information System (VIS) : regulation (EC) no. 767/2008 of the European Parliament and of the Council of July 9, 2008 concerning the Visa Information System (VIS) and the exchange of data between Member States on short-stay visas (VIS Regulation) , OJ L L218/60, 13.08.2008.
55. Council decision 2008/615/JHA of June 23, 2008 on the stepping up of cross-border cooperation, particularly in

combating terrorism and cross-border crime, OJ, L 210/1, 6.08.2008 (*Acts adopted under the EU Treaty).*

56. See Chapter 2 online access and follow-up requests, section 1 DNA profiles or section 2 on Dactyloscopic data.
57. Ph. Bonditti, Biométrie et maîtrise des flux: vers une géo-technopolis du vivant-en-mobilité *?* in *Cultures & Conflicts*, N°58, Summer 2005, 131-154 ; A. Ceyhan, Enjeux d'identification et de surveillance à l'heure de la biométrie in *Cultures & Conflicts*, no. 64, Winter 2006, pp.33-47.
58. S. and Marper v. The United Kingdom, 4.12.2008, 30562/04 and 30566/04.
59. S. and Marper v. The United Kingdom, 4.12.2008, §63.
60. S. and Marper v. The United Kingdom, 4.12.2008, §75.
61. S. and Marper v. The United Kingdom, 4.12.2008: §*78. It is common ground that fingerprints do not contain as much information as either cellular samples or DNA profiles. The issue of alleged interference with the right to respect for private life caused by their retention by the authorities has already been considered by the Convention organs.79. In McVeigh, the Commission first examined the issue of the taking and retention of fingerprints as part of a series of investigative measures. It accepted that at least some of the measures disclosed an interference with the applicants' private life, while leaving open the question of whether the retention of fingerprints alone would amount to such interference (McVeigh, O'Neill and Evans (no. 8022/77, 8025/77 and 8027/77, Report of the Commission of March 18, 1981, DR 25, p.15, § 224).*
    Having regard to these findings and the questions raised in the present case, the Court considers it appropriate to review this issue. It notes at the outset that the applicants' fingerprint records constitute their personal data (see paragraph 68 above) which contain certain external identification features much in the same way as, for example, personal photographs or voice samples".
62. Heinz Huber v. Deutschland, 16.12.2008, C-524/06.
63. Amann v. Switzerland, 16.02.2000, (Application no. 27798/95) : §65: *"...the storing of data relating to the "private life" of an individual falls within the application of Article 8 § 1 (see the Leander v. Sweden judgment of 26 March 1987, Series A no. 116, p. 22, § 48). It points out in this connection that the term*

"private life" must not be interpreted restrictively. In particular, respect for private life comprises the right to establish and develop relationships with other human beings; furthermore, there is no reason of principle to justify excluding activities of a professional or business nature from the notion of "private life" (see the Niemietz v. Germany judgment of 16 December 1992, Series A no. 251-B, pp. 33-34, § 29)".

64. Amann v. Switzerland, 16.02.2000, (Application no. 27798/95): §69: "*The Court reiterates that the storing by a public authority of information relating to an individual's private life amounts to an interference within the meaning of Article 8. The subsequent use of the stored information has no bearing on that finding (see, mutatis mutandis, the Leander judgment cited above, p. 22, § 48, and the Kopp judgment cited above, p. 540, § 53)."; § 71: "Such interference breaches Article 8 unless it is "in accordance with the law", pursues one or more of the legitimate aims referred to in paragraph 2 and, in addition, is "necessary in a democratic society" to achieve those aims*". Leander v. Sweden, 26.03.1987, (Application no. 9248/81) : Kopp v. Switzerland, 25.03.1998, (13/1997/797/1000).
65. Amann v. Switzerland, 16.02.2000, §50: "*The Court draws attention to its established case-law, according to which the expression "in accordance with the law" not only requires that the impugned measure should have some basis in domestic law, but also refers to the quality of the law in question, requiring that it should be accessible to the person concerned and foreseeable as to its effects (see the Kopp judgment cited above, p. 540, § 55)*".
66. Brannigan and McBride vs. The United Kingdom, 25.03.1993 (Application no. 14553/89; 14554/89), §43.
67. P6_TA (2009)0019: European Parliament resolution of January 14, 2009 on the situation of fundamental rights in the European Union 2004-2008, §29.
68. *A. Amicelle, Etat des lieux de la lutte contre le financement du terrorisme : entre critiques et recommendations,* Cultures & Conflicts, *no. 71, Autumn 2008, 169-176 ; T.J. Biersteker, S.E. Eckert (eds.),* Countering the Financing of Terrorism, *New York: Routledge, 2007, p.344 ; I. Warde,* Propagande impériale et guerre financière contre le terrorisme, *Marseille / Paris, Agone / Le Monde diplomatique, 2007, p.320; M. Pieth, «Criminalizing*

the Financing of Terrorism» in Journal of International Criminal Justice, *2006, 1074s.*

69. Friends of Al-Aqsa et the Palestine solidarity Campaign have been closed without being registered on any list of suspects : Faisal AL-YAFAI, "Palestinian aid groups' accounts closed" in *The Guardian*, January 3, 2005.
70. CommDH/IssuePaper(2008)3, December 4, 2008, Th. Hammarberg, the Commissioner for Human Rights, Protecting the right to privacy in the fight against terrorism. https://wcd.coe.int/ViewDoc.jsp?id=1469161&Site=COE. Retrieved on July 21, 2010.
71. D. Harris, *Profiles in Injustice; Why Racial Profiling Cannot Work*, New York: The New Press, 2002, p. 16-23 ; Center for Human Rights and Global Justice, New York University School of Law, *Irreversible Consequences: Racial Profiling and Lethal Force in the "War on Terror"*, New York, May 2006. This briefing paper could be retrieved at http://www.chrgj.org/docs/CHRGJ percent20Irreversible percent20Consequences.pdf as of July 21, 2010.
72. CommDH/IssuePaper (2008)3, 4 December 2008, CommDH/IssuePaper(2008)3, 4 December 2008.
73. The Presidency of the European Union requested on September 3, 2008 an opinion of France within its mandate on the proposed Council Framework Decision on the use of Passenger Name Record (PNR) data for law enforcement purposes: http://www.libertysecurity.org/IMG/pdf_FRA_opinion_PNR_en.pdf , retrieved on July 21, 2010.
74. P6_TA (2008)0561, European Parliament resolution of November 20, 2008 on the proposal for a Council framework decision on the use of Passenger Name Record (PNR) for law enforcement purposes, § 22 and23.
75. "Statement on Racial Discrimination and Measures to Combat Terrorism" (2003), § 5. The CERD is a body of independent experts that monitors implementation of the Convention on the Elimination of All Forms of Racial Discrimination by its State Parties of the United Nations.
76. CERD, General Recommendation no. 30 (Non-Citizens), § 6.
77. Recommendation (2001)10, September 19, 2001, of the Committee of Ministers to member states on the European Code of Police Ethics, Appendix, Art. 40.

4

Rights of Multiculturalism, Muslims and Europe

S.A.M. Pasha

The contemporary face of Western Liberalism, in its interplay with multiculturalism, has many a dilemma to grapple with, and eventually to overcome: in its classical form, liberalism's adhesion to individual-in-society as a criterion in extending rights and liberties to him has not transcended the individual to also take into account vortex, group or collectivity for purposes of rights and liberties. The idea of citizenship connoting legally enforceable claims and concomitant responsibilities remained stationary in its application to individual citizen as an autonomous entity. To delimit the recipients of rights, the discourse that was addressed only to the atomized individual, bereft of his locale in collectivity, is to run counter to holism and mutualism that govern human life. The Western ways of looking at society and the individual persons as its components has been at variance with how the non-West perceives it. There exists a dissonance between the two—the West and the non-West, in particular, the Islamic/Muslim constituent—in so far as their respective understanding of society is concerned. Muslim communities, hailing from non-liberal political regimes, and having already settled down in Western states on a permanent footing, need to inculcate and develop an attitude of conscientization towards Western values, and to the extent of the latter's discrepancy with those of their own, dialogue.

Theoretical debates concerning the notion of multiculturalism, citizenship and the multicultural policy formulations as evidenced by respective state practices (as a component part of statecraft function) pursued by West European states, need to be viewed from an integrationist perspective. The existing conspectus between orthodoxy germane to multiculturalism needs to be revisited. Reformulating the tenets of liberalism in the light of the requirements of contemporary verities is occasioned, *inter alia,* by transborder movement of peoples, especially the one whose religious identity is informed by Islam. The post-War reconstruction and resuscitation of West European economies necessitated the importation of third world labour force from the countries far and near of Afro-Asian continents as well as other parts of Europe. The size of the Turkish segment of this labour force continues to be, comparatively speaking, greater than the other labour manpower.

Originally, their stay in the receiving/host countries was supposed to be temporary; as developments unfolded, they became permanent residents of the host countries, as this has been a defining feature of the Turkish guest workers (*Gestarbeiter)* in the then Federal Republic of Germany (West Germany). Later, as time passed, a few descendents of the first Turkish arrivals acquired German citizenship; a considerable number of Turks obtained permanent resident status. Immigration and citizenship laws in Germany are tougher in relation to its other European counterparts; laws of citizenship are, in particular, still more stringent, as they are governed by ties of blood, called as laws of consanguinity. The unification of two Germanys, made possible with the demise of Cold War, had ironically made worse the state of Turks living permanently on the soil of the unified entity. The successful story of post-War West German economic fortune was, apart from other catalytic agents, made feasible by the lower-paid wage-earning manual tasks performed by the Turkish workforce. However, unlike Great Britain, Holland, and France, there is no colonial past informing the relations between the Turkish community and Germany.

The dilemma and crisis of multiculturalism has dovetailed

into the so-called war on terror, adding further complications to the already complex phenomenon. The politics of the war on terror whose targets, more often than not, happen to be the members of a specific religion, runs counter to the universally acclaimed and accepted norms of rule of law, due process of law, fair play and other assorted values. The birthplace of major political ideologies and values, as the world has come to know about them, has been the soil of Europe, wherein they have been implanted. Their transplantation beyond their locale and their subsequent extension to almost all nooks and corners of the world has been facilitated historically by colonialism, and contemporaneously by globalization. Akin to transplanted human organ creating complications in the human body, transplanted ideologies in the Muslim world, have not led to the desired benign outcome. The upshot of the aforesaid is that Western experiences—be they ideological, political, social, economic and others—are not tantamount to universal experiences. Problems will be galore when the two are conflated.

Islam, and derivatively Muslims, its followers and adherents, are not new to Europe: the latter, in its historic endeavour to define itself, has sought to do so by juxtaposing itself against the "other", the "Muslim Other". The latter has successfully served the purpose of enabling the West to define itself, albeit negatively. This is a debt which the West owes to the "Orient", that too a historic one, in its attempt at self-description. However, this self-description is not devoid of problems, as the current debate about the nature of the European Union (EU) constitution testifies: whether the EU is a union of values or a community characterized by Christianity or Christian heritage. The fate of the Republican Turkey as a potential, future member of EU is contingent upon the collective voice of the EU member states on these twin issues, besides many others.

Issues of multiculturalism are perceived as emanating from the inability of Muslim communities living in Europe to successfully integrate themselves into the host societies. This unilinear way of looking at issues does not make sense, because multicultural issues are also equally issues of power relations in society. The asymmetric nature of the latter is quite obvious when one takes the Muslim predicament into cognizance.

Given the dark clouds enveloping the ties between the West and the Muslim world, is incumbent upon us to remind ourselves of the stellar contribution made by Muslims to world civilization in the manifold realms of human life. In an attempt to remove cobwebs of misconceptions, prejudices, hatred, and ill will that seem to underline the West-Muslim interaction in the context of the continuing war on terror (even though the latter phraseology is kept on hold by the Obama Administration), it is perhaps worth while to recall the Muslim contribution to world civilization. In an editorial prologue to a book [1], the following, in a capsule form, is highlighted:

Arab Muslims transmitted the zero from India to the world; Leonard Da Vinci studied the Arabic numeral system and introduced it to Europe; algorithm (algorism) was invented by Al-Khawarizmi in the ninth century and Abu al-Wafa developed trigonometry. Ibn al–Haytham developed optics, proving that rays pass from object into the eye, and wrote about optical illusions, binocular vision, mirages, rainbows, and halos. Jabbir Ibn Hayyan prepared sulfuric acid and classified chemicals in the eight century. Paper- manufacturing technology was brought by Muslims in the ninth century and spread to the Middle East and Europe, leading to an expansion in the publication of books. The Muslim scholar Ibn Khaldun is credited with founding the discipline of sociology. Al- Idrisi, who lived in Sicily, compiled a book on medieval history and geography of Europe, producing seventy maps of the world. Al- Bayruni and Ibn Batutah were famous travellers and historians, whose scholarly works are still regarded as pioneering contributions to history and geography. [2]

Muslim scientists and scholars introduced scientific

knowledge to Europe at a time when Europe was enveloped in what is known as "Dark Ages." Muslim scholars were the leading lights of scientific development between 700 and 1500 AD, and exercised a profound influence upon the history of mankind. Their scientific legacy laid the foundations for the progress of science and technology in Europe in the second millennium. Indeed these scholars played a vital role in the evolution of human civilization and served as the true harbingers of Europe's Renaissance. Their works were used as textbooks in many European universities until 1600 AD. The works of Muslim scholars in Arabic were translated into Latin and other European languages and students flocked from all over Europe to study at the universities of Baghdad, Spain, Syria, Cairo and Iran, which became the major teaching centers of the world. One might even say that the Muslim world encompassing these centers, acted as the knowledge superpower, to borrow the political language of the globalization- informed present century. The writings of famous physicians, like al-Razi and Ibn Sina's encyclopaedic work on medicine, were taught in European universities until the sixteenth century. [3]

Robert Briffault writes: What we call science arose as a result of new methods of experiments, observation and measurement which were introduced into Europe by Arabs. Modern science is the most momentous contribution of the Islamic civilization, which was made accessible to all regardless of gender, race, creed, or national origin. [4] Deliberate distortion of history has covered up contributions of Islam and Muslims to human civilization. [5]

Issues of Muslim immigration into Europe have become security oriented, thanks to 9/11, being followed by the war on terror. It has been integrated as a component of policy debate in Europe. The Muslim phenomenon in Europe is being perceived in terms of Islamophobia and or Islamofascism, to borrow the lexicon of the Straussian ideology of neo-conservatism which held under its sway the George W. Bush administration and his ilk. Some sections of the European academia have duly documented the Muslim role in the European civilizational and cultural advancement in its historical trajectory. However, the political class of Europe has been sluggish in endorsing this irrefutable historical verity. Political recognition of the latter has a potential to overcome the psychic cobwebs that seem to govern the state of West-Muslim interplay. It will usher in a new era of concordance between these two entities.

Among the prominent issues that multiculturalism debate brings to the fore is the place of religion in the public sphere and the salience to be accorded to considerations of ethnicity in law. Multiculturalism is potentially capable of unsettling the pre-eminence of secularism as a perceived ubiquitous entity in the socio-political life of Western societies. Indeed, there is a widespread perception that Muslims are making politically exceptional, culturally unreasonable or theologically alien demands upon European states. [6] Their challenges expose the taken-for-grantedness of secularism in most European countries. [7] They press politicians and intellectuals to rethink what is secularism, whether it has ever truly characterized modern European societies and most importantly why and to what versions it is still desirable. [8]

The west claims that it is the birthplace of notions such as rule of law, citizenship, due process of law, and of epoch-making movements epitomized in Magna Carta, French Revolution's embodying values of liberty, equality, and fraternity, inclusive of the epoch-making Rights of Man and Citizen. Besides, it is the home of Renaissance (which was effected through the intermediary role played by Muslims as cited in the foregoing), Reformation, Enlightenment (banishing religion, in this case, Papal Christianity from the public sphere), Capitalism, Communism, and Secularism. Reformation entailed a struggle to liberate the individual from the control of religious authorities, namely the Catholic Church.

In the same vein, it is also incumbent upon the academia to underline that the West also gave to the world practices such as colonialism, imperialism (and its various manifestations), racism, anti-Semitic pogroms such as Holocaust and slavery. Prolonged internecine religious wars also characterized the socio-political history of Europe in the past. Such a dark past of Europe has few parallels in the rest of the world. Against this backdrop, the *raison d'etre* for underlining human rights discourse in Europe, and its salience for the rest of the world, makes a great and healthy sign. The importance of the promotion and protection of human rights and fundamental freedoms within and beyond Europe is all the more noteworthy. However, there is a need to graduate beyond rhetoric and the latter has to be converted into praxis. It is precisely in the realm of praxis that the major lacunae in the sphere of human rights lie. Concerning the international legal regime of human rights, few deficiencies are identifiable. It is, of course, predominantly programmed by the *weltanschauung* of liberalism and its offshoots, about which non-liberal ideological systems may have legitimate ideational grievances.

France has a very strong tradition of *laicism,* establishing an iron-clad distinction between public and private spheres. It houses Europe's biggest Muslim minority, numbering five to six million. It expects immigrants, or their descendents, of all faiths to adapt to French ways, not the other way round. [9] Muslims, carrying their religious and cultural baggage from the countries of origin, and immigrating to and settling down in France, find it difficult to conform to the rigid requirements of *laicism.*

In the French political ideology, *laicism* is a very powerful praxis. Striking a balance between personal and religious freedom and the ideals of common citizenship is proving to be an enormous test for all European countries with large Muslim populations—especially when some seem destined to assert, or even caricature, the practices of their homelands.

There exists a functional arrangement between secularism

and official religious establishment in countries such as England, Denmark, Greece, Netherlands and Germany. The variegated secular orders found in these countries, has a potential to accommodate the multicultural demands being voiced by Muslim communities in these and other countries. Secular pure and simple—secularism *simpliciter*—is not what exists in the world. The country-by-country situation is more complex, and indeed, far less inhospitable to the accommodation of Muslims than the ideology of secularism might suggest. [10] There is a need to unearth the potential and give it a concrete, practical shape with a view to addressing the demands germane to multiculturalism. To expect that Muslims will leave their adopted countries in Europe and go back to their homelands is a mirage. They are now an integral part of the West and are there to stay. Yet, the interactions between Western Muslims and the institutions of their countries have been strewn with many a problem.

The French state does not define itself according to minorities. Power is derived from the citizens, whose atomized individuals constitute the nation; the French Republic is the conglomeration of its citizens, not an assemblage of communities. Issues germane to multiculturalism—be they *hijab,* state-funding of faith- based schools, *halal* food and many others—need to be addressed from the perspective of governance. The latter is, *inter alia*, constituted by such values as respect for human dignity, freedom, democracy, equality, the rule of law, and human rights. State accommodation of Muslim religious practices is an increasingly important political issue across Western Europe. [11]

More than ten million Muslims currently live in Western Europe, which makes them the largest religious minority in the region. Islam is a significant social and religious force in Western Europe. [12] The Muslim presence in Europe has forced the academia and policy community to revisit the hitherto-assumed settled nature of religion-state interplay, culminating in the secular ascendance over public sphere, following the internecine wars of religion in Europe a century ago. To the degree that Muslims want the state to recognize and accommodate their religious values, then, they confront the secular tide of these states that have religion and state moving farther apart, not closer together. [13]

Diversity marks Europe's Muslim communities; they are divided along ethnic, sectarian, and socioeconomic lines. They are also characterized by different levels of integration into the societies in which they have settled, their ideological orientations, and the nature of their relations both with the host societies and with their countries of origin. Despite some progress and some bright spots, most of Europe's Muslim communities constitute an underprivileged class, clustered in ghetto-like neighbourhoods imbued with a culture of deprivation and alienation and with antisocial propensities. [14] Their access to socio-economic development indicators remains much to be desired. A wide gap exists between them and the natives in this regard.

In future, the Muslim presence in Europe is likely to proliferate in terms of quality and quantity. Eventually, Islam is likely to find its niche in the social, cultural and political milieux of Europe. Prior to that, in the absence of an essential mutual contract between natives and settled Muslim communities necessary to bring that about, there will be tension and strife governing their relations. Moreover, the latter will neither be uniform nor linear in all the countries.

The Muslim experience hitherto in Western Europe indicates that their acculturation by way of conversion to the values of the West will not automatically lead to assimilation as many have expected it. The underlying idea is that Muslim integration means their adoption of the secular values of the West. As Tariq Ramadan notes, this implies that Muslims should "be Muslims without Islam, for there exists a widespread suspicion that to be too much a Muslim means not to be really and completely integrated into the Western way of life and its values." [15]

To highlight the aforesaid, it is necessary to quote at length the statement of the European Commission:

It is essential to recognize that integration is a two-way process involving adaptation on the part of both the immigrant and of the host society. The European Union is by its very nature a pluralistic society enriched by a verity of cultural and social traditions, which will, in the future, become even more diverse. There must therefore be respect for cultural and social differences but also of our fundamental shared principles and values: respect for human rights and human dignity, appreciation of the value of pluralism and recognition that membership of society is based on a series of rights but brings with it a number of responsibilities for all of its members be they *nationals* or *migrants* [emphasis supplied]. [16]

Surveys on the Muslim Situation

A survey conducted by Open Society Institute (OSI) in 2009 entitled *Muslims in Europe: A Report on 11 EU Cities* [17] (At Home in Europe Project) brings out with glaring vividness the conditions of Muslims with respect to education, employment, housing, health care, policing and security, civil and political participation, media depiction, and other allied issues. It is necessary to highlight a few salient features of this survey with a view to diagnosing the infirmities with which Muslims in Europe are afflicted. Such diagnostics may help public policy community to resort to remedial treatment.

The OSI asserts that Muslims in Europe are currently under "heightened suspicion and scrutiny". [18] It suggests that "religious discrimination against Muslims remains a critical barrier to full and equal participation in society... Europe-born Muslims, particularly women, were more likely to receive higher levels of religious discrimination than Muslims born abroad. Europe-born Muslim men identify the police as a key source of unfair treatment and discrimination. The persistent discrimination and prejudice impair Muslims' sense of national belonging." [19]

For some Muslims, religion plays an important role in supporting and encouraging education. Parental support constitutes a strong predictor of future educational attainment. Across all cities, there is an increasing recognition of the importance of pre-school education in ensuring that pupils from minority and other disadvantaged backgrounds do not start formal schooling under-prepared. [20] Some Muslim pupils continue to suffer racism and prejudice at schools and their instructors have low expectations from them. [21] Most Muslims want to live in mixed communities, challenging the claims that the geographical concentration of Muslims reflects their desire to live among their own kind. Discrimination in housing confronts many Muslims and restricts their choices. [22] Muslims are not integrated into the mainstream labour market. They suffer from higher unemployment and poverty rates than the general population. Those who are employed are often in marginal and low-paid jobs, thus carrying a greater risk of unemployment. Low- paid jobs also lead to segregated or parallel working lives. [23]

The OSI survey further highlights stereotypical and prejudice-filled media portrayal of Muslims. [24] Such negativistic approach propelled the Muslim individuals, civil societies, and public entities to counter them with greater engagement in media discussions.

On civil and political participation in the eleven EU cities, the OSI says that those Muslims who are not EU citizens remain disenfranchised, especially in Germany and France, where they do not have the voting right in local elections. [25] Those Muslims endowed with voting right feel that they can effect change in their city than those who are not. Ethnic and religious political parties do not command the confidence of Muslim voters. Increasing number of Muslims are standing for political office, but face additional scrutiny and questions because of their ethnic and religious profile. [26]

A plethora of research studies reinforce and endorse the foregone conclusions. One of the representative cases is a

Ph.D. work submitted to the University of Toronto, Canada, in May 2005 by Rikke Andreassen, a Danish national. [27] Andreassen, in his 327 page thesis, concludes that the news media's representation of visible minorities during 1971 to 2004, contributed a stereotypical image of visible minorities, i.e., the Muslims. [28] Further, these images depict a scary scenario: 'immigrants who arrive as floods to Denmark', 'the criminal immigrants', 'the oppressed immigrant women', 'the veiled women', 'the sexually aggressive Muslim male', and 'the unintegrated immigrant'. [29]

After presenting the constructed stereotypical images by Danish electronic and print media, the author has sought to deconstruct them by juxtaposing them with actual facts, which proved that they were the figments of imagination of the former. The author says that the function of media depiction of Muslim minority is to reinforce and eulogize Danish nationality and ethnic Danes' self–perception, and to install an 'us-them' binary division between the Danes and Muslims. The potential of this thesis to transcend the case study of Denmark and to envelop the wider European/Atlantic context cannot be gainsaid. At the epilogue of this study, the author has hinted at such a feasibility: "it will be interesting to compare this dissertation's result with similar Scandinavian and European media representations. Some surveys already, e.g. from Sweden and Holland, and others might need to be carried out before comparisons can take place". [30]

Closely related to the elevan EU cities study/survey conducted by the OSI as outlined in the aforesaid, there also exists another survey titled *Ethnic Profiling in the European Union: Pervasive, Ineffective, and Discriminatory*, published by the same organization in 2009. This study covers three broad dimensions: Ethnic Profiling in Ordinary Policing, Ethnic Profiling in Counterterrorism since 9/11, Alternatives to Ethnic Profiling, besides the customary epistemic practice of defining the concept in vogue in the study. Without dwelling upon the nitty-gritty of the study, it suffices to highlight a few findings of the study which are likely to throw radiance on the broad theme of this paper: the rights of multicultural citizenship germane to Muslims in Europe.

The 2009 study emphatically asserts that ethnic profiling by police in Europe is a "common, long-standing practice that has intensified in recent years. Evidence from countries across the European Union shows that police routinely use generalizations about ethnicity, religion, race, or national origin in deciding whom to target for identity checks, stops, and searches. Contemporary concerns about terrorism underlie a rising interest in ethnic profiling in Europe, which many see as an effective way to identify terrorist suspects". [31]

In a scathing critique of the aforesaid presuppositions, the OSI Study demonstrates that "ethnic profiling by police in Europe may be pervasive, but it is inefficient, ineffective, and discriminatory [emphases supplied]. Fortunately, in the opinion of the OSI, better alternatives exist". [32] To authenticate the survey's findings, the OSI draws our attention to some facts on the ground: "since the 9/11 attacks in the United States, 32 per cent of British Muslims report being subjected to discrimination at airports. Police carrying machine guns have conducted identity checks on elevan-year olds at German mosques. Moroccan immigrants have been called "*moro de mierda*" ("Arab shit") [emphasis in original] by the Spanish police. The personal data of 8.3 million people were searched in a massive German data mining exercise which targeted ...people who were Muslim, and which did not identify a single terrorist." [33] The OSI characterizes ethnic profiling in terms of description, pervasiveness, discrimination, ineffectiveness, and finally, alternatives.

The OSI Definition of Ethnic Profiling

The OSI study explains ethnic profiling as "the use by law enforcement of generalizations grounded in ethnicity, race, religion, or national origin—rather than objective evidence or individual behaviour—as the basis for making law enforcement and/or investigative decisions about who has been or may be involved in criminal activity". [34] Ethnic profiling often results in police personnel's decisions about whom to stop, demand identity documents, question, search, and sometimes incarcerate. Ethnic profiling may spring from the racist behaviour of individual police officers, or from the institutionalized bias ingrained in many police forces. [35] It is obvious from the above that ethnic profiling is quite contrary to the principle of rule of law as a cherished value of civilized societies.

Ethnic profiling brings to the fore some malign outcomes. Through ethnic profiling, innocent people are stopped, searched, and even arrested; actual criminals, who do not conform to the established profile, are overlooked; stigmatization of communities ensures; and alienation of those people; who could work with police to reduce crime and prevent terrorism, takes place. [36]

The OSI survey reports in detail the pervasiveness of the practice of ethnic profiling. The European general public, following the so-called war on terror post-9/11, considers the profiling and targeting of Muslims as a "matter of common sense". [37] Armed with the latter, the logic of the public runs as follows: young Muslim men destroyed the World Trade Center in New York, blew up Madrid's Atocha train station, and bombed the London underground, so they should be the targets of police attention. With so much at stake, ethnic profiling may seem like smart law enforcement. [38]

In an increasingly surcharged political and security environment in Europe after 9/11, being epitomized by "war on terror", law enforcement personnel in the United Kingdom, Germany, France, Italy, and other European countries, have resorted to a variety of tools that specifically targeted Muslims. In Britain, stops and searches of Asians; in Germany, mass identity checks outside major mosques; in France and Italy, raids on homes, business, and mosques, were common phenomena. In all these countries, religiously observant

Muslims bore the brunt of these tools. Numerous studies since 2001 have documented "a growing perception among Muslim leaders and communities across Europe that they are being stopped, questioned, and searched not on the basis of evidence and reasonable suspicion, but on the basis of "looking Muslims". [39] Very significantly, the OSI survey underlines the fact that the resort to ethnic profiling is "more of a public relations tool than a reasoned response to crime and terrorism". [40]

Ethnic profiling leads to discrimination and is a gross violation of basic human rights norms. By relying on ethnic, racial, or religious stereotypes, ethnic profiling breaches one of the most fundamental principles of law: that each person must be treated as an individual, not as a member of group.

The European Convention on Human Rights proscribes discrimination and secures the full and equal enjoyment of right in respect of, among other things, the administration of justice. [41] The European Court of Human Rights has declared that ethnic profiling is *per se* unlawful. The European Commission against Racism and intolerance (ECRI) has unceasingly expressed concerns with ethnic profiling across a wide range of European Union member-states. ECRI's General Policy Recommendation Number Eight on Combating Racism While Fighting Terrorism (2004) urges governments to "pay particular attention to…checks carried out by law enforcement officials within the countries and border control personnel. [42] Unfortunately, neither the EU nor any European government has outlawed ethnic profiling till date. [43]

Ineffective Nature of Ethnic Profiling

The OSI survey clearly asserts that there is no factual basis to suggest that ethnic profiling stops crime or prevents terrorism. Separate studies in the UK, the US, Sweden, and the Netherlands have all concluded that ethnic profiling is ineffective. [44] Stops and searches conducted under counterterrorism powers in Europe have produced few charges on terrorism offences and no terrorism convictions to date. [45]

When law enforcement officers engage in ethnic profiling, they are, wittingly or not, contributing to a growing sense of marginalization in minority and immigrant communities. Ethnic profiling stigmatizes entire racial, ethnic, or religious groups as more likely to commit crimes and thereby signals to the broader society that all members of that group constitute a threat.

The OSI survey is galore with findings that ethnic profiling does not improve police efficacy, but that in all likelihood it reduces it, both in countering terrorism and addressing common crime. When police operate on the basis of their personal judgments—that is, with a high level of discretion- they rely more on stereotypes and focus disproportionate attention on minorities, which reduces their effectiveness. [46] Ethnic profiling in fact creates a direct incentive for terrorist organizations to recruit persons who do not fit the profile.

Ethnic profiling strikes at the heart of the social compact linking law enforcement agencies with the communities they serve. It wastes police resources, discriminates against whole groups of people, and leaves everyone less safe. New practices of policing based on intelligence rather than prejudice need to be adopted. They are more efficient than the existing ones. Ethnic profiling is more a problem than a solution; it should be expressly banned in law; unless this is done, the damage it wreaks will only deepen. [47] In a Europe under threat from terrorism and characterized by increasing xenophobia, it is essential that those entrusted to enforce the law do so with maximum effectiveness and full respect for the basic principles of equal justice.

As the foregoing demonstrates, ethnic profiling, besides being pervasive in the European Union, is inefficient, ineffective, and discriminatory too. Its deleterious impact on human rights is also explicit. It is discriminatory both in sprit and substance that focuses disproportionate law enforcement attention on specific individuals and communities, premised on generalizations about religion and ethnicity, instead of individual's patterns of behaviour. This is ironic in view of Europe's historic principle of non-discrimination, derived from the notion of rule of law and ideology of liberalism. Europe needs to pay obeisance to its ethos, the unfolding of which has been paid very dearly in history. That legacy deserves to be cherished and nourished in the current times. Lessons of history can be forgotten only at peril to the present and future.

Ethnic profiling encroaches upon a multitude of civil and political rights: individual's right to liberty and security, freedom from arbitrary detention and imprisonment; a fair trial; respect for private and family life; home and correspondence; freedom of thought; conscience and religion; freedom of expression; and freedom of assembly and association.

Europe is and will continue to be a continent of immigrants. The latter came from all over the world following new developments necessitating migration. Some of them settle and acculturate themselves to new environment, resultantly enriching the local culture and variety of ethno-cultural identities. Others also maintain transnational links and activities. The size of immigrants and immigration origin populations in European cities is likely to proliferate in the future. As a result, new ways of life, new religions, new visions of the world, new cultures are constantly being introduced into the European social fabric.

Developments in Europe, similar to their counterparts elsewhere in the world, need to be contextualized and put in perspective. In the context of the EU, any attempt to chalk out a European immigration policy has to go hand in hand with framing a European integration policy. Issues such as economic and employment integration, public goods sharing, ethnic and cultural diversity, social and political participation, should be subjected to discursive public policy treatment. A holistic approach is clearly required in order to consider the complexity of the migration and post-migration situations in the EU. No consensus exists on a shared definition of integration similar to terrorism, either in academia or in the European policy-formulating circles. There is, likewise, no consensus on the ideal integrated European society for tomorrow either. To put it differently, there is no consensually agreed upon EU blueprint of immigrant integration. Resultantly, the European policy debates, discussions and policy–making on integration occur without a clear definition of integration and without a clear vision of the end result to be arrived at through European policy-making.

Cultural Diversity and Social Justice

The recognition and promotion of ethnic identities and cultures and the struggle against socio-economic exclusion and exploitation should go in a symbiotic fashion. In other words, the politics of recognition, anti-discrimination and anti-racism are originally related to one another though, analytically speaking, they are distinct. It defies common sense to separate issues related to cultural diversity and issues germane to social justice. To promote a cultural citizenship through special cultural rights for minorities without granting them a full socio-economic citizenship and an equal access to the labour market, education, health and housing could be counterproductive and impractical.

Whereas Europe is *de facto* increasingly multicultural and multi-identitarian, institutional visions of multiculturalism, identity and culture in Europe remain mired in the past as it is supposed to have forged the national identities and cultures of the EU member states. European institutional multiculturalism rests on a substantial approach of culture and identity that conditions to a significant extent the opportunities of incorporation within European citizenship of other groups and communities.

France

In the annals of human history, France occupies a pivotal space in terms of cataclysmic, revolutionary transformations, which subsequently transcended their original locale and clime, and finally engulfed the rest of the world. The American War of Independence against British colonialism is indebted to the French Revolution in terms of the latter's sprit symbolized in such human values as liberty, equality, and fraternity. France is a nation that prides itself on its egalitarianism and universal democratic culture, is struggling to live up to its principles and fully integrate its Muslims into all sectors of national life. [48] It is home to the largest Muslim population in the continent, who constitute seven to eight per cent of the total French population. Ironically, more than 50 percent of France's prisoners are Muslims.

France's experience with integration has been shaped by a unique combination of history, philosophy and contemporary concerns, which together have produced a stop and start immigration policy and wariness about Islam. They are faced with a form of discrimination fuelled by nativism and a deep distrust of Islam that has made it harder for them to find homes and jobs. [49] In the French statecraft model, ethnic and/or religious empathies in the public sphere have no role to play, and that they are viewed as divisive of social solidarity. Further, they are considered antithetical to *laicism*, the French State's official secularism. In the name of egalitarianism, French law proscribes even identifying citizens on the basis of national origin, race, or religion.

The real particularity of *laicité* is the place it occupies in the French collective imagination, so much so that it acquired the status of a civil religion. [50] It is in the backdrop of this radical, ultra-modern *weltanschauung* of *laicism* that the presence of Islam and Muslims in France needs to be comprehended. "If the Catholic Church has been considered problematic in France, Islam has been much more so. In fact, religion may be as enduring a fault line in France as race in the

United States. Islam has been distrusted in Europe since the Middle Ages…" and in the specific context of France, "Islam was as a barrier to Frenchness—and in one way or another it still is to day". [51] France's expectation has been that its immigrants, or their off-spring, of all faiths, should adopt French ways, not the other way round. It was in the name of *laicité* that France banned the *hijab* in state schools in 2004. The French commitment to a strict separation between church and state made it more difficult for French Muslims to gain public recognition for their religious practices. [52]

In France's political ideology, *laicité* is a very powerful political reality. France has followed the logic of *laicité* by rejecting multiculturalism as an appropriate educational model. As an ideological construct, *laicité* makes it difficult for Muslims to do much beyond fighting rearguard actions on symbolic, though significant, issues such as the wearing of the *hijab*. Opponents of state recognition of Muslim rights inevitably appeal to *laicité* as a justification for their refusal to countenance state recognition for Muslim religious practices. [53]

Muslims in Europe are the permanent minority residents of non-Muslim majority states that profess liberal, democratic ideologies. They need to explore the possibility of evolving a thought that fuses the organizing principles of governance in Islam and the reigning principles of liberalism that govern the present-day western societies. Such a thought has to take into its vortex their status, rights, loyalties, duties and well-being. "Given that Muslims today comprise a significant and growing proportion of the citizenry of contemporary liberal democracies, it is natural to take interest in the way Muslims regard the liberal conception of citizenship." [54] Such an interest may go deeper encompassing sociological, hermeneutical or epistemological issues. Efforts to bring about epistemic convergence between Islamic and Western civilizations are afoot: Tariq Ramadan may be counted as one of the pioneering scholars among them; he is claimed as the progenitor of "Euro-Islam."

Striking a balance between personal and religious freedom on the one hand, and the ideals of common citizenship on the other, is proving to be an enormous test for all European countries having sizeable Muslims population in their midst. The treatment meted out to Muslim minorities in the EU member-states is, *inter alia*, a function of interplay among multitudinous political forces and parties of various hues. This is particularly true in the case of France, Britain, Germany, Belgium, Denmark, Italy, and Spain. Whatever the multicultural model a given EU member state has adopted - Britain, France, and Germany, to name only the three—the end result has been the same: each model is strewn with complications. There is nothing for any objective observer to emulate from among the available models–Britain, France, and Germany.

Veil (*hijab)* in Europe's political discourse, has acquired a politically sensitive and controversial character. It lends itself to a variety of meanings and tendentious interpretations, contingent upon beholder's eye. The increasing practice of veiling among Muslim women in Western societies has been viewed in the broader context of modernity, globalization and social change and that the practice is a result of complex personal, religio-political, class or local affiliations. The complexity intrinsic to the *hijab* means that it cannot be reduced to a single unitary meaning. Muslim women wear the *hijab* for a variety of reasons and that to make generalizations about its use is bound to infringe upon the universal right to freedom of expression for those Muslim women who wear it as an act of personal religious belief or conviction. [55] As contended by the International Helsinki Federation for Human Rights (IHF) "for many Muslim women wearing a headscarf is a deeply personal choice and a sign of their religious conviction and has nothing to do with Islamic Fundamentalism." [56]

By Way of Epilogue

The continuing presence of Muslims in Western Europe tends to impel the policy-making community to revisit and revise the supposedly settled dichotomy between the respective roles of public and private spheres. The "Muslim question" in Western Europe seems to question the very binarization of their twin spheres.

Both the polities and societies of Europe do have a lot of apprehensions about the nature of Muslim religious institutions with particular reference to their proclivity to construct mosques and *madrasas* with a view to fulfilling their religious duties and convictions. The recent case of prohibiting the construction of minarets in Switzerland constitutes a case in point.

European Muslims have suffered from different problems. Racism and Islamophobia have made it difficult for Muslims to integrate professionally and to move up the economic ladder, and have contributed to the development of minority ghettos mired in poverty and alienation. Their dwelling units are situated away from the mainstream native populations. European Muslims are more socially conservative than their majority non- Muslim counterparts, particularly on such issues as abortion and homosexuality, which points to the possibility of a social and political coalition of orthodox religionists who wish to preserve a public space for religious expression. [57]

In the long run, equitable public policy on the rights of religious believers is a good recipe for political stability and the successful social incorporation of European Muslims. [58] Respect for human rights is among the founding principles of the EU treaties. The situation for most Western liberal democracies and their Muslim minorities is far from ideal, if the media reports are anything to go by. Most of the EU member states are not able to live up to their cherished liberal ethos with regard to the treatment meted out to their minorities. In Britain, the state's blasphemy law protects the Christian religion; attempts by Muslims to extend the law to cover Islam have failed. Britain has an established church, the Church of England; which enjoys certain benefits from the state. Clerics in the Church of England have guaranteed positions in the House of Lords; there are no formal membership provisions for leaders of any other religious tradition.

Notes

1. M. Basheer Ahmad, MD. , ed., et al., *Muslim contributions to Civilization*, Herndon, Virginia: The International Institute of Islamic Thought, 2005, pp. xx+151.
2. *Ibid.*, p. xviii.
3. *Ibid.*, p. xix.
4. Robert Briffault, *The Making of Humanity*, 1938; reproduced in *Islamic Science in the Medieval Muslim World*, Pakistan: Khawarizmi Science Society, November 2001.
5. Norman F. Cantor, *The Encyclopaedia of the Middle Ages*, New York: Viking, 1999, pp. 349-350.
6. Anna Traindafyllidon, et al; "European challenges To Multicultural citizenship: Muslims, Secularism and Beyond," in Tariq Modood, et al; *Multiculturalism, Muslims and Citizenship: A European Approach*, London: Routledge, 2006, p. 3.
7. *Ibid.*, p. 3.
8. *Ibid.*, p. 3.
9. *The Economist*, London, vol. 395, no. 8682, May 15-21, 2010, p. 67.
10. Tariq Modood and Riva Kastoryano, "Secularism and the Accommodating Muslims in Europe," in Tariq Modood, et al., *Multiculturalism , Muslims and citizenship: A European Approach*, London: Routledge, 2006, p. 173.
11. Jod S. Fetzer and J. Christopher Soper, *Muslims and the State in Britain, France, and Germany*, Cambridge: Cambridge University Press, 2005, p. 1.
12. *Ibid.*, pp. 1-2.
13. *Ibid.*, p. 17.
14. Shireen T. Hunter, ed., *Islam, Europe's Second Religion: The New Social, Cultural and Political Landscape*, Praeger: Connnecticut, 2002, p. 274.
15. Tariq Ramadan, *To Be a European Muslim*, Leicester: UK,

Islamic Foundation, 1999, pp. 184-185.

16. Peo Hansen,"A Superabundance of Contradictions: The European Union's Post- Amsterdam Policies on Migrant 'Integration', Labour Immigration, Asylum, and Illegal Immigration," in *Occasional Paper and Reprints on Ethnic Studies*, Norrkoping, Sweden: Centre for Ethnic and Urban Studies (CEUS), March 2005, p. 15.
17. These eleven European cities are Leicester and London (UK), Amsterdam and Rotterdam (Holland), Hamburg and Berlin (Germany), Copenhagen (Denmark), Stockholm (Sweden), Antwerp (Belgium), and Paris and Marseille (France). For details, see website www.soros.org/initiatives/home. Retrieved on July 20, 2010.
18. Open Society Institute, *Muslims in Europe: A Report on 11 EU Cities* (At Home in Europe Project), New York, 2009, p. 22. www.soros.org/initiatives/home. Retrieved on July 20, 2010.
19. *Ibid.*, pp. 22-23.
20. *Ibid.*, p. 23.
21. *Ibid.*, p. 23.
22. *Ibid.*, p. 24.
23. *Ibid.*, p. 24.
24. *Ibid.*, p. 25.
25. *Ibid.*, p. 25.
26. *Ibid.*, p. 25
27. for details, see his unpublished Ph.D. thesis, *The Mass Media's Construction of Gender, Race, Sexuality and Nationality: An Analysis of the Danish News Media's Communication About Visible Minorities From 1971 to 2004*, Department of History, University of Toronto, 2005, p. 327.
28. *Ibid.*, p. 277.
29. *Ibid.*, p. 277.
30. *Ibid.*, p. 292.
31. Open Society Institute, *Ethnic Profiling In The European Union: Pervasive, Ineffective, and Discriminatory*, Open Society Institute, 2009, p. 7.
32. *Ibid.*, pp. 7-8.
33. *Ibid.*, p. 7.
34. *Ibid.*, p. 8.
35. *Ibid.*, p. 8.
36. *Ibid.*, p. 8

37. *Ibid.*, p. 8
38. *Ibid.*, p. 8.
39. Quoted in *ibid.*, p. 9.
40. *Ibid.*, p. 9.
41. *Ibid.*, p. 10.
42. Quoted in *ibid.*, p. 10.
43. *Ibid.*, p. 10
44. *Ibid.*, p. 11.
45. *Ibid.*, p. 11.
46. *Ibid.*, p. 11.
47. *Ibid.*, pp. 12-13.
48. Stephanie Giry, "France and Its Muslims" in *Foreign Affairs*, Vol. 85, No. 5, September-October 2006, p. 87.
49. *Ibid.*, p. 88.
50. *Ibid.*, p. 90.
51. *Ibid.*, p. 90.
52. J. Christopher and Soper and Joel S. Fetzer, "The Practices of Their Faith : Muslims and The State in Britain , France and Germany", in Abdulkader H. Sinno,ed., *Muslims in Western Politics*, Bloomington: Indiana University Press, 2009, p. 39.
53. *Ibid.*, p. 42.
54. Andrew F. March, "The Demands of Citizenship: Translating political Liberalism into the Language of Islam", *Journal of Muslim Minority Affairs*, London: Routledge, Vol. 25, No. 3, December 2005, p. 321.
55. Sveda Clark, "Female Subjects of International Human Rights Law: The Hijab Debate and the Exotic Other Female," in *Global Change, Peace and Security*, vol.19. no. 1, February 2007, p. 39.
56. IHF...,"A French Ban on Religious Symbols Would Violate International Protection of Freedom of Religion," 2003. http//www.ihf-hr.org/viewbinary/viewhtml.php?doc_id=525997. Retrieved on July 20, 2010.
57. Christopher et al., n. 52 , p. 45.
58. *Ibid.*, p. 46.

Section II

Dialogue between National Constitutions and the European Convention

5

The Principle of Sustainable Development in France: The Charter of Environment in the French Constitution

Robert Etien

The French Charter for the Environment has come to complete, within the very heart of the preamble to the Constitution of October 4, 1958, the whole set of proclamation of fundamental rights and liberties. By chronologically successive touches, fundamental rights and liberties have been asserted with the 1789 Declaration of Rights of Man and Citizen, the preamble to the Constitution of 1946 bearing on collective economic and social rights and finally and more recently the environmental rights based on the Constitutional Charter of 2004. [1]

The question that has been raised with regard to the latter concerns not only the universality of these rights and liberties but the global or integral nature of these as part of a whole set of rights applicable to all.

While, as an observer aware of the necessity of the impact of emerging nations on the international scene, one can be satisfied with the reticence of a good number of such nations as India and China, and to a lesser extent Brazil and Russia [2] to accept the compatibility between economic and environmental development. As a citizen sensitive to the future of our international community and the evolution of the planet, one can only worry about it. It is not a matter of coincidence that in the view of a good many Western countries, the Copenhagen Summit has failed, considering the preponderance and the weight of these two giants, India and China. [3]

Parallel to this, it is symptomatic to see a natural alliance emerge in this area between these countries and the United States. [4]

If the French Charter for the Environment is a remarkable text which has specified the contours of new environmental rights, its application has not yet been effective. Indeed, we are far from it. Perhaps it is necessary to add new rights pertaining to political regimes, the exercise of power, and regime of democracy to this compilation of declarations of liberties. But undoubtedly we are witnessing here a veritable reconstruction which is set in a new and universal perspective that takes into account the impact of emerging nations. [5]

I. The Constitutional Construction of Fundamental Rights and Liberties, the Place of Sustainable Development in France

Along with the Declaration of Rights of Man and Citizen of August 26, 1789, the preamble to the Constitution of October 3, 1958 enshrines the fundamental individual rights of Man. The preamble to the Constitution of October 27, 1946 proclaims new social and economic rights. One had to wait till 2004 to see new rights concerning environment and sustainable development in particular, affirmed. [6]

A.The Multiple Layers of French Fundamental Rights

In course of time and by successive layers, France integrated a whole set of fundamental rights and liberties in its preamble to the 1958 Constitution, i.e., rights of Man and Citizen, social and economic rights, and environmental rights (Charter adopted on June 24, 2004 and promulgated on March 1, 2005). All these documents form a whole that has constitutional value. [7] The Declaration of Rights of Man and Citizen was made in a particular context, that of the French Revolution. It had to do with the transformation of the French society and was meant to put an end to monarchy and prepare a universal social project. [8]

The Declaration of 1789 announced the drafting of a new

constitution as was done in the United States that had become newly independent. It was intended to be universal. The declaration proclaimed natural, inalienable and sacred rights of Man and Citizen. It guaranteed fundamental rights and the separation of powers. The declaration is short (17 Articles) and well written. It enumerates the individual rights of Man. It lays down the principle of equality between men and women, announces fundamental rights such as liberty, property, security and resistance to oppression, defines and protects them. It evokes the basis of legality, the role and definition of law, the protection of citizens, the principle of the lawfulness of the notions of offences and punishments, the presumption of innocence, the liberty of opinion, the freedom of expression, the necessity for public order, the control of taxes and public agents by the citizens.

The preamble to the Constitution of 1946 is ensconced in a context of national construction after the Second World War as well as a determination to develop social and collective ideas on the economic and social planes. [9] The 1946 Preamble contains eighteen paragraphs. It solemnly repeats and reaffirms the rights and liberties of Man and Citizen enshrined in the Declaration of the Rights of Man and Citizen of 1789. [10] It integrates "the fundamental principles recognized by the law of the Republics" (Second Republic 1848-1852, Third Republic 1875-1946 with the suspension between 1940-1944) such as the separation of the State and the Church and freedom to assemble. [11] It enounces new political, economic and social principles particularly necessary for our times [12] These principles concern equality between men and women, the right to asylum, the obligation to work and the right to get an employment, trade union freedom, the right to strike, the protection of the rights of the family and those of particular categories, children, mothers, aged workers, the handicapped, the persons in difficulty. The Constitution guarantees the training of the child, the adult and the right to secular and free education. [13] It reaffirms the principles of international public law and in particular the organization and defence of peace, the development of the French Union and the refusal of any system of colonization founded upon arbitrary rule. [14]

This long list of fundamental rights and liberties shows the necessity to integrate new economic and social rights that are juxtaposed to the fundamental rights and liberties of the individual.

B. Sustainable Development Enshrined

The Charter intervened in 2004. It stemmed out of the work of the commission presided by the paleontologist Yves Coppens. The Commission consisted of eighteen members of whom two CEOs, i.e, the CEO of Lafarge and that of Proctor and Gamble France and a representative from the insurance sector, while only four out of the eighteen members represented the field of environment. This composition raised criticisms at the outset. After many tribulations, Jacques Chirac was able to impose the adoption of this project on his stubborn majority. A lot of preparatory work was done and resulted in multiple reflections on the enshrining of new rights.

With regard to the principle of Sustainable Development, [15] the French speak about "durable" development, while the English prefer the word "sustainable". The Italians like the English use "sviluppo sostenible". Between the development we can sustain and that which is durable, the distinctions are apparently significant in depth, while on the surface they seem to be very light. For the French, the concept of development connotes future in terms of progress. The fact that they want it to be "durable" qualifies this development in its reality and in their wish to see to it that it be a true development in the short as well as long terms. France speaks about the idea of development which has a social and economic origin with some reticence. France as ancient colonial power is indeed marked by the underdevelopment of countries that have become newly independent and which are maintained in poverty.

The affirmation of "sustainable development" at the same

time takes on a global dimension and in fact, opposes economic development, which, in reality, is far from being permanent. "Sustainable development" takes into consideration the environmental dimension, in other words, whatever surrounds the planetary space of the individual. Humanity is nowadays obliged to think upon how to preserve the environment efficiently. Sustainable development has become the current paradigm of any debate on the question of environment.

New rights have been enshrined in the Charter for Environment of 2004. [16] The definition of "sustainable development" of the Brundtland Report has been fully absorbed in the typically French notion of "durable development" including the preventative and precautionary principles as well as the notion of responsibility in case of damages to the environment ("polluter pays"), access to information and participation in the public decision making process already developed at the international level. Besides, Article 6 recalls the content of Article 37 of the Charter of Fundamental Rights of the European Union signed in Nice in 2000 and considers "durable development" as a fundamental organizing principle of national public policies to come: "Public policies shall promote sustainable development. To this end they shall reconcile the protection and enhancement of the environment with economic development and social progress". This norm has to be read conjointly with what is contained in Article 10: "This Charter shall inspire France's actions at both a European and an international level". What ensues is that "durable development" is not only a goal of France's domestic public policy but also its foreign policy.

If we want to further deepen our analysis of the Charter for Environment, we could say that it repeats a certain number of rights called "third generation rights" (The Human Rights of 1789 belong to the first generation and the social rights of the twentieth century to the second generation) already enshrined in legislative texts and more often in international conventions.

The Charter of Fundamental Rights enshrines a new individual right, that of "each person's right to live in a balanced environment which shows due respect for health" (Article 1). A legal innovation resides also in the notion of duty, to participate in preserving and enhancing the environment. It is the first time the idea of duty appears in a constitution. The 1946 Constitution mentions the obligation to work, but this is the first time that a duty takes on a normative value. This was criticized, especially by the advocates of the conception of subjective law for whom the only duty the citizen has is to respect the rights of other citizens.

The Charter also elevates other principles to the level of the constitution. These already existed in the body of legislation but acquire a greater force in the Charter. For instance, the idea of environmental responsibility covers the principle of "polluter pays" and gives it a larger scope. The one who pollutes is obliged to pay damages and interests and re-establish the previous situation. [17]

II. Necessary Construction and Universalization of Fundamental Rights and Place of Sustainable Development in New International Relations.

It has become clear that hereafter economic development and sustainable development must go hand in hand. The Copenhagen summit has obviously shown that this was not the case and that the opposite case might exist. [18] The failure of the summit negotiations shows that necessity to write a new charter of fundamental rights which will have a universal reach.

A. Absence of a Common Position between Developed and Emerging Nations

The blatant failure of the Copenhagen summit which took place from December 7 to 18, 2009 showes a series of disagreements between totally opposed positions. The long and minute preparation of the summit since the Kyoto protocol (on the reduction of greenhouse gases, signed on December 11,

1997, and which entered into force on February 1, 2005), [19] environmental awareness, involvement of ecologists, the need for and the obligation of a minimum accord, the will to defend the planet and think about future generations–all these let us believe with the minimum of optimism that the international community was about to reach a consensus. Indeed, there was none and the disillusion was all the more stronger. Manifestly there was a series of stumbling blocks and opposed points of view, which resulted in power struggle that prevailed. [20]

The debate about economic development and sustainable development has not been closed. Many Europeans thought that any economic development would have to henceforth include a new form of development—sustainable development. In fact, it did not occur. Emerging nations, especially China and India, threw all their weight in order to defend economic development, even if it means entailing pollution of the planet and climate change. The development of emerging nations and the place they occupy in the world scene is above all due to their economic growth.

China and India, therefore, do not accept to revise their objectives that will help them contend with industrialized nations and reach their level. Accepting sustainable development boils down to reducing economic growth which neither China nor India wants. In spite of the efforts of Brazil, which with its Amazon rain forests and natural riches, is aware of the limits of economic development without taking into consideration the sustainability of that development, the two Asian giants remained firm in their position. It was all the easier because their standpoint was shared by the US. [21]

America's support for China [22] and directly for India showed that it was in the interests of the two big powers of the world not to consider the environmental dimension. For a series of comparable reasons, numerous emerging nations in Africa have understood that the Chinese emergence should entail a general movement in favour of emerging nations that might concern them. Russia also entered the fray. The principle of sovereignty of states did the rest.

Only Europe had vague desires for environment. Moreover, it was not part of the most polluting countries. Its multiple internal divisions and the American charm dealt the final blow and showed that on this subject a divided and timid Europe was incapable of asserting itself on the international level. [23] As a result, the signed agreement does not meet the expectations and bridles environmental orientations. Ecologists obviously look at this as disappointment and disillusionment.

B. The Redrafting of a New World Charter of Fundamental Rights

The deep disagreements between the countries and the opposition between Western states have showed that due to economic crisis we are witnessing a return to the priority of nation states that defend, above all, their own interests. The very idea of international community seems to have been forgotten in a world where individualism dominates and money reigns supreme. Liberalism, capitalism and merchandization, a certain absence of ethics, do the rest. The absence of American preponderance, the emergence of economic powers with a strong potential like China, India and Brazil, the future that is particularly positive—all these factors prompt the emerging nations to reconsider their position and pass from a dominated to dominating state. They exclude even the least sacrifice in terms of development considering that their economic growth will allow them to position themselves on the international scene.

The renewal of international power balance, the place of emerging nations and of BRIC (Brazil, Russia, India, and China), the repercussion of this dynamism on other states must, on the contrary and in this egalitarian and at least identitarian perspective, be an occasion to start a new dialogue which is not inscribed in the usual framework of a power struggle in which developing nations are dominated. [24]

In this context, a complete redrafting of the world charter of fundamental and universal rights which will be binding on all would be both necessary and salutary. It would no longer be a question of imposing a text dear to the old continent, but on the contrary, giving all the protagonists the opportunity to express themselves.

Discussions will have to be restarted and the three generations of Human Rights and in particular environmental rights, integrated into a whole. This corresponds exactly to the three texts that figure in the preamble to the French Constitution: The 1789 Declaration on the defence of individual rights, the preamble to the 1946 Constitution concerning collective social and economic rights and at last, the environmental rights mentioned in the 2004 Charter for the Environment, including the principles of sustainable development and precaution.

These three series of declarations might naturally appear universal. The writing is simple, clear and strict. The question of political regimes, the place of democracy, the role of the opposition and political pluralism need to be evoked. On this fourth point, the agreements must take place at all costs among the states. These can be made with regard to the goals to attain. The emerging nations have a role to play. They have political regimes that are diversified to say the least, but are characterized by a certain form of presidentialism, political parties that are multiple, a strong political regime where the basis is election, democracy as a goal even if, by definition, democracy does not mean unanimous agreements. For currents of opinion and the place of opposition, a door can be opened partway, while preserving the possibility for countries like China to keep their original structures but evolve. The necessity for a universal charter [25] is felt because of the multiplicity and wide variety of available current reference texts. The United Nations must be able to reconstruct the set of fundamental rights that have been affirmed with regard to individual rights, collective economic and social rights and environmental rights. The disparity in political regimes implies at least the existence of a tendency to defend democracy and respect citizens.

In conclusion, it is easy to note that France has shown how to put in place a complex system which reflects all its preoccupations with regard to the defence of Human Rights- economic, social and environmental. [26] To make them universal, what are missing perhaps are the inclusion of political regimes and the defence of the plurality of opinion and democracy that we find within the 1958 Constitution itself. The path is quite long - as long as there remain divergences among the European countries, the US and the emerging nations. But the end of American preponderance and its wish to represent itself in a less provocative and dominant profile encourages us to think that the conducive moment to update the diverse texts and arrive at a universal charter for the rights of man and citizen, collective rights and environmental rights has come. Indeed, the time has come.

—Translated from French by Geetha Ganapathy-Doré

Notes

1. See appendices.
2. The abbreviation BRIC for Brazil, Russia, India and China was put forward by Goldman Sachs in 2001.
3. The international balance of power seems to be rebalanced.
4. The US as represented by Obama is different from that represented by George Bush.
5. Cf Robert Etien, *Droit public général*, Paris: Foucher, 2008, pp. 46-49.
6. All these three texts form part of what is called the constitutional block.
7. Preamble which has a constitutional value after the ruling of the State Council of 16th January 1971.
8. Rich revolutionary period which was particularly recognized abroad and whose Declaration of 1789 remains a reference for the world.
9. The preamble to the 1946 Constitution is also a monument with regard to the declaration of economic and social rights.
10. Which allows for a certain continuity.

11. The reference to these principles is essential once again for the sake of continuity.
12. The formulation is significant.
13. Indeed we are witnessing the true birth of social rights.
14. These principles of international law form the very basis of the formulation of this right.
15. It is a new formulation in so far as any development is by nature ephemeral.
16. This Charter for the Environment like the Declaration of 1789 and the Preamble to the 1946 Constitution is well drafted, concise and precise.
17. The polluter pays principle is an acquired principle of responsibility hereafter.
18. Many observers did not expect the maintenance of this division.
19. A protocol yet to be ratified by the US.
20. The disillusion is certain particularly for the ecologists.
21. China and the US are major polluters.
22. Barack Obama had other worries at the time of the Copenhagen summit: getting a reform bill on social security passed.
23. Europe was found to be quite disappointing in its inability to defend a common position.
24. Indeed the current situation of the international community which involves the decline of the United States and Russia and the rise of emerging nations can be considered salutary.
25. It is high time that the international community set to work. The time is ripe and the necessity is considerable.
26. A remarkable construction that tends to be forgotten.

Appendix 1

Declaration of the Rights of Man and of the Citizen

(Approved by the National Assembly of France on August 26, 1789)

The representatives of the French people, organized as a National Assembly, believing that the ignorance, neglect, or contempt of the rights of man are the sole cause of public calamities and of the corruption of governments, have determined to set forth in a solemn declaration the natural, unalienable, and sacred rights of man, in order that this declaration, being constantly before all the members of the Social body, shall remind them continually of their rights and duties; in order that the acts of the legislative power, as well as those of the executive power, may be compared at any moment with the objects and purposes of all political institutions and may thus be more respected, and, lastly, in order that the grievances of the citizens, based hereafter upon simple and incontestable principles, shall tend to the maintenance of the constitution and redound to the happiness of all. Therefore the National Assembly recognizes and proclaims, in the presence and under the auspices of the Supreme Being, the following rights of man and of the citizen:

Articles:

1. Men are born and remain free and equal in rights. Social distinctions may be founded only upon the general good.
2. The aim of all political association is the preservation of the natural and imprescriptible rights of man. These rights are liberty, property, security, and resistance to oppression.
3. The principle of all sovereignty resides essentially in the nation. Nobody nor individual may exercise any authority which does not proceed directly from the nation.
4. Liberty consists in the freedom to do everything which injures no one else; hence the exercise of the natural rights of each man has no limits except those which assure to the other members of the society the enjoyment of the same rights. These limits can only be determined by law.

5. Law can only prohibit such actions as are hurtful to society. Nothing may be prevented which is not forbidden by law, and no one may be forced to do anything not provided for by law.
6. Law is the expression of the general will. Every citizen has a right to participate personally, or through his representative, in its foundation. It must be the same for all, whether it protects or punishes. All citizens, being equal in the eyes of the law, are equally eligible to all dignities and to all public positions and occupations, according to their abilities, and without distinction except that of their virtues and talents.
7. No person shall be accused, arrested, or imprisoned except in the cases and according to the forms prescribed by law. Any one soliciting, transmitting, executing, or causing to be executed, any arbitrary order shall be punished. But any citizen summoned or arrested in virtue of the law shall submit without delay, as resistance constitutes an offence.
8. The law shall provide for such punishments only as are strictly and obviously necessary, and no one shall suffer punishment except it be legally inflicted in virtue of a law passed and promulgated before the commission of the offence.
9. As all persons are held innocent until they shall have been declared guilty, if arrest shall be deemed indispensable, all harshness not essential to the securing of the prisoner's person shall be severely repressed by law.
10. No one shall be disquieted on account of his opinions, including his religious views, provided their manifestation does not disturb the public order established by law.
11. The free communication of ideas and opinions is one of the most precious of the rights of man. Every citizen may, accordingly, speak, write, and print with freedom, but shall be responsible for such abuses of this freedom as shall be defined by law.
12. The security of the rights of man and of the citizen

requires public military forces. These forces are, therefore, established for the good of all and not for the personal advantage of those to whom they shall be entrusted.

13. A common contribution is essential for the maintenance of the public forces and for the cost of administration. This should be equitably distributed among all the citizens in proportion to their means.
14. All the citizens have a right to decide, either personally or by their representatives, as to the necessity of the public contribution; to grant this freely; to know to what uses it is put; and to fix the proportion, the mode of assessment and of collection and the duration of the taxes.
15. Society has the right to require of every public agent an account of his administration.
16. A society in which the observance of the law is not assured, nor the separation of powers defined, has no constitution at all.
17. Since property is an inviolable and sacred right, no one shall be deprived thereof except where public necessity, legally determined, shall clearly demand it, and then only on condition that the owner shall have been previously and equitably indemnified.

    (Retrieved from http://www.hrcr.org/docs/frenchdec.html on April 26, 2010)

Appendix 2

Preamble to the October 27, 1946 Constitution

In the morrow of the victory achieved by the free peoples over the regimes that had sought to enslave and degrade humanity, the people of France proclaim anew that each human being, without distinction of race, religion or creed, possesses sacred and inalienable rights. They solemnly reaffirm the rights and freedoms of man and the citizen enshrined in the Declaration of Rights of 1789 and the fundamental principles acknowledged in the laws of the Republic.

They further proclaim, as being especially necessary to our times, the political, economic and social principles enumerated below:

1. The law guarantees women equal rights to those of men in all spheres.
2. Any man persecuted in virtue of his actions in favour of liberty may claim the right of asylum upon the territories of the Republic.
3. Each person has the duty to work and the right to employment. No person may suffer prejudice in his work or employment by virtue of his origins, opinions or beliefs.
4. All men may defend their rights and interests through union action and may belong to the union of their choice.
5. The right to strike shall be exercised within the framework of the laws governing it.
6. All workers shall, through the intermediary of their representatives, participate in the collective determination of their conditions of work and in the management of the work place.
7. All property and all enterprises that have or that may acquire the character of a public service or de facto monopoly shall become the property of society.
8. The Nation shall provide the individual and the family with the conditions necessary to their development.

9. It shall guarantee to all, notably to children, mothers and elderly workers, protection of their health, material security, rest and leisure. All people who, by virtue of their age, physical or mental condition, or economic situation, are incapable of working shall have to the right to receive suitable means of existence from society.
10. The Nation proclaims the solidarity and equality of all French people in bearing the burden resulting from national calamities.
11. The Nation guarantees equal access for children and adults to instruction, vocational training and culture. The provision of free, public and secular education at all levels is a duty of the State.
12. The French Republic, faithful to its traditions, shall conform to the rules of international public law. It shall undertake no war aimed at conquest, nor shall it ever employ force against the freedom of any people.
13. Subject to reciprocity, France shall consent to the limitations upon its sovereignty necessary to the organization and preservation of peace.
14. France shall form with its overseas peoples a Union founded upon equal rights and duties, without distinction of race or religion.
15. The French Union shall be composed of nations and peoples who agree to pool or coordinate their resources and their efforts in order to develop their respective civilizations, increase their well-being, and ensure their security.
16. Faithful to its traditional mission, France desires to guide the peoples under its responsibility towards the freedom to administer themselves and to manage their own affairs democratically; eschewing all systems of colonization founded upon arbitrary rule, it guarantees to all equal access to public office and the individual or collective exercise of the rights and freedoms proclaimed or confirmed herein.

(Retrieved from http://www.elysee.fr/elysee/anglais/the_institutions/founding_texts/preambule_to_the_27th_of_october_1946_constitution/preambule_to_the_27th_of_october_1946_constitution.20243.html on April 26, 2010).

Appendix 3
Charter for the Environment

2. The French People, Having considered that Natural resources and equilibria have conditioned the emergence of mankind;
3. The future and very existence of mankind are inextricably linked with its natural environment;
4. The environment is the common heritage of all human beings;
5. Man exerts ever-increasing influence over the conditions for life and over his own evolution;
6. Biological diversity, the fulfilment of the individual and the progress of human societies are affected by certain types of consumption or production and by excessive exploitation of natural resources;
7. The safeguarding of the environment is a goal to be pursued in the same way as the other fundamental interests of the Nation;
8. In order to ensure sustainable development, choices designed to meet the needs of the present generation should not jeopardise the ability of future generations and other peoples to meet their own needs,

Hereby Proclaim

1. Art 1: Each person has the right to live in a balanced environment which shows due respect for health.
2. Art 2: Each person has a duty to participate in preserving and enhancing the environment.
3. Art 3: Each person shall, in the conditions provided for by law, foresee and avoid the occurrence of any damage which he or she may cause to the environment or, failing that, limit the consequences of such damage.
4. Art 4: Each person shall be required, in the conditions provided for by law, to contribute to the making good of any damage he or she may have caused to the environment.

5. Art 5: When the occurrence of any damage, albeit unpredictable in the current state of scientific knowledge, may seriously and irreversibly harm the environment, public authorities shall, with due respect for the principle of precaution and the areas within their jurisdiction, ensure the implementation of procedures for risk assessment and the adoption of temporary measures commensurate with the risk involved in order to deal with the occurrence of such damage.
6. Art 6: Public policies shall promote sustainable development. To this end they shall reconcile the protection and enhancement of the environment with economic development and social progress.
7. Art 7: Each person has the right, in the conditions and to the extent provided for by law, to have access to any information pertaining to the environment in the possession of public bodies and to participate in the public decision-making process likely to affect the environment.
8. Art 8: Education and training with regard to the environment shall contribute to the exercising of the rights and duties set out in this Charter.
9. Art 9: Research and innovation shall contribute to the preservation and development of the environment.
10. Art 10: This Charter shall inspire France's actions at both European and international level.
    (Retrieved from
    http://www.assemblee-
    nationale.fr/english/8ab.asp#Charter on April 26, 2010).

6

European Convention for the Protection of Human Rights vis-à-vis Fundamental Rights under Indian Constitutional Law

Pawan Kumar

Introduction

The European Convention for the Protection of Human Rights and Fundamental Freedoms (herein after referred to as the Convention) was signed in Rome in 1950 by the then member states of the Council of Europe considering the Universal Declaration of Human Rights of 1948, which aims at securing the universal and effective recognition and observance of the rights declared therein. The Convention intended to achieve greater unity among its member states and further realisation of human rights and fundamental freedoms by reaffirming the members' profound belief in them which are considered the foundation of justice and peace in the world. It was a first step taken towards the collective enforcement of certain of the rights stated in the Universal Declaration. The High Contracting Parties declared that they wanted to secure to everyone within their jurisdiction these rights and freedoms, whereas on November 26, 1949, the people of India *inter alia* solemnly resolved through the preamble to the Indian Constitution [1] to secure to all its citizens:

- JUSTICE, social, economic and political;
- LIBERTY of thought, expression, belief, faith and worship;
- EQUALITY of status and opportunity;
- and to promote among them all FRATERNITY assuring the dignity of the individual and the Unity and *integrity* [2]

of the Nation. In order to realize the above objectives, a full part on Fundamental Rights was enumerated in the Indian Constitution namely Part III, which contains Articles 12 to 35 guaranteeing certain fundamental rights.

According to M.P. Jain, "a few good reasons made the enunciation of the Fundamental Rights in the Constitution rather inevitable. For one thing, the main political party, the Congress, had for long been demanding these Rights against the British rule. During the British rule in India, human rights were violated by the rulers on a very large scale. Therefore, the framers of the Constitution, many of whom had suffered long incarceration during the British regime, had a very positive attitude towards these rights. Secondly, the Indian society is fragmented into many religious, cultural and linguistic groups, and it was necessary to declare Fundamental Rights to give the people a sense of security and confidence. Then, it was thought necessary that people should have some Rights which may be enforced against the government which may become arbitrary at times. Though democracy was being introduced in India, yet democratic traditions were lacking, and there was a danger that the majority in the legislature may enact laws which may be oppressive to individuals or minority groups, and such a danger could be minimized by having a Bill of Rights in the Constitution." [3] The purpose of this study is to compare provisions contained in the Convention with those of the Indian Constitutional law, [4] especially Fundamental Freedoms.

Right to Life

Section 1 of the Convention contains rights and freedoms which are enumerated in Articles 2 to 18. Article 2 of the Convention states that (1) everyone's right to life shall be protected by law. No one shall be deprived of his life intentionally save in the execution of a sentence of a court following his conviction of a crime for which this penalty is provided by law. (2) Deprivation of life shall not be regarded as inflicted in contravention of this Article when it results from the use of force which is no more than absolutely necessary: (a) in defence of any person from unlawful violence; (b) in order to effect a lawful arrest or to prevent the escape of a person lawfully detained; (c) in action lawfully taken for the purpose of quelling a riot or insurrection. On the other hand, Article 21 of the Indian Constitution states that no person shall be deprived of his life or personal liberty except according to procedure established by law and Article 20 states that (1) No person shall be convicted of any offence except for violation of a law in force at the time of the commission of the act charged as an offence, nor be subjected to a penalty greater than that which might have been inflicted under the law in force at the time of the commission of the offence. (2) No person shall be prosecuted and punished for the same offence more than once. (3) No person accused of any offence shall be compelled to be a witness against himself.

Article 21 of the Indian Constitution is applicable to everyone like Article 2 of the Convention. Article 2 of the Convention soundly protects the right to life in comparison with Article 21 of the Indian Constitution, in the light of the judgment of the Supreme Court of India (herein after referred as the Supreme Court) in the A.K. Gopalan Case [5] which held that in Article 21, the phrase 'procedure established by law' meant procedure as laid down in the law as enacted by the legislature. It became obvious that in India, a person could be deprived of his 'life' in accordance with the procedure laid down in the pertinent law and the court has merely to see that the procedure established in the pertinent law been followed. However in the Smt. Maneka Gandhi case [6], the Supreme Court held that the procedure which deals with the modalities of regulating, restricting or even rejecting a fundamental right falling within Article 21 has to be fair, not foolish, carefully designed to effectuate, not to subvert, the substantive right itself. [7] Thus, understood, the 'procedure' must rule out anything arbitrary, freakish or bizarre. The 'procedure' in

Article 21 means fair, not formal, procedure. Law is reasonable law, not any enacted piece. [8] The principle of reasonableness, which legally as well as philosophically, is an essential element of equality or non-arbitrariness, pervades Article 14 and the procedure contemplated by Article 21 must answer to the test of reasonableness in order to be in conformity with Article 14. [9] It must bc "right and just and fair" and not arbitrary, fanciful or oppressive; otherwise it would be no procedure at all and the requirement of Article 21 would not be satisfied.

In the Chameli Singh case, [10] the Supreme Court observed that "Right to life guaranteed in any civilised society implies the right to food, water, decent environment, education, medical care and shelter". [11] In the Narmada Bachao Andolan case, [12] the Supreme Court held that water is part of right to life as enshrined in Article 21. The People's Union for Civil Liberties filed a writ petition in April 2001 under Article 32 of the Constitution for seeking right to food under Articles 21 and 47. [13] The Court by an interim order of November 28, 2008 directed all State Governments to introduce cooked mid-day meals in primary schools. The Court by another interim order of October 7, 2004 issued *inter alia* following directions: [14]

1. The efforts shall be made that all Scheduled Castes/ Scheduled Tribes hamlets/habitants in the country have Anganwadi Centres (herein after referred as AWCS) as early as possible *in view of the fact that Integrated Child Development Services (herein after referred as ICDS) has provision of food to children in age group 0-6 years through AWCS.*
2. The Contractors should not be used for supply of nutrition in Anganwadis and preferably ICDS funds shall be spent by making use of village communities, self help groups and Mahila Mandals for buying of grains and preparation of meals.
3. All State Governments/Union Territories shall put on their website full data for the ICDS schemes including where

AWCS are operational, the number of beneficiaries category-wise, the funds allocated and used and other related matters.

4. All the State Governments/Union Territories shall allocate funds for ICDS on the basis of norm of one rupee per child per day, 100 beneficiaries per AWS and 300 days' feeding in a year i.e. on the same basis on which the Centre makes the allocation.
5. Below Poverty Line shall not be used as an eligibility criterion for ICDS.
6. All sanctioned projects shall be operationalised and provided food as per these norms and wherever utensils have not been provided, the same shall be provided. The vacancies for the operational ICDS shall be filled forthwith.
7. All the State Government/Union Territories shall utilize the entire State and Central allocation under ICDS and under no circumstances, the same shall be diverted and preferably also not returned to the Centre and, if returned, a detailed explanation for non-utilisation shall be filed in this Court.
8. All States/Union Territories shall make earnest efforts to cover the slums under ICDS.
9. The Centre and the States/ Union Territories shall ensure that all amounts allocated are sanctioned in time so that there is no disruption whatsoever in the feeding of children.

The Honourable Supreme Court on November 28, 2001, further directed *inter alia* as follows: [15]

1. The States are directed to complete the identification of Below Poverty Line families, issuing of cards and commencement of distribution of twenty five kg grain per family per month latest by January 1, 2002 *under Targeted Public Distribution Scheme (TPDS).*
2. We direct the States and the Union Territories to complete identification of beneficiaries, issuing of cards and

distribution of grain under *Antyodaya Anna Yojana* latest by January 1, 2002.

3. We direct the State Government/Union Territories to implement the Mid-Day Meal Scheme by providing every child in every government and government-assisted primary schools with a prepared mid-day meal with a minimum content of 300 calories and eight to twelve grams of protein each day of school for a minimum of 200 days. Those Government providing dry rations instead of cooked meals in all government and government-aided primary schools in half of the districts of the State (in order of poverty) and must with a further period of three months extend the provision of cooked meals to the remaining parts of the State.
4. The States/Union Territories are directed to identify the beneficiaries under the Annapurna Scheme and distribute the grain latest by January 1, 2002.
5. We direct the State Government/Union Territories to implement the ICDS in full and to ensure that every ICDS disbursing centre in the country shall provide as under:

- each child up to six years of age to get 300 calories and eight to ten grams of protein;
- each adolescent girl to get 500 calories and twenty to twenty five grams of protein;
- each pregnant woman and each nursing mother to get 500 calories and twenty to twenty five grams of protein;
- each malnourished child to get 600 calories and sixteen to twenty grams of protein;
- to have disbursement centre in every settlement.

6. We direct the State Government/Union Territories to implement the National Maternity Benefit Scheme by paying all BPL pregnant women ₹ 500 through the Sarpanch eight to twelve weeks prior to delivery for each of the first two months.
7. We direct the State Governments/Union Territories to implement the National Family Benefit Scheme and pay a

BPL family ₹ 10,000 within four weeks through a local Sarpanch, whenever the primary breadwinner of the family dies.

8. We direct that a copy of this order be translated in regional languages and in English by the respective States/Union Territories and prominently displayed in all gram panchayats, government school buildings and fair price shops.
9. In order to ensure transparency in selection of beneficiaries and their access to these Schemes, the gram panchayats will also display a list of all beneficiaries under the various Schemes. Copies of the Scheme and the list of beneficiaries shall be made available by the gram panchayats to members of public for inspection.
10. We direct Doordarshan and All India Radio to adequately publicise various Schemes and this order.

The Honourable Supreme Court on December 13, 2006, further directed inter-alia as follows: [16]

1. The Government of India shall sanction and operationalised a minimum of fourteen Lakh AWCS in a phased and even manner starting forthwith and ending in December 2008. In doing so, the Central Government shall identify Scheduled Castes and Scheduled Tribes hamlets/habitants for AWCS on priority basis.
2. The Government of India shall ensure that population norms for opening of AWCS must not be revised upward under any circumstances. While maintaining the upper limit of one AWC per 1000 population, the minimum limit for opening of a new AWC is a population of 300 may be kept in view. Further, rural communities and slum-dwellers should be entitled to an "Anganwadi on demand" (not late than three months) from the date of demand in cases where a settlement has at least forty children under six but no Anganwadi.
3. The unversalisation of ICDS involves extending all ICDS services (supplementary nutrition, growth monitoring,

nutrition and health education, immunization, referral and pre-school education) to every child under the age of six, all pregnant women and lactating mothers and all adolescent girls.

4. All the State Governments and Union Territories shall fully implement ICDS by, *inter alia*,

- allocating and spending at least ₹ 2 per child per day for supplementary nutrition out of which the Central Government shall contribute one rupee per child per day;
- allocating and spending at least ₹ 2.70 for every severely malnourished child per day for supplementary nutrition out of which the Central Government shall contribute ₹ 1.35 per child per day;
- allocating and spending at least ₹ 2.30 for every pregnant woman, nursing mother/adolescent girl per day for supplementary nutrition out of which the Central Government shall contribute v 1.15.

The foregoing history shows that case law has largely extended the meaning of fundamental rights as defined in the Constitution.

Right against Inhuman Treatment

Article 3 of the Convention states that no one shall be subjected to torture or to inhuman or degrading treatment or punishment. In the Indian Constitution there is no such provision. However, the Supreme Court in the Francis Coralie Mullin case [17] observed *inter alia* that any form of torture or cruel, inhuman or degrading treatment would be offensive to human dignity and constitute an inroad into this right to live and it would, on this view, be prohibited by Article 12 unless it is in accordance with procedure prescribed by law, which authorises such punishment and no procedure prescribed by law, which leads to such torture or cruel, inhuman or degrading element can ever be the test of reasonable and non-arbitrariness. It would be plainly unconstitutional and void as being violative of Articles 14 and 21. It could be seen that there is implicit in Article 21 the right to protection against torture or cruel, inhuman or degrading treatment which is enumerated in Article 5 of the Universal Declaration of Human Rights and guaranteed by Article 7 of the International Covenant on Civil and Political Rights. [18] In the Sunil Batra I case, [19] the petitioner, a convict under death sentence, through a letter to one of the Judges of the Supreme Court, alleged that he was kept in solitary confinement and torture was practised upon another prisoner namely Prem Chand by a jail warder, to extract money from the victim through his visiting relations. The letter was converted into a habeas corpus proceeding.

The Court found that prisoner Prem Chand was brought by prison authorities for treatment before Dr. Kapoor, who had made an entry in the hospital register and told that a prisoner named Prem Chand s/o Prehlad who was produced before him had suffered physical abuse. The Court observed that inflictions may take many protean forms, apart from physical assaults, pushing the prisoner into a solitary cell, denial of a necessary amenity, and more dreadful sometimes, transfer to a distant prison where visits or society of friends or relatives may be snapped, allotment of degrading labour, and the like, may be punitive in effect. Every such affliction or abridgement is an infraction of liberty or life in its wider sense and cannot be sustained unless Article 21 is satisfied. There must be a corrective legal procedure, fair, reasonable and effective. Such infraction will be arbitrary under Article 14, if it is dependent on unguided discretion, unreasonable under Article 19, if it is irremediable and unappealable and unfair under Article 21, if it violates natural justice. The Supreme Court also held solitary confinement a cruel and inhuman treatment being violative of Article 21. In the Charles Sobraj case, [20] the Court held that putting prisoner into bar fetters is cruel and inhuman treatment amounting to violation of Article 21.

Abolition of Slavery

Article 4 of the Convention states that (1) no one shall be

held in slavery or servitude. (2) No one shall be required to perform forced or compulsory labour. (3) For the purpose of this Article the term "forced or compulsory labour" shall not include: (a) any work required to be done in the ordinary course of detention imposed according to the provisions of Article 5 of this Convention or during conditional release from such detention; (b) any service of a military character or, in case of conscientious objectors in countries where they are recognized, service exacted instead of compulsory military service; (c) any service exacted in case of an emergency or calamity threatening the life or well-being of the community; (d) any work or service which forms part of normal civic obligations. On the other hand, Article 23 states that (1) traffic in human beings and beggary and other similar forms of forced labour are prohibited and any contravention of this provision shall be an offence punishable in accordance with law. (2) Nothing in this Article shall prevent the State from imposing compulsory service for public purposes, and in imposing such service the State shall not make any discrimination on grounds only of religion, race, caste or class or any of them.

Therefore, on the face of it, Article 23 of the Indian Constitution is wider in scope than Article 4 of the Convention. Slavery is not mentioned in Article 23 of the Indian Constitution. However, the Calcutta High Court in the Dubar case [21] held that there is no doubt the expression 'traffic in human beings' would cover it. The Supreme Court in the People's Union for Democratic Rights case [22] (famously known as the Asiad Workers case), where non-payment of minimum wages to construction workers was challlenged, *inter alia*, for the violation of Article 23, held that the prohibition against 'traffic is human beings and beggary and other similar forms of forced labour' is 'a general prohibition, total in its effect and all pervasive in its range'. The Court held that all unwilling labour is forced labour, whether paid or not, and is therefore prohibited. [23] The Court held that where someone works for less than minimum wages the presumption is that he is working under some compulsion. [24] The Court concluded that any factor which deprives a person of a choice of alternatives and compels him to adopt one particular course of action may properly be regarded as 'force' and if labour or service is compelled as a result of such 'force', it would be forced labour. [25] The Supreme Court in the Bandhua Mukti Morcha case, [26] declared bonded labour as a crude form of forced labour prohibited by Article 23.

Right to Liberty and Security of Person

Article 5 of the Convention states that (1) everyone has the right to liberty and security of person. No one shall be deprived of his liberty, save in the following cases and in accordance with a procedure prescribed by law: (a) the lawful detention of a person after conviction by a competent court; (b) the lawful arrest or detention of a person for non- compliance with the lawful order of a court or in order to secure the fulfilment of any obligation prescribed by law; (c) the lawful arrest or detention of a person effected for the purpose of bringing him before the competent legal authority on reasonable suspicion of having committed an offence or when it is reasonably considered necessary to prevent his committing an offence or fleeing after having done so; (d) the detention of a minor by lawful order for the purpose of educational supervision or his lawful detention for the purpose of bringing him before the competent legal authority; (e) the lawful detention of persons for the prevention of the spreading of infectious diseases, of persons of unsound mind, alcoholics or drug addicts or vagrants; (f) the lawful arrest or detention of a person to prevent his effecting an unauthorised entry into the country or of a person against whom action is being taken with a view to deportation or extradition. (2) everyone who is arrested shall be informed promptly, in a language which he understands, of the reasons for his arrest and of any charge against him. (3) Everyone arrested or detained in accordance with the provisions of paragraph 1.c of this Article shall be brought promptly before a judge or other officer, authorised by law, to exercise judicial power and shall be entitled to trial within a reasonable time or to release pending trial. Release may be conditioned by guarantees to appear for trial. (4) Everyone who is deprived of his liberty by arrest or detention shall be entitled to take proceedings by which the lawfulness of his detention shall be decided speedily by a court and his release ordered if the detention is not lawful. (5) Everyone who has been the victim of arrest or detention in contravention of the provisions of this Article shall have an enforceable right to compensation.

Article 6 of the Convention states that (1) in the determination of his civil rights and obligations or of any criminal charge against him, everyone is entitled to a fair and public hearing within a reasonable time by an independent and impartial tribunal established by law. Judgment shall be pronounced publicly but the press and public may be excluded from all or part of the trial in the interests of morals, public order or national security in a democratic society, where the interests of juveniles or the protection of the private life of the parties so require, or to the extent strictly necessary in the opinion of the court in special circumstances where publicity would prejudice the interests of justice. (2) Everyone charged with a criminal offence shall be presumed innocent until proved guilty according to law. (3) Everyone charged with a criminal offence has the following minimum rights: (a) to be informed promptly, in a language which he understands and in detail, of the nature and cause of the accusation against him; (b) to have adequate time and facilities for the preparation of his defence; (c) to defend himself in person or through legal assistance of his own choice or, if he has not sufficient means to pay for legal assistance, to be given it free when the interests of justice so require; (d) to examine or have examined witnesses against him and to obtain the attendance and examination of witnesses on his behalf under the same conditions as witnesses against him; (e) to have the free assistance of an interpreter if he cannot understand or speak the language used in court.

Coming to India, Article 22 states that (1) no person who is arrested shall be detained in custody, without being informed, as soon as may be, of the grounds for such arrest nor shall be denied the right to consult, and to be defended by, a legal practitioner of his choice. (2) every person who is arrested and detained in custody shall be produced before the nearest magistrate within a period of twenty four hours of such arrest excluding the time necessary for the journey from the place of arrest to the court of the magistrate and no such person shall be detained in custody beyond the said period without the authority of a magistrate. The Supreme Court in the A.K. Gopalan case [27] interpreted the expression 'personal liberty' in a very narrow sense by concluding that 'personal liberty' was confined to freedom from detention or physical restraint. For the first time the meaning and scope of 'personal liberty' came up for consideration before the Supreme Court in the Karak Singh case. [28]

The Court held that an unauthorised intrusion into a person's home and the disturbance caused to him thereby violated personal liberty as enshrined in Article 21. The Supreme Court in the Satwant Singh Sawhney case [29] held that right to travel abroad is included within the expression 'personal liberty' according to procedure established by law. The Court in the Prabhakar Pandurang case [30] held that the right to personal liberty includes the right to write a book and get it published and when this right is denied to a detainee without the authority of law, it amounts to violation of Article 21 of the Indian Constitution. The Court in the Joginder Kumar case [31] concluded that no arrest can be made in a routine manner on a mere allegation of commission of an offence made against a person. It would be prudent for a police officer in the interest of protection of the constitutional rights of a citizen and perhaps in his own interest that no arrest should be made without a reasonable satisfaction reached after some investigation as to the genuineness and bonafide of a complaint and a reasonable belief both as to the person's complicity and even so as to the need to effect arrest.

According to Justice Krishna Iyer [32], Article 22 (1) does not mean that a person who is not under arrest or custody can be denied the right to consult an advocate of his choice. The spirit and sense of Article 22 (1) is that it is fundamental to the rule of law that the services of a lawyer shall be available for consultation to any accused person under circumstances of near custodial interrogation. The Supreme Court in the Bhim Singh case [33] has criticized the conduct of a magistrate who passed an order remanding the accused to police custody without the accused having been produced before him personally and acted in a very casual way. The Court considered it as a pity that the magistrate acted without any sense of responsibility or genuine concern for the liberty of the subject. The police officer acted deliberately and mala fide and the magistrate aided him either by colluding with him or by his casual attitude. The Court ordered the State to pay ₹ 50,000 to the concerned person as monetary compensation for the gross violation of the constitutional rights of the accused under Articles 21 and 22 (2).

In *Vishaka v. State of Rajasthan* [34], the Supreme Court has declared sexual harassment of a working woman at her place of work as amounting to violation of rights of gender equality and right to life and personal liberty which is a clear violation of Articles 14, 15 and 21 of the Constitution. The Court has observed, "The meaning and content of the fundamental rights guaranteed in the Constitution of India are of sufficient amplitude to encompass all the facets of gender equality including prevention of sexual harassment or abuse". [35]

Further, the Court accepted the proposition that the international conventions and norms are to be read into the fundamental rights when there is no inconsistency between them, and there is a void in the domestic law. The Court issued certain directions placing certain obligations on the employers or other responsible persons in work places and other institutions "whether in the public or private sector." The

Court reiterated the Vishaka case ruling in *Apparel Export Promotion Council v. A.K. Chopra.* [36] The Court has observed, "There is no gainsaying that each incident of sexual harassment, at the place of work, results in violation of the fundamental right to gender equality and the Right to life and liberty- the two most precious Fundamental Rights guaranteed by the Constitution of India...In our opinion, the contents of the fundamental rights guaranteed in our constitution are of sufficient amplitude to encompass all facets of gender equality, including prevention of sexual harassment and abuse and the courts are under a constitutional obligation to protect and preserve those fundamental rights. That sexual harassment of a female at the place of work is incompatible with the dignity and honour of a female and needs to be eliminated...". [37]

Protection in Respect of Conviction for Offences

Article 7 of the Convention states that (1) no one shall be held guilty of any criminal offence on account of any act or omission which did not constitute a criminal offence under national or international law at the time when it was committed. Nor shall a heavier penalty be imposed than the one that was applicable at the time the criminal offence was committed. (2) This Article shall not prejudice the trial and punishment of any person for any act or omission which, at the time when it was committed, was criminal according to the general principles of law recognised by civilised nations. Article 20 (1) of the Indian Constitution states that no person shall be convicted of any offence except for violation of a law in force at the time of the commission of the act charged as an offence, nor be subjected to a penalty greater than that which might have been inflicted under the law in force at the time of the commission of the offence. In *Rao Shiva Bahadur Singh v. State of V.P.* [38], the accused was tried for certain offences alleged to have been committed in February, March and April 1949, under provisions of the V.P. Ordinance No. 48 of 1949, which was enacted on September 11, 1949. It was provided in Section 2 of the

Ordinance that it should be deemed to have been in force in Vindhya Pradesh from August 9, 1948. The Court held that Section 2 violated Article 20 (1).

Right to Privacy

Article 8 of the Convention states that (1) everyone has the right to respect for his private and family life, his home and his correspondence. (2) There shall be no interference by a public authority with the exercise of this right except such as is in accordance with the law and is necessary in a democratic society in the interests of national security, public safety or the economic well-being of the country, for the prevention of disorder or crime, for the protection of health or morals, or for the protection of the rights and freedoms of others. The Supreme Court in the Govind case [39] contemplated that right to personal liberty guaranteed under Article 21 of the Indian Constitution includes a right to privacy. The Court in the R. Raj Gopal case [40] held that the right to privacy includes the right to be left alone and a citizen has the right to safeguard the privacy of his own, his family, marriage, procreation, motherhood, child-bearing and education among other matters. The Court in the PUCL case [41] held that right to privacy includes telephone conversation and telephone-tapping amounts to its violation unless it is permitted under the procedure established by law.

Right to Religious Freedom

Article 9 of the Convention states that: (1) Everyone has the right to freedom of thought, conscience and religion; this right includes freedom to change his religion or belief and freedom, either alone or in community with others and in public or private, to manifest his religion or belief, in worship, teaching, practice and observance. (2) Freedom to manifest one's religion or beliefs shall be subject only to such limitations as are prescribed by law and are necessary in a democratic society in the interests of public safety, for the protection of public order, health or morals, or for the protection of the rights and freedoms of others. On the other hand, Article 25 of the Indian Constitution states that (1) Subject to public order, morality and health and to the other provisions of this Part, all persons are equally entitled to freedom of conscience and the right to freely profess, practise and propagate religion. (2) Nothing in this Article shall affect the operation of any existing law or prevent the State from making any law: (a) regulating or restricting any economic, financial, political or other secular activity which may be associated with religious practise; (b) providing for social welfare and reform or the throwing open of Hindu religious institutions of a public character to all classes and sections of Hindus. In *S.P. Mittal v. Union of India*, [42] taking into account the denials of Sri Aurobindo that he was establishing a religion, the Supreme Court of India took a restricted view of religion by holding that the teachings of Sri Aurobindo constituted a philosophy and not religion even if his followers, claimed them to be their religion. In *Bijoe Emmanuel v. State of Kerala* [43], the Supreme Court upheld the religious belief of the Jehovah's Witnesses not to sing the National Anthem under Article 25 of the Indian Constitution.

Right to Freedom of Speech and Expression

Article 10 of the Convention states that (1) everyone has the right to freedom of expression. This right shall include freedom to hold opinions and to receive and impart information and ideas without interference by public authority and regardless of frontiers. This Article shall not prevent States from requiring the licensing of broadcasting, television or cinema enterprises. (2) the exercise of these freedoms, since it carries with it duties and responsibilities, may be subject to such formalities, conditions, restrictions or penalties as are prescribed by law and are necessary in a democratic society, in the interests of national security, territorial integrity or public safety, for the prevention of disorder or crime, for the protection of health or morals, for the protection of the reputation or rights of others, for preventing the disclosure of information received in confidence, or for maintaining the authority and impartiality of the judiciary. Article 19 (1) (a) states that all citizens shall have the right to freedom of speech and expression. In *Romesh Thapper v. State of Madras* [44], the Supreme Court observed:

"Freedom of speech and of the press lies at the foundation of all democratic organizations, for without free political discussion no public education, so essential for the proper functioning of the process of popular government, is possible. A freedom of such amplitude involves risks of abuse. But the framers of the Constitution may well have reflected with Madison, who was the leading spirit in the preparation of the First Amendment of the Federal Constitution, that it is better to leave a few of its noxious branches to their luxuriant growth than by pruning them away, to injure the vigour of those yielding the proper fruits...". [45]

Article 11 of the Convention states that (1) everyone has the right to freedom of peaceful assembly and to freedom of association with others, including the right to form and to join trade unions for the protection of his interests. (2) no restrictions shall be placed on the exercise of these rights other than such as are prescribed by law and are necessary in a democratic society in the interests of national security or public safety, for the prevention of disorder or crime, for the protection of health or morals or for the protection of the rights and freedoms of others. This Article shall not prevent the imposition of lawful restrictions on the exercise of these rights by members of the armed forces, of the police or of the administration of the State. Clause (1) (b) of Article 19 of the Indian Constitution states that all citizens shall have the right to assemble peacefully and without arms and Clause (1) (c) states that all citizens shall have the right to form associations or unions. In *Babulal Parate v. State of Maharashtra* [46], the Supreme Court observed that the right of citizens to take out processions or to hold public meetings flows from the right in Article 19 (1) (b) to assemble peacefully and without arms and the right to move anywhere in the territory of India.

Article 12 of the Convention states that men and women of marriageable age have the right to marry and to found a family, according to the national laws governing the exercise of this right. There is no such corresponding Article in Indian Constitution but all these rights are facets of right to life as extended by the Supreme Court of India.

Right to Effective Remedies

Article 13 of the Convention states that everyone whose rights and freedoms as set forth in this Convention are violated shall have an effective remedy before a national authority notwithstanding that the violation has been committed by persons acting in an official capacity. Article 14 states that the enjoyment of the rights and freedoms set forth in this Convention shall be secured without discrimination on any ground such as sex, race, colour, language, religion, political or other opinion, national or social origin, association with a national minority, property, birth or other status. Articles 32 and 226 of the Indian Constitution provide remedy for enforcing the fundamental rights enshrined in Part III of the Constitution. Clause (1) of Article 32 states that the right to move the Supreme Court by appropriate proceedings for the enforcement of the rights conferred by this Part is guaranteed and Clause (2) provides that the Supreme Court shall have power to issue directions or orders or writs, including writs in the nature of habeas corpus, mandamus, prohibition, quo warranto and certiorari, whichever may be appropriate, for the enforcement of any of the rights conferred by this Part. Article 226 (1) states that notwithstanding anything in Article 32, every High Court shall have power, throughout the territories in relation to which it exercises jurisdiction, to issue any person or authority, including in appropriate cases, any Government, within those territories, directions, orders or writs, including writs in the nature of habeas corpus, mandamus, prohibition, quo warranto and certiorari, or any of them, for the enforcement of any of the rights conferred by Part III and for any other purpose.

The Supreme Court has further strengthened this right through the Bandhu Mukti Morcha case [47] by stating that the Court can allow any member of the public acting bonafide to espouse the cause of persons who on account of their poverty or disability are unable to do so. Therefore, Public Interest Litigation may be filed by any bona fide individual or group for the gross violation of fundamental rights if any. In Labourers Working on the Salal Hydro-Project case, [48] the People's Union for Democratic Rights addressed a letter to Justice D.A. Desai, enclosing a copy of a news item carried by the Indian Express dated August 26, 1982, that a large number of migrant workmen from different states including the State of Orissa were working on the Salal Hydro-Project in difficult conditions and they were denied the benefits of various labour laws and were subjected to exploitation by the contractors to whom different portions of the work was entrusted by the Central Government. [49]

Justice Desai was requested to treat the letter as a writ petition so that justice may be done to the poor labourers working in the Salal Hydro Electric Project. [50] The letter was placed before a bench of the Supreme Court and it was treated as a writ petition. [51] The Court directed that "the Union of India and the Chief Labour Commissioner (Central) shall ensure that hereafter minimum wage is paid directly by the Central Government or the contractors as the case may be, to the workmen employed by them without the intervention of any sub-contractors or jamadars or Khatedars and without any deduction whatsoever except such as may be authorized statutorily". [52] The Court also directed the Central Government to take immediate steps for enforcement of the provisions of the Inter-State Migrant Workmen (Regulation of Employment and Conditions of Service) Act, 1979 in regard to Inter-State migrant workmen employed in the project work as the final report of the Labour Commissioner (J&K) clearly shown that Oriya workmen employed on the project site were recruited by Khatedars from their villages in Orissa. [53]

The Court also directed the Central Government to take immediate steps for ensuring that Canteens, rest rooms and washing facilities are provided by Contractors to the workmen employed by them in accordance with the requirement of sections 16, 17 and 18 (c) of the Contract Labour (Regulation and Abolition) Act, 1970 read with Rules 41 to 50 and 57 of the Contract Labour (Regulation and Abolition) Central Rules, 1971. [54] The Court also observed that the Central Government would do well to persuade the workmen to send their children to a nearby school and arrange not only for the school fees to be paid but also provide free of charge, books and other facilities such as transportation. [55]

Fundamental Freedoms during Emergency

Article 15 of the Convention states that (1) in time of war or other public emergency threatening the life of the nation any High Contracting Party may take measures derogating from its obligations under this Convention to the extent strictly required by the exigencies of the situation, provided that such measures are not inconsistent with its other obligations under international law. (2) No derogation from Article 2, except in respect of deaths resulting from lawful acts of war, or from Articles 3, 4 (paragraph 1) and 7 shall be made under this provision. (3) Any High Contracting Party availing itself of this right of derogation shall keep the Secretary General of the Council of Europe fully informed of the measures which it has taken and the reasons therefore. It shall also inform the Secretary General of the Council of Europe when such measures have ceased to operate and the provisions of the Convention are again being fully executed.

On the other hand, Clause (1) of Article 358 states that while a Proclamation of Emergency declaring that the security of India or any part of the territory thereof is threatened by war or by external aggression is in operation, nothing in Article 19 shall restrict the power of the State as defined in Part III to make any law or to take any executive action which the State would, but for the provisions contained in that Part, be competent to make or to take, but any law so made shall, to the extent of the incompetency, cease to have effect as soon as the Proclamation ceases to operate, except as respects things done or omitted to be done before the law so ceases to have effect. Article 359 (1) states that where a Proclamation of Emergency is in operation, the President may by order declare that the right to move any court for the enforcement of such of the rights conferred by Part III (except Articles 20 and 21) as may be mentioned in the order and all proceedings pending in any court for the enforcement of the rights so mentioned shall remain suspended for the period during which the Proclamation is in force or for such shorter period as may be specified in the order.

Conclusion

This comparative analysis clearly shows that the framers of Indian Constitution took cognizance of the legal system of the world including American Constitution by conferring Fundamental Rights to the people of this Country and the Indian Higher Judiciary has enormously extended these rights by liberally interpreting these rights especially after the Maneka Gandhi case in 1978. The Indian Constitution takes care of women and children by making special provisions for them under Article 15 (3) and the Supreme Court has even upheld reservation in jobs under the State for women under this Article, whereas, there is no such provision under the European Convention. The Indian Constitution also makes special provisions for the advancement of socially and backward classes under Articles 15 (4) and Article 16 (4).

However, the reality remains that for majority of the people of this country these rights are available only in books as they are not aware of these fundamental rights as demonstrated by the fundamental right to food but at the same time hunger death reports feature regularly in newspapers and journals and malnutrition is common among Indian children. There are many people who are aware of their fundamental rights but do not have means to enforce them. The Supreme Court has evolved a remedy in the form of Public Interest Litigation to secure fundamental rights to the people, who have no means to enforce their fundamental rights, which is foreign to the European Convention. However, Public Interest Litigation has been converted by the people into Paise Interest Litigation or Personal Interest Litigation or Publicity Interest Litigation. There is fundamental right to education from the age of six to fourteen years but around thirty-three children out of every hundred in the above age group hardly find their way to schools. The Prisoners have been conferred fundamental rights, but there are regular reports of violations of their fundamental rights by jail authorities. There is fundamental right to equality under Indian Constitution, but it is hardly visible either on political or economic or social fronts. There is need on the part of State to be more vigorous to secure these fundamental rights to a large section of the people of this country by empowering them economically and politically.

Notes

1. P.M. Bakshi, *The Constitution of India*, Delhi: Universal Law Publishing Co., 2008, p. 1.
2. The word in italics was inserted by the Constitution (42nd Amendment) Act, 1976.
3. M.P. Jain, *Indian Constitutional Law*, Nagpur: Wadhwa and Company, 2003, vol. I, p. 972.
4. According to K.C. Wheare, "the Constitution of a country seeks to establish its fundamental or basic or apex organs of government and administration, describe their structure, composition, powers and principal functions, define the inter-relationship of these organs with one another, and regulate their relationship with the people, more particularly, the political relationship. The term "Constitutional law" is broader than the term "Constitution", as it comprises of the "Constitution", relevant statutory law, judicial decisions and conventions." Quoted by Jain, *op.cit.*
5. A.K. Gopalan v. State of Madras, AIR 1950 SC 27.

6. Maneka Gandhi v. Union of India, AIR 1978 SC 597.
7. *Ibid*, as per Justice Krishna Iyer.
8. *Ibid.*
9. *Ibid*, as per Justice P.N. Bhagwati.
10. Chameli Singh v. State of Uttar Pradesh, (1996) 2 SCC 549; Also see, Kishen Pattnayak v. State of Orissa, (1989) 1 SCC 528.
11. *Ibid.*, 555.
12. Narmada Bachao Andolan v. Union of India, (2000) 10 SCC 664.
13. Writ Petition (Civil) 196 of 2001, PUCL v. Union of India and others.
14. People's Union for Civil Liberties v. Union of India, (2004) 12 SCC 104; Also see, People's Union for Civil Liberties v. Union of India, (2004) 12 SCC 108.
15. People's Union for Civil Liberties v. Union of India, (2007) 1 SCC 728.
16. People's Union for Civil Liberties v. Union of India, (2007) 1 SCC 719.
17. Francis Coralie Mullin v. Union Territory of Delhi, AIR 1981 SC 746.
18. *Ibid.*
19. Sunil Batra v. Delhi Administration, AIR 1978 SC 1675.
20. Charles Sobraj v. Superintendent, Central Jail, New Delhi, AIR 1978 SC 1514.
21. Dubar v. Union of India, AIR 1952 Cal 496.
22. People's Union for Democratic Rights v. Union of India, (1982) 3 SCC 235.
23. *Ibid.*, 258.
24. *Ibid.*, 259.
25. *Ibid.*
26. Bandhua Mukti Morcha v. Union of India, (1984) SCC 161.
27. See n. 4.
28. Karak Singh v. State of Uttar Pradesh, AIR 1963 SC 1295.
29. Satwant Singh Sawhney v. A.P.O., New Delhi, AIR 1967 SC 1836.
30. State of Maharashtra v. Prabhakar Pandurang, AIR 1966 SC 424.
31. Joginder Kumar v. State of Uttar Pradesh, AIR 1994 SC 1349.
32. Nandini Satpathy v. P. L. Dani.

33. Bhim Singh v. State of Jammu and Kashmir, AIR 1986 SC 494.
34. AIR 1997 SC 3011.
35. *Ibid.*
36. AIR 1999 SC 625.
37. *Ibid.*
38. AIR 1953 SC 394.
39. Govind v. State of M.P., AIR 1975 SC 1378.
40. R. Raj Gopal v. State of T.N. (1994) 6 SCC 632.
41. People's Union for Civil Liberties v. Union of India, AIR 1997 SC 568.
42. AIR 1983 SC 1.
43. AIR 1987 SC 748.
44. AIR 1950 SC 124; Also see, Brij Bhusan v. State of Delhi, AIR 1950 SC 129; Virndra v. State of Punjab, AIR 1957 SC 896; R. Rajagopal v. State of T.N. (1994) 6 SCC 632; Communist Party of India (M) v. Bharat Kumar, AIR 1998 SC 184.
45. *Ibid.*
46. AIR 1961 SC 884.
47. Bandhua Mukti Morcha v. Union of India, AIR 1984 SC 802.
48. Labourers Working on Salal Hydro-Project v State of J & K, AIR 1984 SC 177.
49. Id at 178.
50. *Ibid.*
51. *Ibid.*
52. *Ibid.*
53. *Ibid.*, 181.
54. *Ibid.*, 183.
55. *Ibid.*

Section III

The Convention Seen through the Prism of International Relations

7

Human Rights Dimensions of European Foreign and Development Cooperation Policies: A Case Study of India-EU Relations

B. Krishnamurthy and S. Jeeva

EU's Human Rights Policy

The European Union (EU) is projected by leaders like Joseph Fischer, former Minister of Foreign Affairs of Germany, as a "Community of values" and of "high" standards. [1] Joseph Nye, leading proponent and theorist of soft power, opines that "instruments of soft power include debates on cultural values, dialogues on ideology, the attempt to influence through good example and the appeal to commonly accepted human values" and illustrates the Union as a leading soft power. [2] Ian Manners projects EU as a normative power, which sets norms on the basis of values, images and principles (VIPs) that it holds dear to it and imposes them gently rather than by force on third countries. [3] The EU intends to 'lead' the comity of nations by its example on the issue of protection, promotion and defence of human rights.

Human rights dimensions are quite discernible in the European foreign and development cooperation Policies. Article 177 of the Treaty establishing the European Community (TEC) of 1957 states that "community policy... shall contribute to the general objective of developing and consolidating democracy and the rule of law and to that of respecting human rights and fundamental freedoms". In the 1970s, when the Europeans toyed with the idea of European

Political Cooperation, the leaders reiterated their stand that the Community stood for the promotion and protection of human rights domestically as well as in the third countries.

In June 1991, the Luxemburg Declaration of the European Council maintained that the European concern for human rights and fundamental freedoms 'cannot be considered as interference in the internal affairs of a state and constitute an important and legitimate part of their dialogue with third countries'. Subsequently, in November, the Council for Development and Human Rights issued a resolution that outlined the positive and negative tools for the pursuit of human rights and principles abroad through political, diplomatic, economic and aid means. It also introduced the principle of conditionality, whereby the EU reserved the right to adopt negative measures 'in the event of grave and persistent human rights violations or the serious interruption of democratic processes'.

Article 6 of the Treaty on European Union (TEU) or the Maastricht Treaty of 1992 maintains: "The Union is founded on the principles of liberty, democracy, respect for human rights and fundamental freedoms, and the rule of law, principles which are common to the Member States" and adds: "The Union shall respect fundamental rights, as guaranteed by the European Convention for the Protection of Human Rights and Fundamental Freedoms signed in Rome on November 4, 1950 and as they result from the constitutional traditions common to the Member States, as general principles of Community law." The triptych, human rights-democracy-rule of law, is projected by Article 6 para 1 as the socle of the EU and thus of its three pillars such as the Communities, Common Foreign and Security Policy (CFSP) and the cooperation in the fields of justice and home affairs. The Amsterdam Treaty of June 1997 too maintains that the Union is founded on the principles of liberty, democracy, respect for human rights and fundamental freedoms and the rule of law, principles which are common to the member states.

Human Rights Dimension of CFSP

Again, TEU projects the main objective of the EU in its external relations as safe-guarding "the common value, fundamental value and independence of the Union" and also to "develop and consolidate democracy and the rule of law, and respect for human rights and fundamental freedom." As per Title V, Article J. 1(2) of the TEU, one of the objectives of the CFSP is to develop and consolidate democracy and the rule of law, and respect for human rights and for freedom. Moreover, the EU has taken a stand in Vienna in 1993 that human rights, democracy and development are interdependent and mutually reinforcing and that the promotion of human rights also improves the prospects of peace and security.

The EU is firm on its conviction that all human rights are universal, indivisible, interdependent and interrelated and also committed to the idea that the promotion and protection of human rights is a legitimate concern of the international community. There is a consensus among the member states of the EU that human rights violations are a source of insecurity and the protection of human rights is 'a valuable objective in and of itself'. The fact that the EU promotes human rights is clearly now a significant element of its international image, one which the member states have generally been keen to maintain. [4]

The EU believes that the struggle for the fulfilment of the commitments of the Universal Declaration must be continued and intensified and it is ready to assist countries to live up to their human rights obligations. This forms the main objective of the CFSP (Article 11 of the TEU). The Union maintains systematic coordination on human rights issues within the framework of the CFSP, in particular in the Council's Human Rights Working Group (COHOM), which is composed of human rights experts from the member states and the Commission, as well as in the regional working groups.

Development Cooperation Policy (DCP)

In the field of development cooperation, the Maastricht

Treaty clarifies that 'Community policy...shall contribute to the general objective of developing and consolidating democracy and the rule of law, and to that of respecting human rights and fundamental freedoms', (Article 130u of TEU). As such, TEU explicitly added development cooperation to the Community's remit. The Union places the human being at the centre of its policies and firmly believes that human rights are integral to peace and security, economic development and social equality. It is well aware of the fact that making human rights a reality is a never-ending challenge and welcomes and promotes the growing international trend towards integrating the promotion of human rights, democracy and the rule of law into development cooperation, trade policies and the promotion of peace and security. The EU insists that civil and political or social, economic and cultural rights share many common denominators and hence, subscribes to the interdependence and indivisibility of all human rights and rejects efforts to limit the enjoyment of one set of rights on the pretext that priority attention must be given to another.

The EU seeks as a general aim to include the human rights dimension in all relevant fields of the EU policy. For instance, the EU Code of Conduct on Arms Exports agreed in June 1998 reinforces the criterion of respect for human rights in the country of final destination. Again, in the framework of the EC's scheme of generalized tariff preferences, respect by third countries for international labour standards, including on child labour, is an important criterion for the Union. The 'social incentive clause' of the Generalised System of Preferences provides for additional preference to be extended to countries honouring certain ILO standards.[5] Even, in its approach to counter terrorism, the EU insists that an unremitting and uncompromising struggle against terrorism is and should at all times be compatible with human rights and fundamental freedoms.

The Committee on Foreign Affairs and the Committee on Development Cooperation of the European Parliament deal with human rights issues outside the EU and in its external policy. The EU uses demarches, political dialogues and press declarations to convey its human rights concerns to the third parties and to seek remedial sanctions. In fact, the EU conducts political dialogue with forty eight countries and regional groupings at different levels.

The EU's external trade and cooperation relations have been institutionalized in a series of treaties, bilateral commercial agreements and elaborate association agreements incorporating cooperation in diverse fields. In trade and aid relations, the EU has gradually incorporated human rights clauses. A Council decision of May 1995 spells out the basic modalities of this clause, with the aim of ensuring consistency in the text used and its application. It consists of a provision stipulating that respect for fundamental human rights and democratic principles as laid down in the Universal Declaration of Human Rights of 1948, the Helsinki Final act and the Paris Charter for a New Europe, underpins the domestic and external policies of the parties and constitutes an "essential element" of the agreement. A final provision dealing with non-execution of the agreement requires each party to consult the other before taking measures, except in certain special cases of urgency. An interpretative declaration specifies that cases of special urgency include breaches of an "essential element clause" of the agreement. This has now become a standard clause in all cooperation agreements that the EU concludes with third parties.

Articles 4 and 5 of the Fourth ACP-EC Convention, signed at Lomé on December 15, 1989, as revised by the agreement signed in Mauritius on November 4, 1995, advocate that the work undertaken by the Community and its member states in the framework of ACP-EC Cooperation must be centred on man, the main protagonist and beneficiary of development; respect for human rights is to be recognised as a basic factor of real development and cooperation should be conceived as a contribution to the promotion of these rights. Thus, the EU tries to use the mechanisms of the *Lomé* Conventions to seek remedies for its human rights and democracy related concerns of the contractual partners. As of now, human rights clauses apply to more than 120 countries, including more than seventy countries governed by the *Lomé* Conventions. [6]

Inclusion of this standard clause is to spell out the rights of the Community to change, defer, suspend or terminate an agreement for reasons connected with non-respect of human rights by the third country concerned. The human rights clause simply constitutes a mutual reaffirmation of commonly shared values and principles, a precondition for economic and other cooperation under the agreements and expressly allows for and regulates suspension and even withdrawal in cases of non-compliance with these values.

The EU spends well over a billion Euros every year on development assistance and humanitarian aid. [7] Along with the Member States, the EU provides 55 percent of the total Official Development Assistance (ODA). The EU is the largest multilateral donor/purveyor of development cooperation aid and accounts for well over half of international aid transferred from the developed to the developing world. The Europeans make a deliberate attempt to link their aid programme with the human rights record of the recipient country in order to assist them to live up to their human rights obligations. In case of failure on the human rights front, they threaten to suspend and even completely withdraw the developmental projects. [8] The mid-term review has also introduced specific rules under Article 366a for sanctions to be taken, including suspension of the provisions of the Convention to any country, which violates such principles. They also establish a consultation mechanism, which aims to prevent human rights violations. Moreover, the revised Convention provides financial support for the establishment of good governance and democratic institution building. [9]

As such, the EU has given the protection, promotion and defence of human rights, democracy, rule of law and good governance centre stage in its external policy and relations. It is trying to convert the good will and the hold it has earned on third parties through its development and cooperation policies and programmes into their compliance of international human rights standards. The fact that the EU's approach is based on legal texts, the human rights clauses in agreements and regulations on aid, needs to be taken into consideration. [10]

However, success of this 'linkage' depends upon the economic condition of the recipient country concerned and its economic dependence on the EU's development assistance and cooperation. A strong economy and viable market like China could deal with the EU on its own terms and conditions. In its relations with China, the EU prefers engagement and dialogue rather than criticising it on the human rights ground and alienate it further, which might cost the Union and its members dearly. [11] On the other hand, in the case of 'poor, marginal' African, Caribbean and Pacific (ACP) countries, whose economic dependence on the EU is almost complete, tendency of the latter to resort to negative measures is quite instant and the consequent conditionalities work more successfully. These countries had to take several measures to please the donor, so that the economic assistance continues to flow unhindered. [12] As a result, democracy and other such high principles have become attainable and measurable goals among the ACP countries, since the Union has thrown its weight behind the pursuit of "adjustment with a human face". [13]

Besides, this 'linkage' policy of the EU is being criticised by the third countries and is being taken as interference in their internal affairs. They base their argument on the cultural dependence of human rights and maintain that they need not accept the Western definition of human rights as final and binding and that they have every right to have their own definition and preferences–whether political and civil or socio-economic rights are to be given prominence. [14] By way of countering this criticism, Fischer argues that human rights policy is not a "soft topic" for unworldly moralists, but, is tough *realpolitik*. "In the age of globalization, observing human rights is the best basis for peace and sustainable development" he maintains. [15]

In their Declaration adopted at the Laeken summit, the leaders of the EU indicated that they wanted to create "a democratic and globally engaged Europe", which would like to see democracy, respect for human rights, rule of law and good governance thrive everywhere in the world. In their eagerness to realize the goal, the Europeans try to use the clout that they have developed with third countries through development cooperation assistance. Though this works to a substantial level with weaker economies, it fails miserably with those countries whose economy is not dependent on the economic assistance from the Union. In such cases, the principles are often trumped by other interests, such as security or economics.

Scholars observe noticeable disparity between the European domestic and external human rights policy and accuse that the EU tries to impose certain human rights standards on third states, which the existing member states are yet to achieve. [16] They also refer about the gap between the rhetoric and action and accuse the Union of differential treatment of partners. They maintain that the tension between the treaty-based requirement of consistency and a more policy-based pragmatism runs through the Union's external relations, thus making it susceptible to accusations of 'double standards' or euro-centrism, despite its appeal to the universalism of the principles it preaches. [17]

Human Rights Dimensions of India-EU Relations

After tracing the human rights dimensions of the European foreign and development cooperation policy and action of the EU in general, let us examine India-EU relations and how far they falls in line with the EU's human rights policy. It may be interesting to note that whether India proves itself to be one more China or one among the ACP or Asian and Latin

American (ALA) countries.

India is one among the few countries which had developed diplomatic relations with the European Community since its inception and there have been regular contacts at the political level between the leadership of the Community and the Indian Government. While 'association agreements' were signed with many of the countries of the developing world, India was one among them chosen for 'cooperation agreement'. On January 1, 1973, a Commercial Cooperation Agreement was signed to develop and diversify trade between India and European Economic Community. The European countries tried to balance the economic relations with India with a reinforced political dialogue through the EU-India Partnership Agreement of 1993, first of its kind involving the Union with any Asian country. [18] Again, since 2000, the EU has been holding annual summit level meeting with India, the sixth country to enjoy such a privilege. Both the entities have developed a 'strategic partnership' to realize a new world order, which is expected to be just, fair and peaceful. [19]

In spite of these cordiality and growing partnership, India has not taken to the European human rights policies and postures kindly. For instance, when the Europeans insisted on the inclusion of human rights clause in the India-EU Partnership Programme in early 1990s, the Indian attitude was nothing but negative. There was a ten month delay in the signing of the Memorandum on Political and Economic Cooperation between India and the EU because of the latter's insistence on stipulating certain conditionalities on issues such as human rights and democracy and the Indian stand that "regardless of our credibility in these matters, we should not, even by implication, subject ourselves to external value judgments or certifications". [20] In the end, the Europeans had to relent. The fact that India is one among the top ten recipients of EC development cooperation assistance in 2004-5 clearly reflects political priorities the Union attaches to its cooperation policy in its relationship with India. [21]

This capitulation continues. Though the European Parliament through its 2006 resolution emphasized that it is no longer prepared to give its assent to any international agreements that do not contain a human rights and democracy clause, negotiations with India on a free trade agreement were disrupted in 2007 because of India's objection to the incorporation of the human rights clause. Apparently the European Commission proposed dropping it. [22]

Three recent and relevant case studies are discussed here to substantiate our argument that for EU political priorities matter more than high-sounding principles in its relations with India.

European Stand on Gujarat Communal Violence

The Godhra incident and subsequent sectarian violence in Gujarat in early 2002 resulted in terrible human rights violations and the State's complicity in the violence proved itself to be a matter of great concern. [23] Initially, the European Commission as well as the member states of the Union were highly critical of the unfortunate developments. The EU, in its declaration concluded that "Godhra served as a pretext for triggering the violence that followed in the state; the post-Godhra violence was pre-planned and the pattern suggests that the attempt was to purge Muslims from Hindu areas; the Chief Minister Narendra Modi instructed senior police officers not to intervene in the rioting; the state and central governments failed to meet the immediate humanitarian needs of the victims; and the prime minister visited Gujarat only on April 4, five weeks after the carnage that started on February 27". After all these condemnation, the Europeans tried to strike a conciliatory note by welcoming "the government of India's condemnation of the violence". [24]

The Indian reaction was on expected lines. When the Finnish Foreign Minister gave an interview on Gujarat, the comment of the Indian Ministry of External Affairs was sharp: "India's does not appreciate interference...including utilisation of the Indian media by foreign leaders as well as by visiting dignitaries to make public statements in order to pander to their domestic lobbies". [25] Moreover, the External Affairs Ministry had asked its missions abroad to explain the "unfortunate developments in Gujarat as the work of extremists on both sides". The then Prime Minister Vajpayee accused the international community of meddling in India's internal affairs. "It is an internal affair and there is no doubt about it. External prescriptions from anywhere in the world cannot help in providing the medicine to handle the situation" claimed the spokesperson of the Ministry of External Affairs of the Government of India. India conveyed to its key interlocutors that it was taking steps to redress the situation in Gujarat and that the government made no discrimination on the basis of religion, caste or creed.

In the end, the Europeans had to conceleate and the Union acquiesced to follow an 'agree to disagree' policy. During the visit of the EU troika Senior Officials Meeting on May 2, 2002, India and the EU agreed that the controversy over the strong position taken by the EU on Gujarat was 'regrettable' and decided to push the issue behind them in the interest of their bilateral relations. In its belatedly passed resolution of May 2002 on Gujarat issue, the European Parliament initially condemned "in the strongest possible way all sectarian violence" and called the Government of India and the Government of Gujarat "to bring responsible to justice, irrespective of their positions, religion, identity or political beliefs".[26] But, at the same breath, the resolution maintained that "India is one of the largest secular democratic countries, in which several communities and religions live peacefully together. The fact that troubles in Gujarat have not affected other parts of the Indian Union testifies to the underlying strengths of India's democratic and tolerant society." The resolution was carefully drawn not to name the State of Gujarat specifically. [27]

The European Commission clarified later on that "the

perpetrators of the crimes in Gujarat should be brought to justice, the victims rehabilitated, and the rights of minorities protected", but added that "the Union has agreed to deal with all matters concerning democracy and human rights in India through its regular, on-going constructive dialogue with the Union Government". [28]

EU's Stand on Kashmir

While acknowledging the Indian sovereign and legitimate right to take 'appropriate' measures to tackle any threat to territorial integrity and protecting its population, the Europeans always insisted that those measures must be within the ambit of international human rights and humanitarian law. The European Council adopted on June 22, 2002, a declaration on India and Pakistan which noted "the importance of free, fair and inclusive elections in Jammu and Kashmir". [29] After the Jammu and Kashmir Assembly elections were held in late 2002 'followed' by a number of EU diplomatic staff based in New Delhi, the EU Presidency released a declaration which appreciated "voters used their democratic right to elect local representatives despite terrorist violence and intimidation"; commanded "strenuous efforts of the Indian Election Commission in promoting free and fair elections"; called "on all parties to respect the results of the elections", and hoped "that the future developments will lead to improvements to the governance and human rights situation in Kashmir". [30]

The EU Presidency also stated: "A lasting settlement to the Kashmir issue can only be achieved through an inclusive dialogue, involving the Kashmiri people". However, in deference to the Indian stand that the dialogue has to be bilateral, the European leaders resolved "to encourage both countries to achieve a lasting settlement of the difference between them through bilateral dialogue". In other words, the EU is ready to facilitate and support a dialogue, but not to mediate, as India wants it to be. Again, while maintaining that the Kashmir issue needed a political resolution, the head of the

European Union's Troika Ambassadors delegation has said that the elections had opened a window of opportunity in Kashmir, which needed to be capitalised upon. Following the Assembly election in 2009, the Europeans once again reiterated their stand that there has been a large participation in the recently held elections but we cannot say that election is the solution. But it can open a window for a solution. [31]

Again, the Europeans were considerate towards India on the issue of sending team of Election Observers to 'follow' elections in third countries to ascertain their free and fairness. While the European Union has sent a eighty eight member Election Observation Mission to Pakistan to monitor the general and provincial elections in 2002, European countries and the European Commission Delegation in New Delhi have just sent a few staff members during the elections in Jammu and Kashmir of October 2002, with a limited mandate, in deference to the Indian sensitivity. [32]

Of late, the Europeans have assumed a stand favourable to India in their relentless struggle against terrorism. In November 2005 the EU named Hizbul Mujahadeen as a terrorist organisation. Moreover, the EU has taken a stand that Kashmir is an integral part of India and Lars-Olof Lindgren, the Swedish Ambassador who led the five-member fact-finding team to Srinagar in November 2006, maintained: "That is the opinion of the European Union. That is our opinion and that is the starting point of the discussion." [33] This pro-Indian stand also reflected in EU Kashmir report (2006) titled 'Kashmir: Present Situation and Future Prospects', of Baroness Emma Nicholson, Member of European Parliament, the EU rapporteur and Vice Chair of the Foreign Affairs Committee. The report was highly critical of Pakistan's role in Kashmir tangle and the situation in POK. [34] Islamabad was particularly irked over the report's dismissal of calls for plebiscite to resolve the Kashmir issue. The original draft report had said that 'continuing calls for a plebiscite on the final status of Jammu and Kashmir are wholly out of step with the needs of the local people and thus damaging to their interests.' [35] As such, Nicolson's report proved itself to be "an extraordinarily pro-Indian document". [36]

Violence against Christians in Orissa

During September-October 2008, there were sporadic incidents of violence in Kandamal district of Orissa against the local Christian population after the assassination of a Hindu religious leader allegedly by the followers/sympathizers of Christianity. Thousands of Christians have fled to the dense jungles to escape from violence. Several other serious violations of human rights and dignity were reported. French President Nicolas Sarkozy along with the chief of the European Union, Jose Manuel Barrosso had strongly raised their concerns with Prime Minister Manmohan Singh in EU-India summit in Marseilles in this regard. The Europeans also sent periodical fact-finding missions. However, the European reaction was muted on the face of vehement Indian reaction which was against foreign interference in their internal matters. The Indian Union Government assumed self-corrective posture and maintained that there was no need for advice from third parties.

Conclusion

Though EU is one among the many actors promoting universal human rights, the way it pursues the human rights objective is more unique. Its preference for persuasion and 'neutrality' distinguishes it from others. Its reluctance to use negative measures for familiar security and commercial reasons, as well as a general scepticism about the efficacy of negative measures is noteworthy.

However, the disparity between the European domestic–external human rights policy and the ever-widening gap in preaching-practice in this regard, though understandable, is quite disturbing. The accusation that the 'global north' practices double standards and punishes or rewards countries of 'global South' based on commercial or strategic interests rather than on actual human rights records, needs to be met with squarely and with full determination.

Regarding human rights factor in India-EU relations, it may be concluded that the EU continues to be supportive of the Indian stand and critical of Pakistan on the issue of abetment of terrorism in India and on democratic deficiency back home. The EU is mild in criticism on India and determined to follow agree to disagree policy. Its readiness to keep contentious issues in back-burner is discernable in all the three case studies elaborated in the foregoing pages. Both India and the EU are not to hurt each other, thereby affecting their cordial relationship. As in the case of China, the European human rights policy is being guided by political and economic considerations of the Union in its relations with India as well.

Notes

1. *EU Annual Report on Human Rights* (henceforth *Report*) *1999* published annually by the European Initiative for Democracy and Human Rights. Statement by Mr. Joseph Fischer, Federal Minister for Foreign Affairs of the Federal Republic of Germany on behalf of the European Union at the 55th Session of the Commission on Human Rights held at Geneva, on March 23, 1999. Annex.10, pp. 73-76.
2. Joseph S Nye Jr., *Soft Power: The Means to Success in World Politics,* New York: Public Affairs, 2004.
3. Ian Manners, "Normative Power Europe: A Contradiction in Terms?", *Journal of Common Market Studies*, 2002, vol. 40, no. 2, p. 236. This idea is further elaborated and the fact that to what extent the VIPs inform the European Common Foreign and Security Policy and Development Cooperation Policy is investigated in Sonia Lucarelli and Ian Manners (eds.), *Values and Principles in European Union Foreign Policy,* Routledge: London and New York, 2006.
4. Karen E. Smith, *European Union Foreign Policy in a Changing World*, Second Edition, Cambridge: Polity Press, 2008, p. 141.
5. *Report 2001,* p. 27. The 'Generalised System of Preferences' (GSP) is a scheme under which the European Community grants autonomous and non-reciprocal trade preferences to developing

countries in order to use trade as an instrument for sustainable development. The benefits can be withdrawn in some cases of unacceptable practices including any form of slavery or forced labour and the export of goods made by prison labour.

6. *Report 1999,* p. 15.
7. Leading by Example: A Human Rights Agenda for the European Union for the year 2000, Philip Alston *et al.*, *The EU and Human Rights*, Oxford: Oxford University Press, 1999, p. 922.
8. *Report 2000*, p. 34 (ACP-EC Partnership Agreement).
9. David Lowe, "The Development Policy of the European Union and the Mid-Term Review of the Lomé Partnership", *Journal of Common Market Studies*, vol.34, August 1996, pp. 16-17.
10. Smith, n. 4, p. 141.
11. B. Krishnamurthy, "Human Rights dimension of the European Common Foreign and Security Policy: The Case Study of EU-China Relations", *Journal of Contemporary Asia & Europe*, vol.1, No.1, January-June 2004, pp. 26-44.
12. *The Hindu* (Chennai) 13/12/2001; 12 and 13/01/2002. To ensure free and fair elections in the African States, the EU offers to send at its own expense a contingent of election observers to those countries, where elections are scheduled. Moreover, it provides assistance for the preparation of elections by supporting National Election Commissions and local election monitoring agencies. In December 2001, President Robert Mugabe rejected the EU's offer of sending observers, saying that they are not welcome. His Government has not carried out the promised reforms and the EU was particularly annoyed by Zimbabwe's Parliament passing bills which will ensure–at least, technically – that Mugabe alone can emerge as victor in the forthcoming March Presidential election and which are aimed at stifling opposition. On the face of defiance, the EU had decided to review its development projects in Zimbabwe worth £ 79 million over five years and also threatened to suspend some Euro 12 million development aid initiated to promote education and to contain HIV/Aids. Finally, Zimbabwe had to accept the EU's demand for independent observers at the elections in March and to agree to a political 'code of conduct' respecting civil liberties. The EU Foreign Ministers reviewed latter, whether Zimbabwe had done enough to avoid "smart sanctions", involving a travel ban on Mugabe and his close circle and a freeze on their

overseas assets, but were not pleased enough. As such the outcome in this case is rather a mixed bag.

13. Olufemi A.Babarinde, "The Lomé convention: An Aging Dinosaur in the European Union's Foreign Policy Enterprise?", Carolyn Rhodes and Sonia Mazey (eds.), *The State of the European Union,* vol. 3, *Building a European Policy?,* Colorado: Lynne Rienner Publishers, Inc., 1995, p. 491.
14. Andreas Thimm, "Development, Human Rights and Democracy", *Law and State*, vol. 52, 1995, pp. 95-96.
15. *Report 1999*, annex 10, p. 76.
16. Alston, n.7, pp. 28-29.
17. Rosa Balfour, "Principles of democracy and human rights-a review of the European Union's strategies towards its neighbours" in Lucarelli and Manners, n. 3, p. 115.
18. B. Krishnamurthy, "India and the European Union-Common Strategy for a Multi-Polar World Order", V.T. Patil and Nalini Kant Jha (eds.), *India in a Turbulent World-Perspective in Foreign and Security Policies,* New Delhi: South Asian Publishers, 2003, pp. 213-14.
19. B. Krishnamurthy and Geetha Ganapathy-Doré (eds.), *Changing World Order: India, EU and US–A Trialogue,* Shipra Publications, New Delhi, 2009, pp. 278-325.
20. J. N. Dixit, *My South Block Years, Memoirs of a Foreign Secretary*, New Delhi: UBS Publishers' Distributors Ltd., 1996. p. 276.
21. Smith, n. 4, p. 61.
22. *Ibid.*, pp. 130-131.
23. Asghar Ali Engineer, "Gujarat Riots in the Light of the History of Communal Violence", *Economic and Political Weekly*, vol. 37, no. 50 (December 14-20, 2002), pp. 5047-5054.
24. Sultan Shahin, "Gujarat: return to the deadly past", http://www.atimes.com/ind-pak/DD26Df03.html April 26, 2002
25. Delhi reflects 'Foreign Interference', *The Hindu*, April 22, 2002.
26. European Parliament Resolution on India, 16 May 2002.
27. Nadia Mushtaq Abbasi, "EU-India: Looking towards Deeper Relations", http://www.issi.org.pk/ss_Detail.php?dataId=275.
28. Commissioner Chris Patten's answer to European Parliament, May 15, 2003.
29. EU Declaration on Pakistan and India, Sevilla, Spain, June 22, 2002.

30. Declaration of the Presidency on Assembly elections in Jammu & Kashmir, October 2002 www.europa.eu.int/comm/external_relations/india/news/decl_10_02.htm).
31. "European Union sees window of opportunity in Kashmir", March 4, 2009. http://worldsikhnews.com/4 percent20March percent202009/European percent20Union percent20sees percent20window percent20of percent20opportunity percent20in percent20Kashmir.htm
32. Jean-Luc Racine, *Majors Powers in South Asia,* Islamabad: Institute of Regional Studies, 2004, pp. 131-162.
33. "Kashmir integral part of India: EU", http://www.defence.pk/forums/world-affairs/39879-j-k-integral-part-india-eu-delegation.html.
34. EU Report on Kashmir Criticises Pakistan, http://www.rediff.com/news/2007/may/25eupak.htm May 25, 2007 03:02 IST. The report was passed by an overwhelming majority with 522 votes in its favour and nine against it.
35. European Parliament committee adopts pro-India Kashmir report Malaysia Sun–March 21, 2007, http://www.charlestannock.com/pressArticle.asp?ID=1560.
36. Bennett-Jones, Owen, "Musharraf's Kashmir Policy", *Asian Affairs*, vol. 38, no. 3, 2007, pp. 315-316.

8

Sovereignty versus Humanitarian Intervention

S. Mohammed Azaad

"There exists perhaps no conception the meaning of which is more controversial than that of sovereignty. It is an indisputable fact that this conception, from the moment when it was introduced into political science until the present day, has never had a meaning which was universally agreed upon." [1]

- LassaOppenheim

Introduction

The last decade of the twentieth century opened and closed with crises that were ended as the result of international interventions, ostensibiy carried out for humanitarian reasons. Operation Desert Storm, which ousted Iraq from Kuwait in January 1991, was an American-led, predominantly Western, military campaign. However, it was mounted with a mandate under Chapter VII of the UN Charter, with the unanimous approval of the Security Council.

Similarly in 1994, the international community fiddled, while Rwanda burned. To the enduring shame of many, the world's most powerful states stood back and watched as genocide was perpetrated against over 800,000 hapless and helpless people. This record of failure was not confined to Rwanda alone. During the 1990's, Somalia, Srebrenica and East Timor, to name but a handful of human catastrophes, became watchwords for international inertia, inaction and incompetence.

Besides this there is no shortage of recent cases where one or more states have intervened in another state (Panama, Grenada, Bosnia, Sierra Leone, Chechnya, Yugoslavia,

Afghanistan and Haiti). Some of these cases involved humanitarian motives, others did not, but all violated the sovereignty of the states and in no case was the intervening state subjected to international disapproval and tangible consequences. The above issue of what is now commonly called "humanitarian intervention" has become one of the most contentious subjects in managing contemporary international relations.

A humanitarian intervention is an armed intervention in another state, without the agreement of that state, to address a threat of humanitarian disaster, particularly those caused by grave and large-scale violations of fundamental human rights. This Article explores the changing character of sovereignty in international law and international relations in the light of armed intervention to defend human rights.

II. Historical Overview

A. Treaty of Westphalia: [2] The Treaty of Westphalia (1648), the agreement which put an end to the Thirty Year's War with the famous dictum, *cuius regio, eius religio* (whoever reigns, his religion), formally recognized the sovereignty and independence of each state of the Holy Roman Empire. The Westphalian principles of sovereignty and independence, and the concomitant principle of non-intervention in the affairs of sovereign nations, have formed the basic foundations of international relations ever since.

B. Concert System: The 'Concert system' created after the 1815 Congress of Vienna modified the Westphalian concept of sovereignty by legitimizing intervention to protect the kind of domestic rule that was accepted by the powerful as being legitimate and conducive to international order. Intervention was seen as a remedy for the threat to the existing international order posed by revolutionary regimes and the principle of self-government.

C. The Rise and Fall of Non-Intervention Norm: The non-intervention norm, though widely viewed as legitimate by the international community, was nonetheless violated on repeated occasions during the Cold War. The two superpowers, the United States and the former Soviet Union, frequently used intervention as an instrument to influence the governments within their spheres of influence throughout the globe. The US interventions in Guatemala (1954), the Dominican Republic (1965), and Vietnam (1967) and of the Soviet Union in Hungary (1956) and Czechoslovakia (1968) illustrate this point.

Still, the principle of non-intervention was reaffirmed by the 1970 UN General Assembly Declaration on Principles of International Law Concerning Friendly Relations and Cooperation Among States [3] which rigorously prohibited any interference by a State against the political, economic, social and cultural elements of another State.

It also referred to intervention in the instance of a civil war, stating, "...every state has a duty to refrain from organising, instigating, assisting or participating in acts of civil strife or terrorist acts in another State, or acquiescing in organised activities within its territory which directed towards the commission of such acts gave support or sustenance to such civil conflict. [4] This principle was further strengthened by the 1975 Final Act of the Helsinki Conference on Security and Cooperation in Europe (CSCE). [5] However, since the 1970s, support for the non-intervention norm has steadily fallen, as "new exceptions which might legitimate the use of military intervention have been claimed." [6]

III. The Progression of Sovereignty and Non-Intervention

'*Rex est imperator in regno sue*' or the 'right to rule in one's own territory' has underwritten the political and economic organisation of the international system ever since its conception at the Peace of Westphalia. The notion that the international community has a responsibility to protect those whose governments are either unwilling or unable to protect them is far from new; indeed Just War theories advocating intervention in limited circumstances are as old as international legal discourse itself.

In 1948, States ratified the '*Convention on the Prevention and Punishment of the Crime of Genocide' [7]* (commonly referred to as the Genocide Convention). The Convention itself reaffirms the long-standing belief that genocide, whether committed during war or peace, is an international crime and asserts that states have a dual duty under international law - to prevent it taking place and to punish those who perpetrate it. [8] This convention has since been adopted by the International Criminal Tribunals for the former Yugoslavia and Rwanda and the Rome Statute of the International Criminal Court, making it an undeniable part of contemporary international law.

It is undisputed that State sovereignty is paramount in international relations and key to this was Article 2(7) of the Charter which declares that "nothing contained in the present Charter shall authorize the United Nations to intervene in matters which are essentially within the domestic jurisdiction of any state..." This is bolstered by other provisions, notably Article 2(4), which is also recognised as customary law [9] and a *jus cogens* norm. [10] Moreover, the 1965 UN General Assembly Declaration on the 'Inadmissibility of Intervention' asserted that "No state has the right to intervene, directly, or indirectly, for any reason, whatsoever, in the internal or external affairs of any other state." [11]

However, the mood had begun to shift in other areas of international law. The rapid rise of the international human rights movement and the conclusion of multilateral human rights treaties [12] gave rise to emerging claims that state sovereignty involved rights, as well as responsibilities. As more and more interventions were ordered, it became clear that state sovereignty and non-intervention were far from inviolable, irrespective of what the Charter's formal terms stated.

IV. The New Interventionism

Inevitably, this new 'interventionism' on the part of the UN and the international community spawned a corresponding debate on the changing limits of state sovereignty and non-intervention. Chapter VII of the UN Charter (permitting intervention for peacemaking) allows for the expansion of admissibility of forcible intervention, [13] and "the belief that governments have a right, even obligation, to intervene in the affairs of other states seems to have gained great currency in recent years." [14] For this reason the major purpose of the UN Charter is the maintenance of international peace and security. [15] This belief has been founded upon a growing awareness and international acceptance of the principles of universal, inalienable human rights.

Furthermore writing in 1992 the then UN Secretary General Boutros Boutros-Ghali, wrote, "[t]he time of absolute and exclusive sovereignty...has passed; its theory was never matched by reality." [16] His report explicitly called for enforcement action to respond to human rights abuse and for nation-building. Indeed, many believed that the apparently increasing willingness of the Security Council to authorise interventions to deal with internal humanitarian crises was a harbinger of a new dawn in multilateral protection.

The reality, as is now well documented, was far different. In 1993 Operation Restore Hope, a UN peacekeeping mission designed to restore order in Somalia, went tragically awry, leading to the deaths of the US soldiers and Somali citizens. Also still stinging from the debacle in Somalia, there was no desire amongst the Permanent Five (P5) members of the Security Council to repeat previous failures and endure the domestic opprobrium which went with it.

V. Ethical Concerns Relating to Humanitarianism

In an Article entitled "The Short, Unhappy Life of Humanitarian War," Charles Krauthammer writes in scathing terms of humanitarian military intervention and concludes by remarking about the "successful" Kosovo intervention, "This is what happens when you win. Which is why there will be no more of it? It is an idea whose time has come and gone." [17] Krauthammer writes from a "realist" perspective (of which more later), but his view is in striking contrast to Fernando Teson's passionate defence of humanitarian war from a human rights perspective.

Teson's real (though qualified) enthusiasm for the idea that Krauthammer regards discredited is captured when he says: "[F]oreign armies are morally entitled to help victims of oppression in overthrowing dictators, provided that the intervention is proportionate to the evil which it is designed to suppress." [18] These contrasting views indicate why the ethics and politics of armed intervention for humanitarian purposes have proved to be among the most theoretically difficult and practically controversial issues facing governments in the past decade of military intervention.

A. The Ethical Dilemmas: The discussion of armed intervention for humanitarian purposes involves multiple ethical dilemmas at many different levels. Foremost among these is the conflict between the desire to respond to situations of humanitarian emergency and gross violation of human rights, and respect for the fundamental principles of sovereignty and non-intervention.

Given that the Security Council holds the sole and exclusive mandate for authorizing the use of force internationally, this dilemma is exacerbated when, due to geo-political considerations, the Security Council finds itself unable to act. However, bypassing the Security Council and acting unilaterally or in some other grouping risks undermining the collective security regime established over the last fifty years. States can take military action outside the established mechanisms for enforcing international law.

Further the UN Secretary-General Kofi Annan asked in his 'Millennium Report' delivered in April 2000 that "if humanitarian intervention is, indeed, an unacceptable assault on sovereignty, how should we respond to a Rwanda, to a Srebrenica—to gross and systematic violations of human rights that offend every precept of our common humanity?" [19]

B. Abuse of State Sovereignty-Checks and Balances: Under international law the international community may not interfere in the domestic affairs of any state. But what happens when the state is unable, or unwilling to offer that protection, or if the state itself is the aggressor against its own people? What are the ethical and legal means by which the international community can call a state to accountability, or intervene to protect human life?

Within the UN framework, place has been provided for checks and balances upon the abuse of state sovereignty, specifically in the area of human rights. Over the years, norms have begun to be established which link the role and responsibility of the state to assure peace, justice and the welfare of its citizens, to accountability to the international community.

Consequently the tension between the principle of non-intervention in the affairs of a sovereign state versus the responsibility of the international community to ensure respect for the human rights and the physical integrity of persons has revealed two things: One is that the concept of sovereignty is in transition and that transition is linked to international accountability. The second is that international law or agreed upon norms have not yet been developed to reflect these changes. In such a situation, it is really a challenging task to balance the legal principle of state sovereignty with the ethical imperative of protecting human life.

C. Humanitarian Intervention–Issues Raised: Armed intervention for humanitarian purposes can only be contemplated when all attempts at preventative diplomacy have failed. These preventative initiatives, and their priority, must always form the context of discussions within which any decision regarding armed intervention for humanitarian purposes is considered or undertaken.

Who Makes the Decision for Intervention and with what authority?

The current limited membership of the Security Council, the veto powers of the five permanent members, its relatively undemocratic character and its highly politicized climate suggest that, in its current form, the UNSC is an unwieldy instrument for formulating timely and effective responses to gross violations of human rights. In the meantime, however, what forum or power should be in a position to authorise intervention for humanitarian purposes if not the UNSC? The risk of misuse of intervention for political purposes looms larger the more the responsibility is removed from a multilateral setting.

What Constitutes a Humanitarian Objective?

Humanitarian action is generally understood as being undertaken according to strictly defined principles: humanity, neutrality, impartiality and universality. In defining the objectives for armed intervention for humanitarian purposes, it is important to define objectives which are linked to the protection of all human life. Particular attention has to be given to assuring that the intervention is truly humanitarian, and not pursuant to political objectives under a humanitarian guise. Amongst other critical questions raised by this study was that:

- In most cases the *casua justa* (just cause) can hardly still be identified because the background for a war lies above all in social and economic injustices, in historically developed enemy images, and in notions of threat.
- The *proportionality* of means is no longer restricted due to the development of military technology, global strategies, and the extension of war to the civil population.
- The *recta intentio* (right intention) is no longer possible under the conditions of modern technology because what should be protected will be getting destroyed.

VI. Evolution of the R2P Doctrine

In 2005, world leaders endorsed a new doctrine called the *'Responsibility-to-Protect' (R2P)* which is designed to provide a moral and legal framework for the international community to respond to mass atrocities. This means that if a state defaults on its responsibility to protect its citizens the international community would assume this responsibility collectively.

For that reason over 170 governments adopted this R2P principle committing states to prevent crimes against humanity –even, if necessary, by military intervention. In striving to prevent a future Rwanda, however, R2P has forced many to re-assess commonly held notions of sovereignty and to focus on the requisite political will and military capabilities necessary to enforce such a precept.

A. The Principle: Prevention, Intervention and Reconstruction

Speaking in September 1999 before the United Nations General Assembly, Kofi Annan, the then UN Secretary General, challenged governments to fill the void in understanding between; the principles of non-intervention and state sovereignty as laid-out by the UN Charter; and on the other hand, the international community's duty to respond to human rights violations such as genocide and ethnic cleansing. Essentially, Annan called for a re-assessment of the balance between the rights of the state and those of citizens.

This challenge was taken-up by the International Commission on Intervention and State Sovereignty (ICISS) [20]–a panel of experts established by the Canadian Government. In conducting its work, the ICISS consulted a host of national governments, regional organisations and Non-Governmental Organisations (NGOs) through a series of roundtable discussions.

With this, the ICISS published its report entitled 'The Responsibility to Protect' [21] which recommended that future crimes against humanity be neutralized through three strategies:

1. Prevention: more should be done to prevent crimes against humanity from occurring in the first place by emphasizing Article 55 of the UN Charter, [22] which calls for higher standards of political, economic and social welfare and respect for human rights and fundamental freedoms;
2. Intervention: if crimes against humanity do occur the international community should attain a UN Security Council (UNSC) [23] mandate to intervene in the first instance, through political measures (e.g. travel restrictions), economic measures (e.g. promises of investment) and legal measures (e.g. International Criminal Court (ICC) trials) and as a last resort, through military measures (e.g. the use of force) [24];
3. Reconstruction: if intervention does occur then the international community has the duty to ensure that post-conflict reconstruction is undertaken including the stabilization of political institutions, the brokering of national reconciliation and assistance with socio-economic development.

B. The Stand of the European Union (EU) After the adoption of R2P, Javier Solana, former High Representative of the EU Common Foreign and Security Policy (CFSP)-stated that "[it] is not enough for the international community merely to say "never again" when atrocities are committed. We have to fulfil our Responsibility to Protect with action to prevent crimes against humanity." [25] While one does not doubt Solana's sincerity, such parlance highlights the complex relationship between sentiment on the one hand and the willingness to act on the other.

This is a dilemma Europe is well-versed in. One only has to recall the portentous "[this] is the hour of Europe" quote made by Jacques Poos–former foreign minister of Luxembourg–during the War in Bosnia (1992) to realize that even if Europe's hour did indeed come, it failed dismally to live up to its convictions.

Fortunately enough for advocates of 'humanitarian

interventionism', numerous NGOs and foreign ministers– such as Bernard Kouchner [26]-keep the R2P debate in the political arena. As was the case when commenting on the humanitarian crisis in Burma, [27] Mr. Kouchner was seen to invoke the R2P concept when he "argued that aid might have to be 'imposed' on Burma if the military regime refused to co-operate." [28] However, the EU seems to be more cautious about the utterance of such words.

The fact that R2P will still have to go through the machinations of UN politics means that the scope for timely intervention is limited–Rwanda and Bosnia are both painful reminders of this. In this sense, while the world has seen the excesses of unilateral military action over the past years, it is quite possible that unilateralism could yet again reach its zenith if multilateral avenues prove unfruitful in implementing R2P in the future.

VII. Intervention in the Future-Some Implications

A traditional conceptualization of sovereignty clearly infers the primacy of the nation-state in international relations since all the interventions were severely contested by the generality of the international community. [29] Hence, humanitarianism has now paved the way for a new form of sovereignty. In such an environment the following insights are fundamental for a humanitarian intervention:

- Military force can only be the last resort after all other means have been exhausted.
- The decision to take military action on humanitarian grounds can only be made by the international community through a commonly-accepted international authority like the Security Council (SC), which has the sole authority to determine when a threat to, or breach of, peace has occurred [30] and thus to authorise the use of force. [31] The decision making process must be transparent and open.
- The use of military action must be limited, proportionate

and defined in relation to the goal of the action, which can only be to protect lives, establish peace with justice and restore respect for human rights. The use of force therefore must be strictly limited in time and scope to the humanitarian aim. [32]

- Military action must have a reasonable chance of achieving its stated aims, so that it does not result in intensification of hostilities.
- Military action cannot be a substitute for other means. It can only be part of a larger effort of humanitarian aid, economic support and the promotion of democratic structures following the conflict.

Thus, it is a red herring to delay or deny humanitarian protection to people under imminent threat of genocide, ethnic cleansing, systematic rape or physical persecution to preserve the sovereignty of failed and illegitimate states and repressive regimes.

While almost all states have signed the various UN declarations and conventions affirming respect for and protection of human rights, nearly no state is willing to take solely their obligations under the documents of international law as a primary reason for stopping or preventing the widespread violation of fundamental human rights in a conflict through humanitarian intervention.

Therefore, we can admit the grains of truth in the cynical slogan, "If you want peace, prepare for war," but the surer path to a more tranquil world is to prepare for peace directly.

Notes

1. See Lassa Oppenheim, *International Law 66,* edited by Sir Arnold D. McNair, 4th edition, 1928.
2. See: http://avalon.law.yale.edu/17th_century/westphal.asp.
3. See: http://www.un.org/documents/ga/res/25/ares25.htm.
4. UN General Assembly Declaration on Principles of International Law concerning Friendly Relations and Co-operation among States in accordance with the Charter of the United Nations, A/RES/25/2625, 24 October 1970.

5. See: http://www.hri.org/docs/Helsinki75.html.
6. Luard, Evan, *Conflict and Peace in the Modern International System*, 2nd edition, (Albany: State University of New York Press, 1988) 49.
7. General Assembly Resolution 260 A (III), December 9, 1948.
8. Article 1 of the Genocide Convention, 1948.
9. See Military and Paramilitary Activities in and against Nicaragua (*Nicaragua v United States of America*) (Merits) [1986] ICJ Rep 14 [Nicaragua case], pp.107-8. ibid. para.190; Randelzhofer, 'Article 2' in Simma (ed.), '*The Charter of the United Nations, A Commentary*', Volume I, 2nd ed. Oxford: Oxford University Press, 2002, p. 112.
10. Nicaragua case, para.190; UNGA GAOR Draft Articles on the Law of Treaties, 'Report of the International Law Commission' 18th Session [1966] II ILC Year book, pp. 247-249, 261.
11. UN General Assembly Declaration on the Inadmissibility of Intervention in the Domestic Affairs of States and the Protection of Their Independence and Sovereignty, A/RES/20/2131 (XX), 21 December 1965.
12. For example the *International Covenant on Civil and Political Rights* and the *International Covenant on Social, Economic and Cultural Rights* both of which were concluded in 1966.
13. Johnson, James Turner, *Humanitarian Intervention, Christian Ethical Reasoning, and the Just-War Idea*, in Lugo, Luis E. (ed.), Sovereignty at the Crossroads? (London: Rowman & Littlefield, 1996), pp. 127-143.
14. Blechman, Barry M., "The Intervention Dilemma", *The Washington Quarterly,* vol. 18, Summer 1995, p. 63.
15. See Edmund Jan Osmanczyk, *Encyclopedia of the United Nations and International Agreements,* London: Routledge, 1985, pp. 836-41 (documenting that the purposes of the United Nations are to "maintain international peace and security" and to encourage "friendly relations" and cooperation between nations).
16. Boutros Boutros-Ghali, *An Agenda for Peace: Preventive Diplomacy, Peacemaking and Peace-keeping* A/47/277-S/24111, 17 June 1992, para 17.
17. Charles Krauthammer, "The Short, Unhappy Life of Humanitarian War," *National Interest,* no. 57, fall 1999, p. 8.
18. Fernando Tesón, *Humanitarian Intervention: An Inquiry into Law and Morality,* New York: Transnational Publishers, 1998,

15. Tesón adds: "A further requirement is that the intervention be welcomed, actually or ideally, by those citizens whose human rights are being violated."

19. Millennium Report, 48.
20. The ICISS was co-chaired by Gareth Evans and Mohamed Sahnoun who led a team of ten experts including Michael Ignatieff, Cyril Ramaphosa, Fidel Ramos and Ramesh Thakur.
21. International Commission on Intervention and State Sovereignty, *The Responsibility to Protect: Report of the International Commission on Intervention and State Sovereignty*, Ottawa, International Development Research Centre, 2001, pp. 1-85. A supplementary volume containing research essays, a bibliography and details of the ICISS' consultations was published alongside the Report.
22. See www.un.org/aboutun/charter/ under Chapter IX.
23. The ICISS Report makes clear that any intervention whether political, economic, legal or military must be mandated by the UNSC in accordance with Article 41 and 42 of the UN Charter. See www.un.org/aboutun/charter/ under Chapter VII.
24. The ICISS Report states that military intervention must be dealt with on a case-by-case basis, must be the absolute last resort with all other UN mechanisms utilized first (e.g. mediation and sanctions) and be conducted by the UN (with funding and troops from member states).
25. Council of the European Union (2008) *Javier Solana, EU High Representative for the CFSP, welcomes today's launch of the Global Centre for the Responsibility to Protect',* Brussels, S058/08.
26. In many ways it can be claimed that the work of Bernard Kouchner, former French Foreign Minister and Mario Bettati, a Law Professor–through *Médecins Sans Frontières* helped plant the seed of the R2P concept.
27. It is to be noted that 'Burma' was officially renamed 'Myanmar' by the Burmese military junta in 1989 under the 'Adaptation of Expressions Law'.
28. See: www.economist.com/world/international/displaystory.cfm?story_id=11376531.
29. UNSC SCOR [4 December 1971] UN Doc S/10416; UNGA Res 2793 [1971] UN Doc A/L.647/Rev.1; UNSC SCOR [11

December 1978] UN Doc S/12962.
30. UN Charter, Art. 39.
31. UN Charter, Art. 24; Cassese, 'International Law in a Divided World', 1st edition, Oxford: Clarendon Press, 1988, p. 215.
32. UK Foreign and Commonwealth Office note to NATO states, 1998.

References

Books

Brownlie, *'Principles of Public International Law'.* 6th ed. Oxford: Clarendon Press, 2003.

Cassese, *'International Law in a Divided World'.* 1st ed. Oxford: Clarendon Press, 1988.

Gray, *'International Law and the Use of Force'.* 2nd ed. Oxford University Press, Oxford 2000.

Hoffmann, Stanley. *The Ethics and Politics of Humanitarian Intervention.* Notre Dame, Ind.: University of Notre Dame Press, 1996.

Kouchner, Bernard and Mario Battati. 1987. *Le Devoir d'Ingerence. Peut-on les laisser mourir?* Paris: Les Edition Denoël.

Luard, Evan, *Conflict and Peace in the Modern International System*, 2nd ed. Albany: State University of New York Press, 1988.

Oppenheim, *'International Law'.* Jennings & Watts (eds). 9th ed. London: Longman, 1992.

Stromseth, *'Rethinking Humanitarian Intervention: The Case for Incremental Change'* in Holzgrefe & Keohane (eds.), *'Humanitarian Intervention: Ethical, Legal, and Political Dilemmas'.* 1st ed, Cambridge University Press: Cambridge, 2003.

Tesón, Fernando. *Humanitarian Intervention: An Inquiry into Law and Morality.* New York: Transnational Publishers, 1998.

Walzer, Michael. *Just and Unjust Wars: A Moral Argument with Historical Illustrations,* 2nd ed. New York: HarperCollins, 1992.

Weiss, Thomas G. *Military-Civilian Interactions: Humanitarian Crises and the Responsibility to Protect.* 2nd ed. Lanham, Md.: Rowman & Littlefield Publishers, 2005.

Articles

Annan, Kofi. "Secretary-General Presents His Annual Report to General Assembly," transcript of speech to 54th United Nations General Assembly, September 20, 1999, press release no.

SG/SM/7136/GA/9596, http://www.un.org/News/Press/docs/1999/19990920.sgsm7136.html.

Bersa, Pavel. "Waging War in the Name of Human Rights? Fourteen Theses about Humanitarian Intervention." *Central European Review of International Affairs* 24 (2005): 5-20.

Boutros Boutros-Ghali. *Supplement to An Agenda for Peace: Position Paper of then Secretary-General on the Occasion of the Fiftieth Anniversary of the United Nations*, A/50/60; S/1995/1, 3 January 1995, p. 4.

Charles Krauthammer, "The Short, Unhappy Life of Humanitarian War," *National Interest,* no. 57, fall 1999, 8.

Coady, C. A. J. "The Ethics of Armed Humanitarian Intervention", United States Institute of Peace, Peace works No. 45, July 2002.

G.I.A.D. Draper, "Humanitarianism in the Modern Law of Armed Conflicts", in *Armed Conflict and the New Law* (Michael A. Meyer, ed. 1989).

Hoffmann, Stanley. "Out of the Cold: Humanitarian Intervention in the 1990s." *Harvard International Review* 16, no. 1, 1993, 8–9, 62.

Mill, John StuArt. "A Few Words on Non-Intervention." In *Collected Works of John Stuart Mill,* vol. 21, *Essays on Equality, Law, and Education.* Toronto: University of Toronto Press, 1984, 111-124.

Smith, Dan. "The Norm of Sovereignty in the Age of Intervention." In *Will World Peace Be Achievable in the Twenty-first Century?* Edited by Young Seek Choue, 185-224. Seoul: Institute of International Peace Studies, Kyung Hee University, Seoul, 1999.

Walzer, Michael. "The Politics of Rescue." *Social Research* 62, no. 1 (1995), 53-66.

Section IV

Some Literary, Philosophical and Pedagogical Approaches to the Convention

9

The Jewish Question and the Lessons to Learn

P. Marudanayagam

The Jews can no longer be considered a persecuted race or a suppressed minority but in the writings cited here, they are to be taken as a metaphor for the marginalized. The atrocities reported to have been perpetrated on them are to be viewed as what the West and Western civilization have done by way of violation of human rights. It was Gayatri Spivak who asked the question, "Can the subaltern speak?" Here is a minority which could speak and write powerfully, have its way and turn even the exile into a fortunate one.

One of the most important Anglophone Canadian writers of this century, Abraham Moses Klein, was leader of the Jewish community in Canada, editor of The Canadian Jewish Chronicle from 1938 to 1955 and an active participant in the labour Zionist movement. As he lived in Quebec, a French Canadian province surrounded by an English-speaking majority, he was aware of his minority status and his Jewish tradition enabled him to view Quebec's French-Canadian conservatism sympathetically. Bent upon exploring the variety of Jewish culture, Klein celebrates the riches of Jewish heritage in Hath Not a Jew, indicts Nazi Germany in The Hitleriad and expresses his Zionism in the novella, The Second Scroll. All his writings witness to his admiration for Jewish folklore and parables as well as to his learning in Jewish law, philosophy, culture and history.

In his poem "Portrait of the Poet as a Landscape", Klein pictures the poet as a lonely figure, as a voice with no hearer. The figure presented is not simply the Canadian artist but the isolated Jew, the modern individual, who is getting frustrated in his attempt to achieve integration and communication in a community without destroying the individuality of the self. The Jewish experience of isolation and the world's indifference to his existence are, throughout the poem, hinted at:

It is possible that he is dead, and not discovered.
It is possible that he can be found some place
in a narrow closet, like the corpse in a detective story,
standing, his eyes staring, and ready to fall on his face,
It is also possible that he is alive
and amnesiac, or mad, or in retired grace,
or beyond recognition lost in love.
...
The truth is he's not dead, but only ignored-
like the mirroring lenses forgotten on a brow
that shine with the guilt of their unnoticed world.
...
He is alone, yet not completely alone.
Pins on a map of a colour similar to his, each city has one,
sometimes more than one;

The complex, expansive metaphors in the poem enable Klein to speak at once of the poet's experience and the Jewish predicament. One also remembers that idealized portraits of the Jewish community are not uncommon in Klein's early poetry.

Irving Layton, rightly, describes Klein as "a poet of the minorities". The Jew, the French Canadian, the Indian and the poet are the minority groups who make their frequent appearance in his poems. Even when Klein writes about the Indians, he identifies them with the French Canadians as well as with the Jews. The short poem, "Indian Reservation; Caughnawaga" describes the vanishing species in the form of childhood recollections.

Where are the braves, the faces like autumn fruit,
Who stared at the child from the coloured frontispiece?

And the monosyllabic chief who spoke with his throat?
Where are the tribes, the feathered bestiaries?
Rank Aesop's animals erect and red,
with fur on their names to make all living things kin-
Chief Running Deer, Black Bear, Old Buffalo Head?

The child's wonder and admiration for the colourful appearance and enchanting names lead to its desire for a similar existence:

Childhood, that wished me Indian, hoped that
One after school I'd leave the class room chalk,
the varnish smell, the watered dust of the street,
to join the clean outdoors and the Iroquois track.

But this spell doesn't last long. There is a painful realization of their present pathetic condition.

Their past is sold in a shop: the bleached shoes,
the sweet grass basket, the curio Indian,
burnt wood and gaudy cloth and inch-canoes-
trophies and scalpings for a traveller's den.

Now also they may occasionally dance but it is not out of joy. The pleasures of a carefree life are lost to them for ever:

Sometimes, it's true, they dance, but for a bribe;
after a deal don the bedraggled feather
and welcome a white mayor to the tribe.

The contrast between their past and present naturally brings to the poet's mind the past of the Jewish community. The present plight of both the groups appears to be almost identical:

This is a grassy ghetto and no home.
And these are fauna in a museum kept.
The better hunters have prevailed. The game,
losing its blood, now makes these grounds its crypt.
The animals pale, the shine of the fur is lost,
bleached are their living bones. About them
watch as through a mist, the pious prosperous ghosts.

By the time the poem ends, the identification of the Indians with the Jews is total and the poet's nostalgia for the good old days of the Jews becomes too evident.

Irving Layton is proud of his Jewish heritage and has a number of poems on many Jewish intellectuals but his self-conscious Jewishness and anti-Christian rhetoric spoil the cause he desperately attempts to champion. In a short poem, he gloats over the victory of Spinoza, Marx and Freud:

Three Jews, three Jews lit a fuse under the bum of Christendom
First, Baruch Spinoza who mixing Ethics with Euclid dropped the lid on the Christ myth
though Pope and priest strain they'll never lift open that lid again
Three Jews, three Jews lit a fuse under the bum of bourgeois Christendom, it's done for, it's had its day; three Jews chomping on cigars puffed it away.

Consciously privileging excess over restraint, vulgarity over decorum and passion over reason, he expressed himself often with a rage that is puerile and fails to overcome ethnic and religious prejudices.

It is a pity even while dealing with the holocaust theme, which is inherently tragic and can easily evoke the emotions of pity and terror, Layton fails to capitalize on that. In a short piece called "You Never Can Tell", for example, he tries to make a poem out of a common joke associating it with the holocaust but fails to create the desired effect:

You fool, keep quiet about the holocaust,
There are Christians
who haven't heard and it might give them ideas.

What is achieved is not a supreme instance of black humour but a sick joke. Another attempt of the same kind meets with the same fate in a poem called "Jew".

Someone who feels himself to be a stranger everywhere, even in Israel. We hear a voice made confident not by vision but by blind fury, even when he chooses to deal with the Auschwitz disaster. It was in Auschwitz, a town in southern Poland, where, between 1942 and 45, some four million people, mostly German and East European Jews, were killed by the Nazis. One of the most tragic themes that history has bequeathed to literature, a deft touch it can be easily endowed with a cathartic effect. But the poet's very belief in violence, retaliation and revenge precludes the possibility of an appeal to enlightened emotions. The poem "After Auschwitz", in the form of an apostrophe to the poet's son, advises him not to entertain any faith in the sacred books of the past but to prepare himself for bloody revenge.

Believe an aging poet of the twentieth century: neither the Old Testament nor the New or
the sayings of the Koran or the Three Baskets of Wisdom or the Dhammapada will ever
modify or restrain the beastliness of men.

In order to provoke his son further, he mentions how the Nazis once made Lampshades from the skins of the murdered Jews. He does not seem to remember that he has already attempted an almost identical ironic presentation of the horrifying event in a short poem called "Proper Reading Light":

You don't understand, my son,
they made lampshades
that they might read the text better.
"Which text father?"
"Love one another".

Unmindful of the loss of effect, the poet repeats the idea with very little change:

Lampshades were made from the skins of a people preaching the gospel of love; the
ovens of Auschwitz and Belsen are open testimony to their folly.

Their Christian enemies may claim that they realize their folly and repent of their sin but the poet is certain their repentance will only be short-lived. His advice to his son, therefore, is to resort to the use of an automatic rifle:

An automatic rifle endures a lifetime.

Forgetting what he has condemned as “beastliness” and “folly”, he is advocating the very same thing to his son. In the poem, there is cliche, there are confusions; the rhetoric of it is frank, passionate but lacks subtlety. The subject matter provides an excellent opportunity to celebrate the power of human endurance; Layton, unfortunately, sacrifices it at the altar of bitterness and malice.

Eli Mandel also has a poem on the Nazi extermination camp in Poland, a post-modernist attempt to recapture the scene of genocide and to describe the effects of psychic shock on the contemplation of horror. In the middle of the poem, with a few impressionistic strokes, an atmosphere of terror is evoked successfully:

this is mother this is father this is the one who is waving her arms like that is the one who like I mean running with her breasts bounding running with her hands here and there with her here and there hands the generals smiling saluting in their mythic uniforms god-like generals uniforms with the black leather with the straps and the intricate leather the phylacteries and the prayer shawl corsets and boots and the leather straps.

This event is beautifully interwoven with the poet’s own violent tendencies. He recalls a scene in which he finds himself as a Jewish youth cheering the cowboy heroes who kill a large number of Red Indians:

While the whitehatted star spangled cowboys shot the dark men and shot the dark men and we threw popcorn balls and grabbed each other and cheered; me Jew boy yelling for the shot down and the falling men.

There is a subtle indication that the Jews are not the only victims of persecution and that they are not absolutely free from aggressive feelings. As a post-modernist piece, the poem is self-reflexive, its evocative descriptions leading to hysterical incoherence of words and phrases:

the poem becoming the body becoming the faint hunger body prowling through words the words the words the poem flickers, fades the four Yarzeit candles guttering one each four million lights dim my words drift.

The poem succeeds because of its objective expression of the poet's experience of bitterness and horror over what man has done to man.

All the three–Klein, Layton and Mandel–are, no doubt, accomplished poets, though they differ from one another in more than one respect. When they treat Jewish themes in poem after poem, their characteristic strengths and weaknesses come to the fore and one cannot help feeling that their success would have been guaranteed had they learnt a lesson or two from a poem like W.H. Auden's "Refugee Blues", whose protagonist is a weary Jewish refugee talking to his wife about their miserable condition as they have been running from pillar to post in search of shelter. Modelled upon the Negro folk songs with their slow jazz rhythm and melancholy words, Auden's poem gives a controlled expression of his bitter anger at Hitler's inhuman policy of wiping out the Jews. Every short stanza of three lines proclaims the Jewish predicament with a telling effect:

Say this city has ten million souls,
Some are living in mansions, some are living in holes:
Yet there is no place for us, my dear, yet there's no place for us.

Once we had a country and we thought it fair,
Look in the atlas and you'll find it there;
We cannot go there now, my dear, we cannot go there now.

In the village churchyard there grows an old yew,
Every spring it blossoms anew;
Old passports can't do that, my dear, old passports can't do that.

The poem makes it clear that the fish and the birds can lead a carefree life but not man because his is the only cursed race and that he alone is responsible for the curse.

Walked through a wood, saw the birds in the trees;
They had no politicians and sang at their ease;
They weren't the human race, my dear, they weren't the human race.

Dreamed I saw a building with a thousand floors.
A thousand windows and a thousand doors;
Not one of them was ours, my dear, not one of them was ours.

It achieves unqualified success because it touches the archetypal in us as the Jewish refugee portrayed is at once a Jew and every man.

The protagonist of Saul Bellow's Ravelstein is a gifted professor of political philosophy at the height of his career and the novel purporting to delineate the last days of his life lived in great luxury deals with a few favourite Bellow themes and some new ones including friendship and jealousy, disease, death and deathlessness, confronting one's own death and cannibalism but it is the Jewish question that predominates.

Both the hero and the narrator–friend happen to be old Jews constantly exchanging their thoughts on Eros and Thanatos, philosophy and history and life and literature. Ravelstein is reported to have become a millionaire by authoring a bestseller about the ideas that sustain or kill mankind and Chick is entrusted with the prestigious task of writing a memoir of his famous friend. Whatever may be the thematic preoccupation, the novel turns again and again to the predicament of the Jewish race. The blacks seem to have been scrupulously excluded from the scene as they have no representative, major or minor and this ensures that the Jew may be the novelist's chief focus of attention.

The reader is never left in doubt as to the racial identity of any of the numerous characters that make their sustained or brief appearance. Ravelstein himself is at times referred to as "the Jewish Comedian", (R: 23) "this large Jewish man from

Dayton, Ohio" (R: 94). He and Chick, during their many friendly gossips over their absent companions and enemies, don't fail to bring in the Jewish question in some form or other.

> *"That's why he wears such a sad and distant look. So what's left?" Ravelstein said. "The Jewish question." "Not to be a Jew was very desirable in those times, a big asset. One never knows. But the big thing with Kurbanski is being French".* (R: 136)

Even a Christian character like Rosamund, the young wife of Chick, is unbelievably made to stress the significance of the Jewish problem. When he tells her that having a Jewish son-in-law poisoned Vel's mother's old age, Rosamund, rather improbably, responds,

> *"Now you've put your finger on the real subject"... "You've given lots of thoughts to all kinds of problems, except the most important one. You began with the Jewish question".* (R: 166-67)

This prompts her husband to give a lecture, though short, on the atrocities perpetrated by Hitler as well as on his rise to power.

> *It was the Jews that were Hitler's ticket to power. He didn't have nor did he need, any other program. He became Chancellor by uniting Germany and much of the rest of Europe against the Jews.* (R: 167)

When Chick talks nostalgically of the bad old days, he comes out with a puzzling statement on the sad plight in which the American Jews find themselves.

> *Well, I had a Jewish life to lead in the American language, and that's not a language that's helpful with dark thoughts.* (R: 167)

It is not clear if this ambiguous utterance is a compliment to English or a satiric comment on its inadequacies. But in this needlessly prolonged dialogue, the old man is goaded into giving a moving account of the fascist concentration camps and of the destruction of "hundreds of thousands of millions" on ideological grounds.

Ravelstein is all admiration for Athens and Jerusalem, "the twin sources of civilization", "the two main sources of higher life" but in his last days it was the Jews he wanted to talk about, not the Greeks". (R: 173)

To the dying Ravelstein, even the green parrots "have a Jew look to them". (R: 170) Though Chick seems to distance himself from his hero's obsession with Judaism, there are occasions when he cannot help being sucked into it. Ravelstein's passion for teaching is defended by him as a typical Jewish trait.

> *We are a people of teachers. For millennia, Jews have taught and been taught. Without teaching, Jewry was impossibility* (R: 101)

There are other minor characters who have no reservations about the validity of Ravelstein's views on the Jewish problem. They also feel equally vehemently that a Jew should take a deep interest in the history of the Jews and that the Jews have nothing of greater value than their religious legacy.

The numerous references to anti–Semitism and anti-semites, not veiled but overt, cover an extremely broad spectrum of men and events. Ravelstein takes it upon himself to tell his Jewish colleagues, friends and admirers that anti-semitism is in the air and to warn them away from Jew-haters. When he is attempting to recover his earnest money from his aristocratic French landlords, he tells his friends.

> *"Especially in this instance, because the tenant is a Jew, and there's a Gobineau in the landlord's family tree. Those Gobineaus were famous Jew-haters... Anyway, they will let a Jew live on their street, but he should pay for it".* (R: 70)

He feels that Chick is anything but risk-averse because he does not mind marrying a Christian woman. Ravelstein is perturbed by his family mementos.

> *As for you Chick, you're making your total declaration of rights, it's very brave of you to do it but it's also off the*

> *wall...For miles around, you're the only Jew. Your neighbours have one another to rely on.*
> *Whom do you have-a gentile wife?* (R: 116)

The implications of his statements are clear. It may be France, Italy or America but no place is safe for a Jew even though constitutional guarantees may be on his side. Chick claims on more than one occasion he doesn't feel threatened by such warnings from a religious zealot but the latter's enthusiasm proves infectious. When Chick is reading J.M. Keynes, he finds himself drawn again and again to the anti-semitic utterances in the book which he reads out to Rosamund. The reputed British economist's description of Lloyd George's treatment of a Jew named Klotz, one of the French ministers, causes a dreadfully upsetting experience.

Lloyd George had always hated and despised him. And now saw in a twinkling that he could kill him. Women and children were starving, he cried, and here was M. Klotz prating and prating of his 'gold'.

> *He leant forward and with a gesture of his hands indicated to everyone the image of a hideous Jew clutching a money bag.* (R: 80)

Some of the Jew-haters come under fire from both the old Jews who, in their 'fun conversations', highlight the stupidity and wickedness of their stand. Ravelstein used to contend that Voltaire was not intellectually serious but now Chick is certain he would have condemned the French philosopher for hating Jews (R: 178). Chick is advised by Ravelstein to drop Kipling from his list of favourites when the former mentions one of the letters by the English writer in which he had stated that while the Jews in general had distorted social reality for their Jewish purposes, Einstein was disfiguring physical reality with his relativity theory. (R: 174)

That Bellow is haunted by the Jewish question is glaringly evident throughout the novel. He might have portrayed the Jew as victim and victimizer in his earlier novels, might have had a gentile hero for a novel, and might have completely ignored the Jews in another novel. But all that belongs to the past. The old man who has authored Ravelstein is a Jew, through and through.

These twentieth century writers may not be considered by some as sincere and serious-minded champions of human rights and their works of art may not be objective dispassionate accounts of what happened to the Jews before and after Hitler.

But in any kind of stock-taking undertaken to find out if the European Convention has served the objective of protecting human rights, the "Jewish witness" of this type has to be taken into account.

References

Saul Bellow, *Ravelstein*, New York, Viking, 2000.

Russel Brown and Donna Bennett, eds., *An Anthology of Canadian Literature in English*, Toronto, OUP, 1982.

Irving Layton, *Fortunate Exile,* Tornto: Meclelland and Stewart, 1987.

10

Forced Marriages in the European Court of Human Rights and the European Court of Justice

Geetha Ganapathy-Doré

As a specialist in literature, I must confess that the idea of working on a topic of this kind had occurred to me while I was studying English romantic poetry. Shelley, who had been married twice and had had several unhappy love affairs, intended writing a book on marriage and had acquired books on the Nairs of Kerala [1] to study other marital customs. His second wife Mary was none other than the daughter of Mary Wollestonecraft, the author of *A Vindication of the Rights of Women.* Later in 1997 Arundhati Roy, a novelist who hails from Kerala, published her one-of-a-kind novel, *The God of Small Things* in which the protagonist Ammu comes back to claim her ancestral property after divorcing her husband and finds her right denied.

In real life, Arundhati Roy's mother Mary Roy had had to take her own case to India's Supreme Court in 1986 to challenge an archaic Travancore Christian Succession Act of 1916 that says that "in case of intestate property, the *daughter* is entitled to 1/4th of the son's share of estate or Rs. 5000, whichever is less". [2] I had later met Novelist Githa Hariharan who again had had to file a case in the Supreme Court in 1999 to challenge the *Hindu* Minority and Guardianship Act of 1956 and Section 19 of the Guardian and Wards Act of 1890, when the Reserve Bank refused to issue 9 per cent Relief bonds for her minor son with her acting as the guardian. According to these laws, the mother could not be the natural guardian of her child unless the father is dead, goes to *vanaprastha* or turns *sanyasi* or is declared unfit by a court. [3] I had then been thinking about how a woman's individual liberty is curtailed, in the legal sense of the term, by marriage. Though India serves as a base for my reflections, my analysis is interdisciplinary and will focus on Europe. [4]

This Article will first look at the tradition of marriage in several cultures and see how it complicates the human rights issue. This involves reviewing some international legal instruments. It will then describe the types of marriages that are now regarded in Europe as going against the principle of human rights and examine some land mark cases that were brought before the European Court of Justice and the European Court of Human Rights. Finally, it will weigh the impact of jurisprudence to see what lessons could be learnt for the protection of the individual faced with the collective weight of society and culture and how women's rights form the foil to human rights in some aspects. This again is a theme that had been dealt with by the French revolutionary Olympe de Gouges who penned the *Declaration of the Rights of Woman and the Female Citizen* which envisaged among other things a law to protect widows and young girls from men who make false promises.

From time immemorial, marriage implied a certain degree of violence for women. The rape of Europa and the abduction of Helen of Troy are some classical examples. Of course, in the Indian tradition of *swayamvara*, the woman was free to choose. But this was a custom practiced generally by royal families and not a common practice among ordinary people. In ancient Indian texts, eight types of marriage [5] are mentioned, depending on which party initiates the union and for what purpose. In the *Brahma* marriage, it is the boy's parents who are on the look out for an eligible bride. In the case of *Prajapatya* marriage, it is the other way round.

The girl can sometimes be forced into a *Daiva* marriage where she marries the priest in the absence of a suitable groom, or an *Arsha* marriage in exchange for two cows, or an *Asura* marriage where she is given over to an unsuitable groom in exchange for wealth. Marriage by kidnapping is called *Rakshasa* marriage and marriage by rape, *Paishacha* marriage. *Gandharva* or love marriage, where the girl and the boy exercise their free will resembles a Western romance. Polygamy in the form of polygyny and polyandry existed in India. However, monogamy has been upheld as a value since the days of Rama. The British reformers passed laws against the practice of Sati (1829), in favour of widow remarriage (1856) and to restrain child marriage (1929).

In spite of modernization by legislators, thanks in particular to the Dowry Prohibition Act 1961, the age-old systems of dowry and bride price persist in India. In popular imagination all over the world, the concept of arranged marriage is forever associated with India, with parents arranging weddings over the continents via the internet. Novelists like Vikram Seth and Chitra Divakaruni Banerjee and movie makers like Mira Nair and Gurinder Chadha have helped romanticize and perpetuate this cliché. Autobiographies such as Baby Halder's *A Life Less Ordinary* add a poignant touch of reality to these embellished stories. Madhu Kishwar, the editor of the feminist journal, *Manushi*, has argued that even love marriages are nothing but self-arranged marriages. [6]

Those who have read the novels of Pearl Buck would know that in imperial China a man was allowed to choose concubines though formal marriage could exist only between one man and one woman. African polygamy is well known. Much less known perhaps is the custom in which when the husband dies, the surviving wife is compelled to marry the brother. This is the levirate marriage practiced in countries like Somalia, Nigeria, Kenya and South Africa. In India, levirate marriages can be found among the Jats of Punjab and Haryana.

Among the Igbo people of Nigeria, there is a tradition of same sex marriage. When her husband dies, a woman is allowed to take another woman as "husband". This change of sexual orientation of one person during the course of her life might appear tribal and disconcerting. However, on a much less scandalous scale, we can find, even in Europe, highly educated and well-heeled women in their fifties whose marriage has failed spending more time in the company of their female friends.

The Koran, paradoxically, gives reciprocal rights to the spouses. Mutual consent is needed. There is a contract and spouses inherit from each. But forced marriages, honour killings and brutal divorces that are unjust towards women occur in several parts of the world where Muslims live and mar this intended ideal picture. As far as Judaism is concerned, the Talmud specifies that a woman could be acquired through money, a contract (*Ketubah*), and sexual intercourse. But she can be acquired only through her consent. It is heartening to note that companionship, love and intimacy are the primary purposes of marriage in the Jewish tradition and not procreation. Though divorce is allowed by Jewish law, intermarriages are not accepted.

In the Western tradition, marriages had been strategic alliances to preserve wealth and power. Research in Renaissance culture shows that a parallel culture of courtesans thrived in Florence which means that love and marriage did not always coincide. [7] When divorce was forbidden by the Catholic Church, King Henry VIII founded the Anglican Church. The French revolution replaced the religious ceremony by a civil and republican one. Though marriages are legally monogamous, an idea inherited from Saint Augustine's thought, social polygamy does exist in the West. Mormon polygyny in the US is also well documented.

However, in the West and in cultures influenced by the West, people hold on to the Shakespearean idea of love at first sight and the fairy tale vision of marriage. In the fairy tale world, marriage marks the beginning of bliss. Fairy stories typically end with the charming prince marrying the fair but ill-treated princess, their living happily ever after and having many children. In his Sonnet 144, even Shakespeare himself talks about

Two loves I have of comfort and despair,
Which like two spirits do suggest me still,
The better angel is a man right fair,
The worser spirit a woman coloured ill.

We have to note that marriage in a modern and patriarchal set-up is less of a sacrament than a socio-economic institution that is increasingly called into question by what are known as civil pacts of solidarity, gay marriages or simply bachelor or spinsterhood. An uneasy category of the "undivorced" [8] and praise of "fissional love" [9] have come into being that further throw light on the troubles that have befallen marriage as institution. Whether customary or religious or secular, marriages create a de facto situation of inequality for women's freedom to choose, to move, to dispose of their body. The degree of violence and distress that sometimes accompanies this deprivation of liberty calls for more reflection and action.

The co-existence of ancient and modern patterns of marriage in the context of international migration has given rise to cultural clashes that are sometimes solved in courts of justice. The basic rights that are at stake are those enshrined in the following legal instruments:

1. The Universal declaration of Human Rights (1948), Article 16 in particular:

- Men and women of full age, without any limitation due to race, nationality or religion, have the right to marry and to found a family. They are entitled to equal rights as to marriage, during marriage and at its dissolution.
- Marriage shall be entered into only with the free and full consent of the intending spouses.
- The family is the natural and fundamental group unit of society and is entitled to protection by society and the State.

2. The document binding on the member states of the

Council of Europe, i.e., the European Convention on Human Rights, Articles 1, 2, 3, 12, 13 and 14 which ensure everyone's rights and freedoms, the right to life, the right to be free of inhuman and degrading treatment, the right to marry and found a family, the right to an effective remedy when these are violated and finally the enjoyment of these rights without any discrimination.

A closer examination of case law shows that Article 12 includes the right not to marry and the requirement of free and full consent to marriage by the intending spouses thanks to the principles of self-determination and human dignity that underlie the Convention. [10]

3. The international Covenant on Civil and Political rights (1966, entered into force in 1976) which states "no marriage shall be entered into without the free and full consent of the intending spouses".
4. The UN Convention on Consent to Marriage, Minimum Age for Marriage and Registration of Marriages of 1962 (entered into force in 1964).
5. The UN Convention on the Elimination of All Forms of Discrimination against Women of 1979 has also emphasized the importance of consent to marriage. "A woman's right to choose a spouse and enter freely into marriage is central to her life and her dignity and equality as a human being".
6. Council of Europe Parliamentary Recommendation 1325 (1997) on traffic in women and forced prostitution, [11] Council of Europe Parliamentary Assembly Resolution 1327 on "So called honour crimes (2003), [12] UN Report on the Elimination of Crimes against Women Committed in the Name of Honour, [13] Council of Europe Parliamentary Assembly Report on Child Marriages and Forced Marriages dated June 20, 2005, [14] Council of Europe Parliamentary Recommendation 1732 (2006) on the Integration of Immigrant Women in Europe [15], EU Guidelines on Violence against Women and Girls and

Combating All Forms of Discrimination against Them, [16] Council of Europe's Future Convention on Ccombating Violence against Women and Domestic V iolence. [17]

To this must be added national legislation of the States parties to the ECHR.

Litigation before the Court of Justice of the European Communities and the European Court of Human Rights has brought new nuances to the old categories of early marriage, forced marriage and marriage of convenience dubbed by the press as bogus or passport marriage. An early marriage is one in which at least one of the spouses is too young to give consent. According to UN guidelines, the minimum age to marry should not be less than fifteen years.

However, as a recommendation, this does not have a binding value and leaves room for granting "dispensation as to age for serious reasons" by competent authorities. "Leaving the minimum age of consent to the discretion of each country and allowing an authority to make exceptions to the minimum age of marriage aggravates the potential for early marriage to become a forced one", as the British NGO Liberty's briefing points out. [18] Some Council of Europe member countries think that early and forced marriages are specific to migrant communities which use them to get passports for non-European spouses.

Denmark and Netherlands used this discretionary power to set the minimum age for marriage at twenty five years for migrants to be able to reside in their territory. Though immigrant women applaud this move because it helps women complete their education and thus make a reasoned choice, it is at discrepancy with the European Convention on Human Rights which should be applied irrespectively to all the residents whether they are nationals of the member states or not. Another measure for control of forced or bogus marriage that goes against the grain of human rights is the UK Asylum and Immigration Act 2004 Section 19 which imposes preconditions for marriage on parties subject to immigration control, i.e., non-European Economic Area nationals. This provision contravenes Article 14 of the European Convention on Human Rights.

The famous *Metock and Others v. Minister for Justice, Equality and Law Reform* judgement rendered in 2008 by the Court of Justice of European Communities has somewhat highlighted this inequality. The ECJ ruled in favour of a Cameroonian national who had married an EU citizen of Cameroonian origin living in Ireland and held that the right of a national of a non-member country who is a family member of a Union citizen to accompany or join that citizen cannot be made conditional on prior lawful residence in another Member State. [19] It is to be remembered that there were two children born before the arrival of the father in Ireland.

The courts make a distinction between arranged marriages and forced marriages. They concede that marriages arranged by parents and families are an established and accepted tradition in some cultures. The Report of the Special Rapporteur Sigma Huda on the Human Rights Aspects of the Victims of Trafficking in Persons, Especially Women and Children," states that, "[a] marriage imposed on a woman not by explicit force, but by subjecting her to relentless pressure and/or manipulation, often by telling her that her refusal of a suitor will harm her family's standing in the community, can also be understood as forced." [20]

In forced marriages, one or both of the partners cannot give free or valid consent to the marriage. "Forced marriages involve varying degrees of force, coercion or deception, ranging from emotional pressure by family or community members to isolation, abduction and imprisonment". [21] In extreme cases, the victim can be subject to physical or sexual abuse, including rape. Forced marriages are generally conducted to protect caste, religious or racial identity and solidarity. Poor parents might use marriage as means to get rid of the girl child as quickly as possible or use it to settle their debt. In the context of immigration where the social mores are permissive, marriage is forced upon the girl to prevent pre-marital sexual relations that might tarnish a girl's reputation. It is not always the girls who are victims of forced marriages. Boys too come under undue family or social pressure to marry a partner not of their choice. [22]

In case of physical violence and rape, forced marriage is held to be a breach of the right to bodily integrity guaranteed in international human rights instruments. Article 3 of the ECHR prohibits torture, inhuman or degrading treatment. In *Ireland v United Kingdom 1978*, the European Court of Human Rights said that the factors that help determine whether there has been a breach or not are: age, sex and vulnerability of the victim. [23] According to the Court, the right guaranteed in Article 3 covers mental as well as physical suffering which exceeds a minimum level of severity. "Forced marriage also contravenes Article 8 of the Convention which includes the right to develop one's personality and to create relationships with others". [24]

While the US has granted asylum to victims of forced marriage, [25] the French State Council has held as late as July 2009 in the case of Mrs A that women who refuse to accept a forced marriage do not form a social group that can be considered a victim of persecution according to Article 1 of the Geneva Convention. [26] Though the suspicion of using marriage to circumvent immigration regulations hangs heavy in Europe, the truth is that forced marriage remains a scourge that plagues the immigrant populations in Europe.

Brought up in a society whose education and culture uphold freedom and human rights, the daughters of immigrant parents, of the second and even third generation, find themselves married by force when they go on a holiday to their country of origin, married to much older men at home sometimes. In some dramatic cases they are killed by their father or brother in what are known as honour killings because they fall in love and exercise their free will to choose their partners in their country.

Human Rights Law puts the onus on the State to implement legal measures which act as an effective deterrent. These measures need not necessarily involve recourse to criminal law. Great Britain has been the first country to take action in this regard and enact The Forced Marriage (Civil Protection) Act 2007. Under this law, individuals and organizations can apply for forced marriage protection orders.

Let us now consider two particular and landmark cases with regard to bodily integrity. The first is a case in marital rape. In C.R. v. United Kingdom 1995, a British subject married and separated from his wife after five years of conjugal life and the birth of a son, was accused of rape and assault, when he tried to force his wife to have sexual relations with him after she had told him that the marriage was over and gone to live with her parents. The accused pleaded immunity citing matrimonial consent and contract and quoted a legal principle from Sir Matthew Hale's *History of the Pleas of the Crown* published in 1736 that "A husband also cannot be guilty of rape upon his wife."

The Crown Court Justice had held that the withdrawal of one party from cohabitation is indication enough of the revocation of consent and charged the husband with the crime of rape. The husband pleaded guilty and was sentenced to three years imprisonment. He lodged an appeal saying that there was neither a court order nor agreement between the parties about the end of their marriage. The Court of Appeal dismissed the appeal and the Apex Court, the House of Lords, upheld the Court of Appeal's judgment.

He took the matter to the European Court of Human Rights and argued that the English courts breached Article 7 of the European Convention according to which no one shall be guilty on account of any act or omission which did not constitute a criminal offence under national or international law at the time when it was committed. But the Court decided in 1995 that "the abandonment of the unacceptable idea of a husband being immune against prosecution for rape of his wife was in conformity not only with a civilized concept of marriage but also, and above all, with the fundamental objectives of the Convention, the very essence of which is respect for human dignity and human freedom". [27]

Such reasoning has led the Council of Europe Parliamentary Assembly to redefine consent as "agreement by choice when having the freedom and capacity to make that choice". [28]

Another important example is the case of marital violence. The case Opuz v Turkey judged by the European Court of Human Rights in June 2009 is a telling example. Ms Opuz started living with her mother's husband's son (step-brother) in 1995 and had three children with him. The husband had repeatedly wounded the wife and her mother with the knife. The victims complained to the criminal courts several times, but withdrew their complaints under threat. Finally the husband shot the mother-in-law in 2002, when the wife decided to leave him.

He was condemned to life imprisonment, but was released on bail and started threatening his wife. Ms Opuz brought the matter before the European Court of Human Rights and alleged that the Turkish authorities failed to protect the right to life of her mother and that they were negligent in the face of repeated violence, death threats and injury to which she herself was subjected. She relied on Articles 2 (right to life), 3 (prohibition of torture and inhuman or degrading treatment), 6 (right to a fair trial within a reasonable time) and 13 (right to an effective remedy). She further complained about the lack of protection of women against domestic violence under Turkish domestic law, in violation of Article 14 (prohibition of discrimination).

The Court therefore concluded that "the national authorities had not shown due diligence in preventing violence against the applicant and her mother, in particular by pursuing criminal or other appropriate preventive measures against H.O in the form of effective deterrence against serious breaches of the applicant's personal integrity by her ex-husband. Ms Opuz had been able to show that domestic violence affected mainly women and that the general and discriminatory judicial passivity in Turkey created a climate that was conducive to domestic violence. Bearing that in mind, the violence suffered by the applicant and her mother could be regarded as gender-based, which constituted a form of discrimination against women". [29]

Convenience or bogus marriages take place when the real purpose of marriage is not founding a family but getting passports. Destitute EU brides from Latvia, Poland and Estonia get paid 10,000 Euros to marry prospective Pakistani or African grooms. At the other extreme of the exploitation of women within the marriage framework is the refusal to grant divorce by some husbands maintaining the wife in a different kind of enslavement. Mrs. Masuma Jarriwalla's case in Britain is case in point. She has divorced her husband under civil law but her husband refuses to accept that as binding on him and refuses to grant her "talaq" basically to prevent her from remarrying. [30]

In an age of accelerated time and constantly shrinking space and increased movement of people and things, cultural practice and economic conditions are altering dramatically. In spite of the spectacular progress made by women, the status of women as "fiduciary signs" as Pierre Bourdieu [31] puts it continues to persist. To give them agency, it is not enough to implement token reforms in sex education and law and set up crisis lines and temporary shelters.

An awareness campaign about life during and after marriage and an effective support system must be put in place whether in India or Europe. Even in France where the mayor recalls the rights and obligations of the spouses before ascertaining their consent, couples are too absorbed in the emotion of the moment to think about the consequences of marriage especially with regard to the matrimonial contract.

An awareness campaign might prove useful to men too, as more and more debates about stay-at-home dads and father's rights are taking the forefront.

The individual freedom to choose paradoxically depends on societal sustenance for that freedom to be viable. While discussing the issue of human rights in view of global imperatives, Amartya Sen remarks that "the force of a claim for a human right would indeed be seriously undermined if it were possible to show that it is unlikely to survive open public scrutiny". [32] At times of crises when states become pauperized and families destitute, happiness, that new measure of progress popularized by Joseph Stiglitz, [33] is compromised.

A balance therefore needs to be found between individual liberties and collective good. It is indeed difficult to find a common ground for social economy and the economy of individual desire. In the context of international migration, this can perhaps take the form of an EU India Forum on Forced Marriage to come up with a new legal instrument and an independent monitoring body. The way shown by Norway, which has set up integration advisors in its embassies in countries where forced marriage is prevalent and minority counsellors in upper secondary schools in its own territory, provides an interesting example.

The theoretically universal aspect and the preoccupation for gender equality that are consubstantial to the human rights reveal some fractures with regard to the rights of women. Whether you call it affirmative action or positive discrimination, special care needs to be taken in the direction of women who remain vulnerable in certain aspects. The taking into consideration of rights of women does not mean promoting one gender to the detriment of the other but enhancing the effectiveness of human rights for all. This is what the French philosopher Michel Serres calls the "soft revolution". [34]

I want to conclude with a quotation from the Tamil poet

Bharati. “Whatever you do, do not get married”, he advised. Why does he exhort his readers to boycott marriage? Was he being selfish? As a poet who was in love with liberty, he was perhaps averse to anything that fettered personal freedom. One way to eradicate forced marriages is perhaps to free marriage itself from the servitudes attached to it. A more realistic approach to marriage based on the knowledge of law might make it less of an entanglement and more of a tie that helps preserve the family. The existence of forced marriages shows that like all human institutions, marriage is a perfectible institution. This is not to undermine the spiritual aspects of marriage we could meditate upon.

Notes

1. Geetha Ganapathy-Doré, "The Indian Woman and the British Romantics" in *Les Cahiers du Sahib*, Presses universitaires de Rennes, no. 3, May 1995, pp. 83-105.
2. Venu Menon, « The Matriarch, The Real McRoy” *Outlook*, November 3, 1997. Retrieved from http://www.outlookindia.com/Article.aspx?204514 on April 12, 2010.
3. Githa Hariharan and another v Reserve Bank of India and another. Retrieved from http://www.githahariharan.com/downloads/write_up_on_case.pdf on April 12, 2010.
4. Indeed The French *Senat* conducted a colloquim on “Forced Marriage and Honour Crimes” on March 8, 2010 and has published the proceedings on line: http://www.senat.fr/rap/r09-408/r09-4081.pdf, retrieved on June 14, 2010.
5. http://www.vivaaha.org/newpage2.htm, retrieved on April 12, 2010.
6. Madhu Kishwar, « Out of the Zenana Dabba–Strategies for Enhancing Women’s Political Representation” in *Manushi*, no. 06, 1996, pp. 21-30.
7. Johan Nils Ringdal and Richard Daly, *Love for Sale, A World History of Prostitution*, New York: Grove/Atlantic, 2004.
8. Pamela Paul, “The Un-divorced” in *The New York Times*, July 30, 2010. http://www.nytimes.com/2010/08/01/fashion/01Undivorced.htm

l?_r=1, retrieved on August 15, 2010.

9. Serge Chaumier, *L'amour fissionnel, le nouvel art d'aimer*, Paris: Fayard, 2004.
10. The right to freedom of association guaranteed by Article 11 of the Convention includes the freedom not to join an association (*Cheall v United Kingdom* (1985) 42 DR 178, at 185), quoted in http://www.liberty-human-rights.org.uk/pdfs/policy07/liberty-briefing-forced-marriage-bill.pdf retrieved on April 12, 2010.
11. http://assembly.coe.int/Main.asp?link=/Documents/AdoptedText/ta97/EREC1325.htm retrieved on April 12, 2010.
12. http://assembly.coe.int/Main.asp?link=/Documents/AdoptedText/ta03/ERES1327.htm retrieved on April 12, 2010.
13. http://daccess-dds-ny.un.org/doc/UNDOC/GEN/N02/467/90/PDF/N0246790.pdf?OpenElement retrieved on April 12, 2010.
14. http://assembly.coe.int/Documents/WorkingDocs/Doc05/EDOC10590.htm retrieved on April 12, 2010. Asks member states to initiate a dialogue with the migrants' countries of origin to prohibit practices which are contrary to human rights, such as polygamy, repudiation, forced marriages, divorce without mutual consent and the automatic granting of custody of children to the father.
15. http://www.coe.int/t/e/legal_affairs/legal_co-operation/Steering_Committees/CDCJ/Documents/2006/CDCJ_BU_2006_10BIL_PA_Rec_1732_2006_2.pdf retrieved on April 12, 2010.
16. http://www.consilium.europa.eu/uedocs/cmsUpload/16173cor.en08.pdf retrieved on April 12, 2010.
17. http://www.epacvaw.org/IMG/pdf/CAHVIO_2009_interim_report_final.pdf retrieved on April 12, 2010.
18. http://www.stopvaw.org/Forced_and_Early_Marriage.html retrieved on April 12, 2010.
19. http://ec.europa.eu/dgs/legal_service/arrets/08c127_en.pdf retrieved on April 12, 2010.
20. http://daccess-dds-ny.un.org/doc/UNDOC/GEN/G07/104/10/PDF/G0710410.pdf?OpenElement retrieved on April 12, 2010.
21. *Ibid.*
22. At the joint colloquium held by Pondicherry and Paris 13 universities, this was pointed out to me by young male students

in the audience.

23. http://www.worldlii.org/eu/cases/ECHR/1978/1.html retrieved on April 12, 2010.
24. Liberty's briefing. See F.no. 7 for the link.
25. http://www.ncdsv.org/images/WaitingforAsylumBatteredWomenStuckLegalLimbo.pdf Retrieved on April 12, 2010. The case of Aruna Vallabhaneni is pending in Chicago.
26. http://www.vosdroitsendirect.com/particuliers-news-661-le-refus-d-accepter-un-mariage-force-ne-peut-ouvrir-droit-au-benefice-du-statut-de-refugie.html retrieved on April 12, 2010.
27. http://cmiskp.echr.coe.int/tkp197/view.asp?action=html&documentId=695832&portal=hbkm&source=externalbydocnumber&table=F69A27FD8FB86142BF01C1166DEA398649 retrieved on April 12, 2010.
28. http://assembly.coe.int/Main.asp?link=/Documents/AdoptedText/ta09/ERES1691.htm retrieved on April 12, 2010.
29. http://cmiskp.echr.coe.int/tkp197/view.asp?item=1&portal=hbkm&action=html&highlight=Opuz percent20 percent7C percent20v percent20 percent7C percent20Turkey&sessionid=51024817&skin=hudoc-en retrieved on April 12, 2010.
30. http://www.epolitix.com/mpwebsites/mpspeeches/mpspeechdetails/newsArticle/mrs-masuma-jariwalla///mpsite/edward-garnier/ retrieved on April 12, 2010.
31. Pierre Bourdieu, *La domination masculine*, Paris: Seuil, 1998, p. 49.
32. Amartya Sen, *The Idea of Justice*, London: Allen Lane, 2009, p. 387.
33. Cf. *Report by the Commission on the Measurement of Economic Performance and Social Progress* (2009) http://www.scribd.com/doc/19784660/Happiness-and-Measuring-Economic-Progress-by-Joseph-Stiglitz retrieved on April 12, 2010.
34. Michel Serres, *Temps des crises*, Paris: Editions Le Pommier, 2009.

11

Human Rights as Glimpsed from the Lens of Post-1968 French Philosophy

Himanshu Damle

"Human Rights are axioms. They can co-exist on the market with many other axioms, notably those concerning security or property, which are unaware of or suspend them even more than they contradict them: "the impure mixture or the impure side by side," said Nietzsche. Who but the police and armed forces that co-exist with democracies can control and manage poverty and the deterritorialization and reterritorialization of shanty towns? What social democracy has not given the order to fire when the poor come out of their territory or ghetto? Rights save neither men nor a philosophy that is reterritorialized on the democratic State. Human rights will not make us bless capitalism. A great deal of innocence or cunning is needed by a philosophy of communication that claims to restore the society of "consensus" to moralize nations, States, and the market. Humans rights say nothing about the immanent modes of existence of people provided with rights." Deleuze and Guattari (1992, 107)

The quote from Deleuze and Guattari's 'What is Philosophy?' nicely sums up the abstraction, pure, empty abstraction that Deleuze calls the party line for odious intellectuals. Deleuze does not pay much heed to the notion of human rights, but, instead broods over life rights.

My intention is not to delve into the Deleuzean version of Human/Life Rights, but to look at the conception of human rights from the point of view of two French philosophers who are beginning to make an impact in the English speaking world of late. The thinkers in question here are Badiou and Rancière who with their delivery of political agencies are not only complexly similar on many grounds, but provide many insights into the differences between one another. Their writings delve into human rights as a base for their versions of political agencies.

The time was February 2008, when a group of the so called new philosophers signed a petition in *Le Monde* calling the practices of the United Nations as diametrically opposed to the ideals of human rights. [1] It was further commented that there was a cause of concern with the institution becoming a caricature. Although we are ensconced in a multicultural world, the level of tolerance could be said to be reaching a nadir of sorts as was substantially proved in the petition detailing religious criticism as a form of racism, thus highlighting the tide against the basic ideas of Human Rights. The petition then called for the return to the Universal Ideals on Human Rights. [2]

It would be far fetched, but still appropriate to call the new philosophers as sandwiched between viewing the ideals of 1948 as problematic with their emphasis on a return to ideals. That the new philosophers are sandwiched between the two poles is attributable to one pole being that of Arendt and Agamben with their insistence on Human Rights as infringing of the political into the private sphere and the other of Badiou and Rancière calling for a political agency critiquing both the view points.

Arendt dismisses the idea of Human rights by calling it necessity based as action by the nation state to impose its control over the huge mass of refugees created in the aftermath of the Second World War, when the refugees that had been rendered stateless had nothing left but their humanity. [3] This way, for Arendt, the nation state gets to determining who gets the rights and who doesn't or who is part of humanity and who is not, thus quashing the ideals meant to protect rights. Despite the good intentions behind the formulation of the Universal

Ideals, it is nothing but an *apparatus* through which, the state exercises its total power over the stateless by making the latter submissive to it and other allied organs of power. This indeed proves the thesis that an interventionist approach is taken up by the nation state into the private sphere.

Arendt's thesis is pressed upon by Agamben, when he calls the peril of our present time as lying alongside an intercourse of the political power into the bare public life as omnipresent. Agamben links the notional intercourse as no different from what the refugees had to face in concentration camps. For him, the human rights act in a totalizing manner as now the most basic human existence is intricately surrendered to power structures thus making existence politicized. To quote Agamben,

"...until a completely new politics—that is, a politics no longer founded on the exception of bare life—is at hand, every theory and every praxis will remain imprisoned and immobile, and the "beautiful day" of life will be given citizenship only either through blood and death or in the perfect senselessness to which the society of the spectacle condemns it." [4]

Ernst Hemel reads the following quote in a dual way. viz, the seizure of private bare life by the structures of power and the deprivations of the individual in engaging with true emancipatory politics. The institutionalization of human rights is therefore seen as a part of the imprisoned and immobile life that somehow fails in its approach to reach the blunt political situation we are all faced up with. This reaches its aporetic limit in a way to invent a new political situation after criticizing the entire idea underlining human rights. So, for both Arendt and Agamben, the codification of the Universal Declaration of human rights is fraught with a critique that runs counter to new philosopher's insistence on attaining the ideal.

Badiou and Rancière both show their aversion to these readings and in their own ways of constructing the political agency exhibit displeasure in treating human rights as an ideal on the one hand and refusing to believe in the all encompassing political dominion on the other. Rancière brilliantly unearths the tautology in Arendt's version of human rights by noting that the rights of man are the rights of the unpoliticized person, or they are the rights of those who have no rights, thus amounting to nothing and rights of man are the rights of the citizen, that is, they are being attached to the fact of being a citizen, thus connoting rights of man as rights of citizens. [5] This in conflation amounts to a tautology. In effect, there is abandonment of human rights in Arendt according to Rancière since it is based on state power who has the discretion of providing rights to those who are excluded. This argument is taken forward to deal with Agamben, wherein it is noted that any kind of emancipatory political action is in retreat. Rancière quotes from his 'The politics of Aesthetics',

"There was at least one point where 'bare life' proved to be 'political': there were women sentenced to death as enemies of the revolution. If they could lose their 'bare life' out of the public judgment based on political reasons, this meant that even their bare life—their life doomed to death–was political. If, under the guillotine, they were as equal, so to speak, as men, they had the right to the whole of equality, including equal participation to political life." [6]

It is only in these situations that the totality is fissured in that there is a sense of inclusion but not belonging that is governed by exclusion that is only brought to light through acts of dissensions. This Rancièrean point is closely linked up with what Badiou has been maintaining with his 'Event'. 'Event' is the coming into being of what was never thought of (accidental) in the conceptual structuring of the present scenario. To explicate on the coming into existence of the 'Event', one needs to change the conceptuality and his idea behind this is borrowed from Cantorian set theory of placing the element inside the set, but at the same time not belonging to the set.

This is philosophically pertinent to the distinction between the political inclusion but non-belonging, in that, inclusion shares the possibilities in the world, whereas belongingness presents a systemic snapshot congruent with the given world view. In the moment of the 'Event', a person is faced with an ethical choice, by either denying what happened as new and trying to fit it in the existing template or by accepting it and building upon new consequences. To draw on these consequences is brought about by the act of naming. For Badiou, the notion of human rights is incapable of accommodating truth and is an attempt on the part of the dominant structure to be able to account for all elements of the set. [7] As he writes,

"The refrain of "human rights" is nothing other than the ideology of modern liberal capitalism: We won't massacre you, we won't torture you in caves, so keep quiet and worship the golden calf. As for those, who don't want to worship it, or who don't believe in our superiority, there's always the American army and its European minions to make them be quiet." [8]

For Badiou, the only universality is that which resists structuring and becomes tangible in the notion of an 'Event'. If Universality be equated with Truth, then according to his thesis in Manifesto of Philosophy, '*Truth makes a hole in knowledge*' and therefore it could now be inferred why for Badiou human rights as a kind of universality in equality, in freedom is anything but a form of dominant western ideology. To quote him again,

"The latest violence, the presumptuous arrogance inherent in the currently prevalent conception of human rights derives from the fact that these are actually the rights of the finitude[...] By way of contrast, the eventual conception of universal singularities requires that human rights be thought of as the rights of the infinite." [9]

So for Badiou, codification of the situations along the prefixed lines of universality results in redundancy alone and little wonder why he admonishes the case for human rights to be thought of as that which is included but not belonging. He takes a similar viewpoint towards justice by claiming the irrelevance of justice in the creation of anything new and thereby is more concerned with the conditions of possibilities of new politics rather than improving the sphere of juridicalness. In a way, what Badiou is looking for is very similar to what Rancière aims at and that being looking at human rights as an affirmative action. For both the thinkers, it is the exclusive situation where the insight into the human rights is to be taken up, to be formulated in a reconstructive manner.

The exclusive situation is normed as disruption by the thinkers and this disruption is then the affirmation for the coming into being of affirmative changes in the socio-political aspect. Since, this aspect of coming into existence is missing in the universal declaration, it becomes non-political in its conception as far as gauging the totality of the situation is concerned. Rancière sees this as the inability of the logic that dictates who is part of the situation, who has the right to voice claims and who forms the basis of political agency. For Badiou, it is the false totality altogether as it is impossible to envisage anything new or radical getting to the surface concretely. Since, there is absence of anything radically new, it is doomed to repeat the dominant power based ideology.

Although there are similarities in the ways the thinkers look at human rights, there are some differences that are stark in nature. For Rancière, it is the un-belongingness that counts cardinally despite the fact of the subject being inclusive in the system under consideration, whereas for Badiou, it is the subject getting called onto witnessing the 'Event' and thereby faced up with the radical choice that is ethical in nature. Badiou's invoking of mathematics to first name the 'Event' and thereafter follow it up to rewrite the radicality of the situation differs from reinterpreting human rights as suggested by Rancière. Most importantly, Rancière uses disruption as a singular revelation in that he is constrained in the expansionary vision/force of the dissensus. Badiou, on the other hand, emphasizes on the extensibility of the 'Event'. Rancière works within the existing system and is not concerned much with restructuring and vacillates between dissensus and consensus thereby giving it a more democratic feel of basing itself on negotiation, where Badiou aims at a revolutionary agency that he calls militant in nature.

The only universal human right that Badiou and Rancière envision is the right to intervene in the name of infinite universality, and they remain far from any institutionalization of universal human rights. Instead, their theories are geared towards a critical evaluation of the underlying presuppositions of doing politics, and providing rights. This critical evaluation is done in preparation of 'truthful' politics, which entails for both Rancière and Badiou a radical break with notions of politics that are defined in terms such as citizenship, freedom of speech or a return to ideal enlightenment values. Politics aims at a constant possibility. [10]

Notes

1. The petition was published in *Le Monde* on February 28, 2008. for full text in French and its translation in English, visit http://www.licra.org/index.php?old_navigator=true&section=detail&start=0&id=3000.
2. Ernst van den Hemel, *Krisis: Journal for Contemporary Philosophy*. Issue 3, 2008, p. 17.
3. Arendt, H. *The Origins of Totalitarianism*. New York: Harcourt Brace Jovanovich Inc., 1973, pp. 31-48.
4. Agamben, G. *Homo Sacer: Sovereign Power and Bare Life*. Stanford: Stanford University Press, 1998, p. 13.
5. Hemel, *Ibid*., p. 23.
6. Rancière, J. *The Politics of Aesthetics*. Continuum: New York, 2004, p. 304.
7. Hemel, *Ibid*., p. 24.
8. Badiou, A. *'On Evil: An Interview with Alain Badiou'* Cabinet Magizine Online, 5, Winter-issue 2001/2002. http://www.egs.edu/faculty/badiou/badiou-on-evil.html.
9. Badiou, A. 'Huit Thèses sur l'Universel'.

http://www.lacan.com/baduniversel.htm2004.

10. Hemel, *Ibid.*, p. 29.

12

Critical Pedagogy in Human Rights Education

Amruth G. Kumar

Introduction

The concept underpinning human rights education is that education should not only aim at transforming individuals into trained and skilled professionals, but also at contributing to their development into individuals who possess the skills to interact in a society. The major aim of human right education is to provide pupils and students with the ability to accompany and produce societal changes. Education is seen as a way to empower people, improve their quality of life and increase their capacity to participate in the decision-making processes leading to social, cultural and economic policies.

The importance of human rights education has long been recognized by the international community. The prominence accorded to it at the Vienna World Conference on Human Rights in 1993, and the fact that the United Nations decided to establish the Decade for Human Rights Education, are evidence of this. According to Amnesty International "learning about human rights is the first step toward respecting, promoting and defending those rights".

The United Nations General Assembly has proclaimed human rights education as central to the achievement of the rights enshrined in the Universal Declaration of Human Rights (UDHR). Article 26.2 of the UDHR states the role of educators in achieving the social order called for by the declaration:

"Education shall be directed to the full development of the human personality and to the strengthening of respect for human rights and fundamental freedoms. It shall promote

understanding, tolerance and friendship among all nations, racial or religious groups, and shall further the activities of the United Nations for the maintenance of peace."

Due to the initiatives of the United Nations in this field there have been considerable attempts across the world to promote human rights education as one of the most important priorities of the states. UNESCO shoulders the responsibility to promote human rights education throughout the world, and was a key organiser of the UN Decade for Human Rights Education. UNESCO attempts to promote human rights education through:

- Development of national and local capacities for human rights education, through its co-operation in development projects and programmes at national and sub-regional levels.
- Elaboration of learning materials and publications and their translation and adaptation in national and local languages.
- Advocacy and Networking Activities.

Following the Decade of Human Rights Education, on December 10, 2004, the General Assembly proclaimed the World Programme for Human Rights Education, and some projects to advance the implementation of human rights education programmes in all sectors:

"Building on the achievements of the United Nations Decade for Human Rights Education (1995-2004), the World Programme seeks to promote a common understanding of the basic principles and methodologies of human rights education, to provide a concrete framework for action and to strengthen partnerships and cooperation from the international level down to the grass roots."[United Nations High Commissioner for Human Rights (www.ohchr.org)]

A proper methodology for teaching human rights education has become always a matter of debate among educators. Since the human rights education can not be confined to class rooms only, the selection of methodology for each target group is a complex process. A methodology which is suited for school students may not be suited for the adults. Teaching strategies for women need some other features to cater to the nature of that group. This problem, treating the heterogeneous group, prevails as a major problem to be solved for the successful implementation of human rights education.

In Search of Strategies for Teaching

The basic aim of teaching human rights is to recognize and develop the freedom that is innate to the individual: individual freedom that recognizes its own worth and the worth of others are characterized by stable moral qualities and the ability to live a fruitful life and by agreement in a multicultural and multinational world. This aim is realized in the process of continuous education of children in accordance with their developing characteristics. At various stages in education the teaching material differs in content (depth, degree of concreteness, level of generalization, etc.), but, at the same time, it retains its overarching challenge to develop the following:

- The ability for co-operation and agreement between individual and group values, using the ability to resolve disputes without force;
- An understanding of the value of freedom as a condition for human self-realization and its link with responsibility and self-regulated behaviour;
- The feeling of individual worth based on a high morality and respect for the rights and worth of people of other nationalities, races and religious beliefs;
- An understanding of the variety, richness and uniqueness of the cultures of peoples of the world;
- An understanding of personal and civil responsibility in conserving the environment in one's own country and on a global scale.

According to the Russian Academy for Upgrading Professional Standards and the Retraining of Educators, teaching human rights in a school includes three stages. At the first stage (primary education) basic moral values and standards of human behaviour are introduced. Children form an understanding of the significance of human dignity and an understanding of their own individuality and the dignity of others. Children learn respect for others, tolerance, the feeling of solidarity, a tendency towards co-operation, and the ability to solve conflicts without force.

The second stage (basic school) formulates a system of values and the principles of human behaviour; younger children acquire knowledge and abilities for future independent life in society. At this stage of the teaching of human rights, respect towards the law and the rights of other people is promoted. There is an enrichment of students' knowledge of the history of the motherland and a perception of legal standards. At the third stage (full middle school), knowledge is broadened about the processes occurring in different spheres of society about the rights of people.

A perception forms around the complex interconnection among philosophical, cultural, political, legal and socio-economic bases, and civil positions of the human and socio-political orientations of students are determined. The task for this stage consists of ensuring that, in the process of social activity, students refine the readiness and ability to defend their rights and the rights of other people, create for themselves standards of activity and behaviour, and build individual and collective activity.

There has been a wide range of pedagogic applications in human rights education at the formal level. The potential of educational technology is widely used for human rights education across the world. Interactive methods are also used to develop the abilities and skills of students. In class room, human rights learning often leads to student projects and activities both inside and outside the classroom. A wide range of extracurricular activities are also used for teaching human rights to children. It has become one of the most powerful methods of human rights education. Activities like work in a micro region, organization of clubs, organization of trips to other towns and cities, to foreign countries, organizing friendship festivals, UN weeks, etc. are widely used by educators to impart human rights.

One of the indispensable conditions of teaching human rights is rebuilding the whole system of education on a democratic basis, introducing democratic relationships into the very fabric of school life. In other words, it is creation of a democratic way of life in school. Though there is a plethora of methods and strategies for human rights education, a democratic way of teaching, which may help the power of critical thinking, has yet to be practically implemented in this field. Here is the need for pedagogy for developing critical thinking of students based on democratic interactions. This paper is an attempt to explore the potential of Paulofrierian philosophy (popularly known as 'Critical Pedagogy') in human rights education.

Paulo Freire and Critical Pedagogy

The Brazilian educator Paulo Freire is the most influential educational thinkers of the late 20th century. His *Pedagogy of the Oppressed* is currently one of the most quoted educational texts (especially in Latin America, Africa and Asia). Freire was able to draw upon, and weave together, a number of strands of thinking about educational practice and liberation. Sometimes some rather excessive claims are made for his work e.g. 'the most significant educational thinker of the twentieth century'.

Throughout the book 'Pedagogy of the Oppressed' and his subsequent works, Fraire argues for system of education that emphasizes learning as an act of culture and freedom. He is most well known for concepts such as "Banking" Education, in which passive learners have pre-selected knowledge deposited in their minds; "Conscientization", a process by which the learner advances towards critical consciousness; the "Culture of Silence", in which dominated individuals lose the means by which to critically respond to the culture that is forced on them by a dominant culture. Other important concepts developed by Freire include: “Dialectic", "Empowerment", "Generative Themes/Words", "Humanization", "Liberatory Education", “Mystification", "Praxis", "Problematization", and "Transformation of the World". Theoretical notions developed by Freire lead to the emanation of pedagogical framework, which became popular as Critical pedagogy.

Critical Pedagogy

Critical pedagogy is deeply related to the work of Paulo Freire for his pioneering efforts to link the development of literacy to forging critical political consciousness among oppressed peoples. The aim is to develop a critical consciousness in the learner and to encourage social action to overcome oppressive social structures. For example, a program to teach illiterate adults to read would be part of a wider effort to overcome the marginal position of most of these people in terms of employment and civil rights. Many Western educational theorists and activists have been inspired by Freire's approach.

Critical pedagogy considers how education can provide individuals with the tools to better themselves and strengthen democracy, with the view to creating a more egalitarian and just society, and thus deploying education in a process of progressive social change. According to Henry Giroux (1994) Critical pedagogy signals how questions of audience, voice, power, and evaluation actively work to construct particular relations between teachers and students, institutions and society, and classrooms and communities. Pedagogy in the critical sense illuminates the relationship among knowledge, authority, and power.

"The fundamental commitment of critical educators is to empower the powerless and transform those conditions which perpetuate human injustice and inequity" (McLaren, 1988).

This purpose is inextricably linked to the fulfilment of what Freire (1970) defines as our "vocation" - to be truly humanized social agents in the world. Hence, a major function of critical pedagogy is to critique, expose, and challenge the manner in which schools impact upon the political and cultural life of students. Teachers must recognize how schools unite knowledge and power and how through this function they can work to influence or thwart the formation of critically thinking and socially active individuals.

"Unlike traditional perspectives of education that claim to be neutral and apolitical, critical pedagogy views all education theory as intimately linked to ideologies shaped by power, politics, history and culture. Given this view, schooling functions as a terrain of ongoing struggle over what will be accepted as legitimate knowledge and culture. In accordance with this notion, a critical pedagogy must seriously address the concept of cultural politics by both legitimizing and challenging cultural experiences that comprise the histories and social realities that in turn comprise the forms and boundaries that give meaning to student lives" (Darder, 1991).

Critical pedagogy studies the role which schools play in maintaining the social stratification of society, and the possibilities for social change through the schools. According to Peter McLaren (1998), *"Critical pedagogy is both a way of thinking about and negotiating through praxis the relationship among classroom teaching, the production of knowledge, the larger institutional structures of the school, and the social and material relations of the wider community, society, and nation state."* Peter McLaren (1998) explains that Critical pedagogy is an approach adopted by progressive teachers attempting to eliminate inequalities on the basis of social class, and that it has also sparked a wide array of anti-sexist, anti-racist, and anti-homophobic classroom-based curricula and policy initiatives.

Common questions for the critical educator include: What knowledge is of most worth? Whose knowledge is most important? What knowledge should be taught, and just as important, what knowledge is not to be taught? How does the structure of the school contribute to the social stratification of our society? What is the relationship between knowledge and power? What does this imply for our children? What is the purpose of schooling? Is it to ensure democracy or to maintain the status quo and support big business? How can teachers enable students to become critical thinkers who will promote true democracy and freedom?

Ira Shor (1992, p. 122) identifies principal goals of Critical pedagogy: "when pedagogy and curricular policy reflect egalitarian goals, they reflect what education can do:

- Oppose socialization with desocialization;
- Choose critical consciousness over commercial consciousness;
- Transform society over reproduction of inequality;
- Promote democracy by practicing it and by studying authoritarianism;
- Challenge student withdrawal through participatory courses;
- Illuminate the myths supporting the elite hierarchy of society;
- Interfere with the scholastic disabling of students through a critical literacy program;
- Raise awareness about the thought and language expressed in daily life;
- Distribute research skills and censored information useful for investigating power and policy in society;
- Invite students to reflect socially on their conditions, to consider overcoming limits.

Critical pedagogy, then, is defined by what it does-as a pedagogy which embraces a raising of the consciousness, a critique of society, as valuing students' voices, as honouring students' needs, values, and individuality, as a hopeful, active pedagogy which enables students to become truly participatory members of a society, who not only belong to the society but who can and do create and re-create that society, continually increasing freedom.

Relation between Human Rights Education and Critical Pedagogy

The relation between human rights education and Critical pedagogy is very strong. We could affirm with no doubt that human rights education is one of the most concrete and tangible expressions of critical pedagogy. In addition to it, human rights education–in order to fulfil its main purposes: to empower people to become subjects of rights–requires a proper educational atmosphere. An educational system based on the principles of Critical pedagogy creates this appropriate environment.

Both, Critical pedagogy and human rights education are very much interested in observing power structures outside and inside the educational system. Critical pedagogy is mainly interested to examine the way in which interaction between educational structure and the curriculum and there by shaping of knowledge. Human rights education is essentially concerned with how educational structure and the curriculum have an effect on moulding the "subject of rights". Educational hierarchy, educational ideology, models of discipline, State norms and school regulations are, among others, expression of power.

The curriculum as a system of power itself reproduces, resists and accommodates these other power systems. The key resource used by the curriculum to promote their interests is the power to create and legitimate knowledge. By its form and content, this knowledge is tied to both the interests of the curriculum designers and to those of powerful groups in society. Human rights educators assuming a critical pedagogy stand should understand, analyze and be aware of how the power component of education and curriculum works and interacts; determining how people are formed and empowered to become subject of rights. By making this analysis human rights education fosters critical living behind any innocent and naïve position.

Critical pedagogy considers freedom to choose, to express, to make decisions, i.e. within the general constraint of the curriculum, the material to be covered, the texts to be used, and the examination questions and essay topics-as an important component of power. When this sort of freedom exists, considerable scope exists for changing the content, to sample a range of viewpoints, to interact openly, etc. A Critical pedagogy demands introducing teaching methods which give students more control over their learning. When students choose what and how they learn, they are more likely to develop critical perspectives. Human rights education cannot operate in an educational atmosphere of restraints, vertical impositions, authoritarian and rigid relations or an environment of no dialogue and communication.

Human rights education as a Critical pedagogy encourages students to become independent learners, no longer dependent on injections from curricula and control by teachers. Human rights education by definition should provide students power and control over their learning. In this perspective human rights education adopts different initiatives, which have been used in teaching: self-paced learning; student choice of topics; student design of learning; student-oriented learning in which students help each other to learn; Work in small groups to promote learning which is egalitarian and self-sufficient (study groups, discussion groups, consciousness-raising groups and community research groups).

Both Critical pedagogy and human rights education aim to empower people to become subjects of rights. A subject of rights is someone with a basic knowledge of fundamental rights of people and who applies them in the promotion and defence of his or her own rights and the rights of others. It's a person who is familiar with the Universal Declaration of Human Rights, and with some of the human rights-related resolutions, covenants, and conventions, domestic and international declarations. The knowledge of these legal rules becomes an instrument of demand and surveillance oriented to the effective exercise of human rights. This subject of rights has also a basic knowledge of the institutions, especially those of its community, that protects its rights, and which it can resort to when its rights are violated.

Critical Pedagogy and Human Rights Education

Critical pedagogy is closely related to critical theory which refers to the work of a group of socio-political analysts associated with the Frankfurt School, whose prominent members included Adorno, Horkheimer, Walter Benjamin, Marcuse and Habermas, among others. They were all interested in the idea of a more just society and in empowering people to be in cultural, economic and political control of their lives. They argued that these goals could only be achieved through emancipation, a process by which oppressed and exploited people become sufficiently empowered to transform their circumstances for themselves by themselves. It is called 'critical theory' because they saw the route to emancipation as being a kind of self-conscious critique which problematises all social relations, in particular those of and within the discursive practices of power, especially technical rationalism.

It is precisely because our society faces so many difficulties—and schools are part of society—that teachers should, through a critical approach, decode and deconstruct their own prior perceptions of this reality. They should be motivated to develop a critical consciousness of problems, to analyse them, to make their cause explicit, to attempt to explore solutions and change conditions, to discover what is possible in confronting and taking action to solve the problem. Through human rights education, teachers are reinforcing the principles of transformative learning that could achieve this purpose. From this perspective, human rights education should be considered ethical and political education. Human rights education considers learning to be an integral aspect of life, rather than something separate from and largely irrelevant to other parts of life.

It should be said that human rights education, particularly in Latin America, started within the social movements or "popular education" movement (peace movements, feminist movements, workers' movements, environmental movements, minority rights movements, etc.), working within Freire's approach where people learn through dialogue and become conscious that they are subjects of rights and learn how to work on their own 'liberation'. Freire′s approach aims not just to give knowledge to the oppressed, but also to link the learning process with the actual social use of the knowledge-tool (empowerment).

Consistent with the basic concepts of Critical pedagogy, it has been always emphasized that teachers need to be conscious of how human rights are manifested and experienced in their day-to-day life as well as in their personal and collective experiences. When we ask teachers to define human rights they generally refer to their personal experiences with human rights—what happens to them on a daily basis with human rights, what is happening in their community.

To them human rights were related to peace and work. In their words they said 'When the militaries and the militants will let us work in our schools, this is then human rights for us'. Human rights education is a moment to realize significant and crucial situations of life. We should encourage teachers to face problems; this means to admit conflicts and to analyze contradictions that are implicit in human rights. We have to remember that, historically speaking, human rights are the result of intensive and incessant struggles of people to fulfil their rights and this struggle is full of contradictions and conflicts. We must be conscious that in human rights education, teachers should comprehend these conflicts.

Critical pedagogy and human rights education involves strategic pedagogic action on the part of classroom teachers, aimed at emancipation from overt and covert forms of domination. It is not simply a matter of challenging the existing practices of the system, but of seeking to understand what makes the system as it performs today, and challenging that, at the same time as remaining conscious that one's own sense of justice and equality are themselves open to question. The problematisation of consciousness and the values rooted in it is therefore the key characteristic of critical pedagogy and human rights education.

Critical pedagogy is a pedagogy designed for the purpose of enabling the learner to become aware of conditions in his life, in society, and to have the necessary skills, knowledge and resources to be able to plan and create change. It is a form of consciousness-raising. Critical pedagogy, as does Critical Theory, strives to help one see the true situation, often being a form of oppression resulting in decreased freedom, and to help one understand that this can be changed; in other words it reveals possibilities, the learner is able to discover the possibilities and then act on them.

Conclusion

The promotion of critical pedagogy is the promotion of the case of human rights and education for a culture of peace. Critical pedagogy is subversive pedagogy as it strives for structural social change. Its principal objectives are the creation of awareness for human rights, the rejection of violation and discrimination against different segments of population. Like human rights, Critical pedagogy is universal and maybe applied everywhere.

Therefore, critical pedagogy, a dialectic un-restful pedagogy is the pedagogy of human rights since it promotes critical social thinking and a challenge to automatic obedience and submission. Yet critical pedagogy is bound to create tensions between values of human rights and nationalistic ideas that put ideals of state's values higher than citizen's well being, national security priority and the perceived rights of the collective at a higher level than the human rights that each and every individual is entitled to.

The struggle to change methods of teaching is a very important challenge, and it needs to be followed with the change of teachers' attitudes. Raising teachers' consciousness is an invisible Sisyphean task. Good methods and pedagogical practices are very important, yet they cannot bypass the teachers. Critical thinking and social awareness must be part of teachers' preparation to compliment the wonderful initiative of endorsing human rights in schools.

References

Antonia D, Marta P. Baltodano and Rodolfo D, T. *The Critical Pedagogy Reader*: Second Edition. London: Routledge, 2008.

Darder, A, ed. *Multicultural Education, Critical Pedagogy and the Politics of Difference.* New York: Suny Press, 1995.

Freire, P. *Pedagogy of the oppressed.* New York: Herder and Herder. 1970.

Freire, P. *Cultural Action for Freedom.* Cambridge: *Harvard Educational Review.* 1970.

Freire, P. *Education for Critical Consciousness.* New York: Seabury Press, 1973.

Henry A. Giroux. "Doing Cultural Studies: Youth and the Challenge of Pedagogy," in *Harvard Educational Review.* 64 (3), 278-308, 1994.

Ira, S. *Empowering education.* Chicago: The University of Chicago Press. 1992.

McLaren, P. "Culture or cannon? Critical pedagogy and the politics of literacy. Review of P. Freire and D. Macedo, *Literacy: Reading the Word and the World*" in *Harvard Educational Review,* 58(2): 213–234, 1988.

United Nations High Commissioner for Human Rights. www.ohchr.org.

Section V

Epilogue

European Convention on Human Rights: Lessons to Learn

B. Krishnamurthy

"Europe has succeeded because it recognizes that the rights of individuals are inalienable and universal and it has created institutions to protect those rights. Only Europe can speak with credibility on the subject of universal human rights. For the sake of all of us, Europe must continue to speak out—even more forcibly than it has in the past."

Joseph E. Stiglitz [1]

I

As Monjal argues in his paper, the Second World War had largely demonstrated the triple failure of the European States: "failure in their capacity to contain aggressive nationalist ideologies, to protect people and property thanks to their parliamentary and judicial institutions and to organize regional diplomatic relations around pacifist values". This failure resulted in unprecedented destruction and devastation of Europe. The Western statesmen and intellectuals reacted to this human tragedy positively and established the United Nations (UN), which stood for universal human rights and was the first to link it with peace and security. Still, the UN could not come out with an implementation mechanism due to lack of unity and mutual trust between the western capitalist democracies and the Eastern Communist/totalitarian regimes. They continued to approach human rights from a different perspective, which, in turn, has given birth to a perpetual debate/dispute on the issue of universality of human rights v cultural relativism. While universality of human rights is spearheaded by Western democracies, Communist countries insisted on their preference to socio-economic rights at the cost of political and civil rights. The integral and indivisible nature of human rights, on which there was a consensus in the late

1940s, was questioned and disputed in the light of the vagaries of Cold War international politics.

However, the human rights system developed under the auspices of Council of Europe (CoE) is successful in bringing both these groups together. The Europeans opt for global peace through the protection and promotion of human rights and are successful in saying 'no' to war and in creating a practical and practicable human rights regime. Adherence to the system thus created is made conditional to the membership of the CoE and subsequently of the European Union (EU).

Consequently, Europe has a successful record in making war as the part of history and no great wars marred the peace of Europe for the past sixty years or so. The EU has achieved a level of economic prosperity which is the envy of others; absorbed the Central and East European countries admirably; is in the process of enlarging towards the South Eastern Europe and continues to prove itself to be a successful international experiment. Scholars take the EU as an example of post-modern or post-Westphalian state, where the borders have blurred and are loosing their significance as an ethical boundary.

Joseph Stiglitz is quite right in attributing this success to the European human rights record. For instance, in the case of death penalty, the number of abolitionist states now stands at ninety five including the entire European continent except Belarus. The EU is working towards impressive changes in the retentionist countries like the US and China and is for achieving global moratorium on executions by 2015.

Still, all is not well with Europe in the human rights front. Violation of the rights guaranteed in the European Convention occurs every now and then. Europe had experienced the phenomenon of international terrorism since late 1960s campaign of terror launched by 'indigenous' as well as foreign terrorist groups, which reached its zenith by mid 70s. According to a US State Department report, in 1984, the highest number of incidents occurred in Western Europe (39 percent of the world total), the same area with the least "war" since 1945. [2] The 1990s have witnessed growing terrorist activities in the member states of the European Union.

As a reaction to the September 11 terrorist attack on the US, the European Council at its extraordinary meeting on September 21, 2001, declared that terrorism is a real challenge to the world and to Europe and that the fight against terrorism will be a priority objective of the EU. The German government changed the law that gave special protection to clubs and groups with a religious character and is determined to tighten laws to crack down on suspected terrorist organisations. Britain introduced a new Anti-Terrorism, Crime and Security Act which allowed foreign suspects to be detained without trial. All these terrorist and counter terrorist measures resulted in severe human rights violations. While preaching others on handling terrorism with humanitarian approach, the Europeans practiced differently and mishandled the whole issue.

Immigration is another area resulting in terrible human rights violations. It often opens the old scars of the European complexes over racial superiority and colonial hangovers. The immigrant communities are perpetually accused of widespread criminality and of dumping down the educational system and prevailing unemployment among the Europeans is attributed to them. There is widespread accusation that the immigrants from Turkey and Arabic countries have more difficulty integrating than other settlers and that Europe must end immigration from other cultures. As maintained by Pasha the European societies have failed to handle their Muslim minorities as per their cherished ideals. The European leaders like Angela Merkel comment that multiculturalism has failed and European workers cannot live "happily side by side" with foreign workers. Earlier Jacques Chirac talked about the 'smell and sound' of the immigrant workers, which was rightly criticized by human rights defenders for its racial overtone. It is rather ironic that even mainstream politicians are pushing a bigoted agenda with racist overtones thus worsening a climate of insecurity for the ethnic minorities in the EU member states. These kind of unfortunate developments certainly diminish the EU's international standing as a power which cares for human rights and welfare.

However, to the credit of the European human rights system, it may be maintained that the member states as well as regional institutions always attempted to rise to the occasion. Subsequent to fires in crowded rundown Paris buildings in 2005, in which almost 50 people lost their life, a new French law was introduced in 2007 making housing a basic, enforceable right like education. [3] The system of checks and balances have immediately been activated and there were genuine efforts to contain and control the situation as in France with regard to the covert quota system based on racial lines in training youngsters for football that was about to be introduced. [4]

Again, institutions like the Council of Ministers of the CoE, European Commission, European Parliament and the European Court of Justice as well as the European Court of Human Rights (EctHR) reacted sharply to any human rights violations on the part of the member states of the CoE or the EU. For instance, the European Parliament's 2001 report on human rights called for the setting up of a permanent working group to continuously monitor the situation of fundamental rights in the EU. [5] The Council of Ministers of the CoE adopted a set of guidelines on counter-terrorism and human rights for its member states. These guidelines, which were the first of their kind to be adopted by an international body, had been drawn up by a group of specialists appointed by the Council's Steering Committee on Human Rights. Based on international human rights treaties and case law of the ECtHR, they established minimum standards for the level of human rights protection that states must ensure when they adopt measures to combat terrorism.

The guidelines stress that all counterterrorism measures must be lawful and that arbitrary or discriminatory implementation of such measures are prohibited. [6] Again, on the introduction of post-September 11 anti-immigration laws in UK or the recent anti-Roma policies and actions of the French Government, the European civil society, human rights activists as well as the European institutions came down heavily and were highly critical of their policies and activities. On the issue of immigration, the Court intervenes meaningfully as and when the situation warrants. The year 2008 alone witnessed a very large increase in requests for interim measures: some 3,200 requests were received, of which almost 750 were granted, mostly in sensitive cases concerning immigration law and the right of asylum. Again, the Court received 3,680 requests for interim measures (Rule 39 of the Rules of Court), a 65 percent increase on the already exceptionally high number of requests received the year before (2,399). 1,440 requests (almost 40 percent) were granted in 2010. [7] All these clearly prove beyond doubt that the restrictive mechanism works well and in time, whenever and wherever any human rights violation occurs in the CoE/EU area.

Still, some scholars do not rate the European human rights system highly, especially the way in which it is being practiced. Monjal argues that in the aftermath of the Second World War, the European States have over-reacted to their historical past, which was full of wars and as such, by implication, resulted in perpetual human rights violations. He maintains that by way of redemption, the European States "have definitely renounced the idea of re-appropriating fundamental rights. It is the Court, which, as ultimate arbiter, dictates the values of the Convention to the member states. This relinquishment, which is undoubtedly justified by the wish of the states to redeem themselves by depriving themselves (through a kind of self-punishment) for ever of the national control of fundamental rights, gives the judges of the ECtHR more power".

Both Monjal and Reiplinger feel that in the European

human rights regime that has developed under the framework of the ECHR and the auspices of the CoE, the States have surrendered their role in protecting and promoting human rights to the European Court. They argue that the human rights institutions have become a burden on the States Parties. Reiplinger remarks that "the European Court is now in a position of giving lessons of liberal democracy to the country where liberal democracy was undoubtedly conceived and born, and which has not, contrary to its neighbours, known any authoritarian regime since the late seventeenth century…".

Still sharper criticism comes from Monjal, who opines that the European Court seemed to make a mockery of the sovereignty of the States parties. Again, Monjal accuses that in the name of the theory according to which "the Convention is a living document, the European Court has freed itself thoroughly from the conventional techniques of interpretation and initial will of the authors of the ECHR". He even goes to the extent of arguing that the European Court by its contestable interpretations and its will to keep enlarging the field of individual rights calls into question the very validity of the Convention.

However, it may be maintained that this is the price the European states had to pay for the uninterrupted peace and prosperity that they enjoy in the post-War period. There is a need to control the State from getting intoxicated with power and its tendency to misuse it. Regarding the issue of interpretation of the European Convention, Phillipe Boillat, Director General of Human Rights and Legal Affairs of the CoE, argues: "The Court is required to interpret the Convention not *in abstracto* but rather in the context of the real-life factual situations found in the cases before it. In addressing these situations and the evidence presented during proceedings, the Court can ensure that the standards of protection afforded by the Convention evolve in line with social attitudes and legal standards both within and across the States parties.

In *Airey v. Ireland,* the Court emphasised that "[t]he Convention is intended to guarantee not rights that are theoretical or illusory but rights that are practical and effective." [8] Again, in his speech delivered on January 30, 2009, on the occasion of the opening of the Judicial Year, Jean-Paul Costa, President of the ECtHR, claimed that "through its interpretation of the Convention, the Court has gradually raised the standards of protection required, which has led via a process of emulation to a harmonization of standards at a higher level". [9]

The European Convention has played a fundamental role not simply in providing a mechanism for protection but also in underscoring the European commitment to human rights and in emphasizing that "such commitment, if taken seriously, involves important concessions which States must make to classical notions of national sovereignty". [10] This compromise is a historical necessity and a minimum price required to be paid for peace and development.

Europe's handling of the problem of terrorism too invites severe criticism from the human rights activists and scholars. Dick Oosting, Director of Amnesty International's EU Office in Brussels, maintains that by introducing emergency legislation to curb terrorist activities, the United Kingdom created a shadow criminal justice system without essential safeguards, and in the process derogated from the European Convention on Human Rights. Amnesty International reiterated its concern that the EU should not in any way compromise on the prohibition, enshrined in its own recently adopted Charter of Fundamental Rights, from surrendering individuals to a country where they may be at risk of suffering serious human rights violations including in particular torture and the death penalty. [11]

Dominique Hiebel too maintains that the EU member states are practicing invasions of privacy of their own citizens in the name of anti-terrorist struggle or actions against serious criminality. She also questions the employment of technologies which enable "profiling" and "data mining" that affects a large numbers of innocent people directly and stigmatizes entire communities on a scale that is unacceptable in a democratic society. After all, "the game is not worth the candle, since such practices seem to work only up to a point and fails to guarantee the security of citizens", remains her line of argument.

ECHR and Charter of Fundamental Rights

The member States of the EU signed the Charter of Fundamental Rights of the European Union on December 7, 2000. This Charter reaffirms the rights as they result from constitutional traditions, treaty provisions and international obligations common to the Member States, such as the European Convention for the Protection of Human Rights and Fundamental Freedoms. Walter Schwimmer, Secretary General of the CoE, while addressing an EPC briefing on February 14, 2001 on the "Council of Europe's Challenges for 2001", claims that the EU's new Charter of Fundamental Rights would not have been possible without the CoE's Human Rights Convention. [12]

The Charter closely follows the European Convention and deliberately avoids any contradiction. Article 52.3 analyses the scope of guaranteed rights under the auspices of the Charter and maintains that the meaning and scope of the rights contained in it, which correspond to rights guaranteed by the Convention for the Protection of Human Rights and Fundamental Freedoms, shall be the same as those laid down by the said Convention. Again, Article 53, which speaks about the level of protection provided under the Charter holds: "Nothing in this Charter shall be interpreted as restricting or adversely affecting human rights and fundamental freedoms as recognised, in their respective fields of application, by Union law and international law and by international agreements to which the Union, the Community or all the Member States are party, including the European Convention for the Protection of

Human Rights and Fundamental Freedoms, and by the Member States' constitutions".

The revised Charter of Fundamental Rights of the European Union (2007) reiterated the stand taken by the earlier Charter. In short, the Charter represents the most modern codification of fundamental rights in the world.

European Union's Accession to the European Convention

European Union's accession to the European Convention remained a hotly debated topic for decades and with the entry into force of the Lisbon Treaty that issue was settled in favour of the Union acceding to the ECHR. Moreover, the EU's Charter of Fundamental Rights has now become legally binding and represents a major step forward in terms of the Union's political commitment to fundamental rights. Viviane Reding, Vice-President of the European Commission responsible for Justice, Fundamental Rights and Citizenship, during her presentation to the Hearing of the European Parliament's Constitutional Affairs Committee on March 18, 2010, maintained that the accession of the EU to the European Convention completed the EU system of protecting fundamental rights.

The EU's accession to the Convention is of a high political and legal significance since the accession will guarantee that any person claiming to be a victim of a violation of the Convention by an institution or body of the Union can bring a complaint against the Union before the Strasbourg Court under the same conditions as those applying to complaints brought against Member States. By acceding to the Convention, the European Union puts its weight behind the Strasbourg system of external judicial control in the area of fundamental rights by integrating its legal order fully and formally to that control system.

This will enhance the credibility both internally and externally of the EU's strong commitment to fundamental rights. Accession to the Convention will ensure that the case-law of both Courts–the Court in Strasbourg and the "Constitutional Court" in Luxembourg–evolves in step. It is therefore an opportunity to develop a coherent system of fundamental rights protection throughout the continent, with a strong promise for a Europe truly united by law and values. Moreover, the Union will have at its disposal all rights that the Convention gives to the Contracting Parties to defend the human rights conformity of its acts before the Strasbourg Court. The Union will also be able to be represented in the Strasbourg Court with an EU judge. As such, the accession of EU to the ECHR reinforces the human rights system this far developed under the auspices of the CoE. [13]

II

South Asia is one of the sub-regions of Asia and having more than one fifth of the world's population. It is most populous and most densely populated regions of the world. [14] Again, South Asia is one of the poorest regions reeling under endemic poverty and the home to half the world's poor. South Asian Countries are at different levels of nation-building processes and are at different stages of economic development. There is severe competition among them in sharing the meagre natural resources (they are meagre not because that they are available in lesser volume, but because there are over billions to share) and in finding markets for their products. Presence of competitive nationalism on the basis of ethnicity, culture, language and religion, further complicates the environment, and cooperative regionalism/internationalism has become a casualty in that scenario.

Endemic poverty, pestilence and poor health condition remain a common feature of the South Asian countries. The UN Human development Index, places them at very low level. In 2008-09, India ranked 132 out of 179 countries, preceded by Bhutan at 131st rank and Sri Lanka at 104. The South Asians face insecurity from traditional and non-traditional sources and are severely afflicted by communalism, casteism, and terrorism, which threaten their very existence and well-being. As a result, the human Rights situation in South Asia continues to remain a question mark. [15]

Political Instability

The Indian Government is being accused of riding roughshod over the human rights of the people of Jammu and Kashmir, denying them the right to self determination. In Pakistan, democracy has failed to take roots and it is precariously vacillating between democracy and military dictatorship by turn. Sri Lanka continues to witness human tragedy in the name of civil war and its aftermath between the majority Sinhalese and minority Tamil communities. Bangladesh is reeling under political instability and natural calamities. Nepal is undergoing political uncertainty. Maldives and Bhutan too were not exceptions to this general rule. Situation in Afghanistan is fluid and hovers between worse and worst. All these result in human rights violations day in and day out.

India-Pakistan relations can very well be characterized as 'rivalry of the siblings'. While, the Indians consider that Pakistan, born out of the two-nation theory, is a serious threat to their secular path of nation-building, the leaders of Pakistan sincerely believe that the former have never reconciled to the division of the Indian sub-continent and given an opportunity they would undo it. Any proposal about the establishment of a 'Confederation in South Asia' from the Indian side causes not just ripples but strong protest voices from the other side. This basic contradiction has developed into the Kashmir issue, which remains the most serious threat to peace in South Asia till date.

Pakistan has its own set of grievances against India, born out of the problems in the respective processes of nation-state building and economic development. History, geo-politics, conflicting economic interests, problems of distribution and management of shared resources which proved to be quite inadequate and ecology remain at the root of internal threat to South Asian region and especially to India and Pakistan.

Another tragedy that has over taken the South Asian region is the terrorist menace which results in the loss of life and infrastructure. India is facing the problem of terrorist violence since the 1980s, first in Punjab, then in the Jammu and Kashmir and the North Eastern region. The Indian situation is further complicated by the support given by its neighbours, notably Pakistan, to the terrorist elements operating in the Indian soil. On the other hand, India was accused of harbouring and training the militants belonging to the LTTE by the Sri Lankan government. Pakistan too raised its accusing finger against India on this count. The scourge of terrorism continues to result in terrible human rights violations by the State as well as by the terrorists.

Lack of Political Freedom

Political freedom continues to be denied to some sections of people in India on the basis of caste, ethnic and religious exclusion. [16] On political freedom, Bangladesh scores the worst in the region. By definition, any care-taker government must function within the ambits of the Constitution and other national laws to facilitate and expedite the installation of a new government with the people's mandate. Instead, after taking power following the imposition of a State of Emergency on January 11, 2007, political freedom was severely curtailed and the care-taker government banned all political activity, including processions, strikes and trade union activities, and banned political discourse (freedom of expression and opinion) including in print and electronic media under the Emergency Powers Rules, 2007 imposed on January 26, 2007. On March 8, 2007, the care-taker government issued a blanket ban on political activities including "indoor politics". In the first 10 months, a total of 4,40,684 people were arrested and of these, only 2,39,480 arrested persons had arrest warrants and only 778 were wanted by the police for alleged criminal offences.

Those arrested included political activists, criminals, businessmen, journalists and alleged corrupt persons. [17]

Violation of Right to Life

On right to life, India's record is worse than Nepal, Bhutan and Maldives. Both the security forces and the Armed Opposition Groups are responsible for widespread violations of the right to life. According to the 2007-2008 Annual Report of the Ministry of Home Affairs (MHA), the National Human Rights Commission (NHRC) received a total of 1,459 cases of custodial deaths during the period from April 1to December 31, 2007. In addition, large numbers of civilians have been killed by a burgeoning number of Armed Opposition Groups.

The Armed Forces (Special Powers) Act of 1958 was enacted with the official objective of enabling Indian security forces to more effectively quell armed rebellion in Nagaland and was later extended to Manipur in 1980. The impunity which the law extended to the Armed forces has indeed resulted in a long and shameful trail of extra-judicial killings, forced disappearances, rape, torture and extortion. Irom Sharmila, a human rights activist from Manipur, began her fast on November 4, 2000, demanding the repeal of the Act.

The Government of India appointed in 2004 a Commission headed by former Supreme Court Judge Jeevan Reddy to enquire whether the law needed to be amended or repealed in order to conform to the government's obligations to human rights. The Commission in 2005 recommended repeal of the law. But the Government of India has chosen not to act in accordance even with the Commission's counsel.

Human rights violations are integral to counterinsurgency operations conducted by the military in the sub-region. Human rights are routinely violated in police detention including the routine use of torture. National security laws tend to be poorly framed, routinely abused and used as blanket cover to silence legitimate dissent rather than tackle security. In India, a pervasive regime of impunity is in vogue, under which human rights violations remain an acceptable operational practice of the security forces. [18]

On the right to life of the Bangladeshis, the Rapid Action Battalion (RAB) was of deep concern. Formed in March 2002 to combat crime, RAB personnel have been responsible for systematic and widespread "extrajudicial executions" euphemistically called "cross-fire" killings in which 184 persons were killed in 2007 alone. On the right to life, Pakistan performed poorly. Hundreds have become victims of enforced disappearances and it was acknowledged by the authorities that 689 persons were held during the war on terrorism and from amongst them, 369 persons have been handed over to the US for money. The security forces continued to engage in extrajudicial executions in the War against Terror in addition to an extraordinary number of custodial deaths. [19]

Human Rights Defenders

Human rights defenders face repression across South Asia. For instance, in Sri Lanka, human rights defenders and aid workers were subject to the highest level of threat from all sides to the conflict. In September 2007, the Asian Human Rights Commission stated that at least forty three aid workers were killed and fourteen others were missing in Sri Lanka since 2006. In no other South Asian country, so many human rights defenders have been done to death. The recent case of Vinayak Sen [20] of India clearly proves the sorry plight of human rights promoters in South Asia.

Judicial System

India is the best human rights performer in South Asia according to the *South Asia Human Rights Violators Index 2008*. Though cases reported from India were more voluminous than other SAARC countries, taking the population of India into consideration while comparing with others, Indian performance is comparatively better. India's judiciary remains more independent than its counterparts in

South Asia but backlog of cases are a noteable problem.

Independence of judiciary remains Maldives weakest point. The then President Maumoon Abdul Gayoom was head of the Judiciary and could rule or overrule on any of the decisions of the High Court, the highest court in the country. [21] Nepal's judiciary was undermined by the Peoples Court of the Maoists and the government's contempt for the Supreme Court and ranked poorly. The independence of the Judiciary was weakened when the Supreme Court has been made accountable to the Prime Minister of Nepal. However, in 2007 the Judiciary demonstrated its independence when on June 1, the Supreme Court ruled on a large number of enforced disappearance cases. The Court ordered the government to immediately investigate all allegations of enforced disappearances. The court ordered that the Commission of Inquiry must comply with international human rights standards.

Women's Rights

Pakistan's performance on discrimination against women remains appalling. Apart from cruel 'cultural' practices, reports of custodial rape were widespread. The application of *Sharia* law and inability of the government to confront cultural practices increased violence against women. Under the Offence of *Zina* (Enforcement of *Hudood*) Ordinance of 1979, a rape victim must produce at least four adult male Muslim eyewitnesses, who must be truthful persons and abstain from major sins (*kabair*) and have physically seen the act of rape in order to prove her case. If unable to prove rape, a woman can further be prosecuted under the *Hudood* Ordinance for adultery. Honour killings and rape of women at the order of *jirga* (traditional court) were common. Between January and December 2007, at least 1,305 people including 792 women and thirty four minor girls were victims of honour killings. [22]

The Maldives' treatment of women remains still appalling.

Women have restricted access to public life. There was increased reporting of sexual violence such as rape, assault, domestic violence etc. There is no law on violence against women. Court judgments were atrociously lenient and did not commensurate with the gravity and barbarity of the crimes committed against women. The punishment for rape is banishment in an island and not imprisonment.

Rights of the Child

India performed poorly on the rights of the child. The National Crime Records Bureau recorded a total of 18,967 cases of crimes against children reported in the country during 2006 as compared to 14,975 cases during 2005, reflecting an increase of 26.7 percent. The establishment of National Commission for Protection of Child Rights, a statutory body of Government of India, in March 2007 has not helped. Most disturbingly, children are increasingly being used by the State and the AOGs in armed conflict situations. [23]

On violations of the rights of the child, Sri Lanka by far had the highest number of child soldiers in South Asia. By the end of December 31, 2007, UNICEF reportedly received 6,248 cases of recruitment of child soldiers by the LTTE and 453 cases by the Tamileela Makkal Viduthalai Pulikal, the Karuna Group. It is the policy of the State to allow the Karuna group and the Eelam People's Democratic Party to recruit child soldiers.

Minority Rights

The condition of minorities - religious, cultural, linguistic and ethnic–in South Asian countries remains pathetic and worrisome. In India, both the majority as well as minority communities compete mutually in creating hard time for each others. Situation is not different in other South Asian countries like Pakistan and Sri Lanka. In Bangladesh, Hindu minorities continued to be targeted and their religious freedoms violated. A new study showed that some 1.2 million or 44 percent of the

2.7 million Hindu households in Bangladesh were affected by the Enemy Property Act, 1965 and the Vested Property Act, 1974, which empower to identify the Hindus as enemies of the State and to seize their properties. On the violations of the rights of minorities, Bhutan has been ranked second behind Sri Lanka. Bhutan continued to have discriminatory laws, policies and practices against the ethnic Nepalese. Since the release of 2005 census report, about 80,000 mainly ethnic Nepalis remains identified as "foreigners". Again, some 70,000 such "foreigners" were reportedly prevented from taking part in the electoral processes. [24]

Rights of the Indigenous/Tribal People

In the South Asian countries discrimination is endemic, institutionalised and in many cases legalised. Over eighty four million indigenous/tribal people of India continued to be disproportionate victims of 'development' and consequent displacement and dispossession–victims of state and non-state actors. According to the 2001 Census, tribal people constituted 8.2 percent of the total population. They represented 55.1 percent of the 8.54 million persons displaced in India by development projects and conflicts from 1950 to 1990. [25]

The Asian Centre for Human Rights (ACHR) published its first Annual Report on Human Rights in India in 2009. ACHR argues that the Indian government must find new answers to the growing security problem arising out of Naxalism. [26] Current security-driven responses are not working; indeed they may even prove to be counter- productive. The report suggests that the root causes of Naxal violence-discrimination, marginalisation and exclusion-must be addressed. There is an imperative need for the government to address security concerns. However, security responses of the government, whether state or central, have been resulting in human rights violations against local populations; this state violence has been feeding support for Naxalism. During 2005-8, more security forces have been killed in naxal violence than in J and

K and North East. [27]

Failure to Eradicate Poverty

At present, the South Asian countries are hooked to the processes of globalization and have become the victims of its evil effects. Respective States have failed miserably in their duty to protect their peoples from national and international capitalist vultures, by ensuring a level playing ground. South Asian countries have failed miserably in their efforts to alleviate poverty and create more equal society.

India's case is something very peculiar in this context. In 2007, there were fifty three Indian billionaires holding wealth to the tune of US$ 335 billion. At the same time, there were 836 million Indians living on less than twenty rupees a day and over 200 million less than twelve rupees. Since 1997, over 2,00,000 Indian farmers have committed suicide, unable to face the onslaught of the globalised world. Indian Life expectancy at birth remains 64.1 years, not a matter of pride. According to the Global Hunger Index compiled by the International Food Policy Research Institute, India ranks 67th among 88 developing countries. Indian failure in converting the national income/wealth into human development remains a blot in the otherwise success story of India as one of the fastest growing economies of the present decade.

III

Though, every SAARC Member State's constitution guarantees fundamental rights for its respective citizens, such constitutional rights are laden with contradictions and exceptions. Some of them have introduced National Human Rights Acts, but, there remains a huge gap between the spirit of the act and the way in which they are implemented. The governments are also known for defending their human rights records on the plea that intervention in the internal matters is unwarranted and unacceptable. Some governments like Bhutan even dare to conjure up "Gross National Happiness" to beguile the international community on the absolute denial of rights. [28]

National Human Rights Institutions

Most of the Member States of SAARC have even failed to establish National Human Rights Commission to supervise and question the governments at the national and state level. India, Nepal, Afghanistan, Maldives and Sri Lanka are perhaps the only South Asian countries to have independent, autonomous statutory National Commission/Court to provide some relief to their citizens. Others have not even bothered to form such an institution at the national level. The Government of India passed the Human Rights Act of 1993 and established the National Human Rights Commission with the retired Chief Justice of the Supreme Court as the Chairman of the Commission on October 12, 1993. The NHRC of India disposed of 85,661cases during the period from April 1, 2004 to March 31, 2005, while 49,548 cases were pending before the Commission as on March 31, 2005. Moreover, State Human Rights Commissions have been established in sixteen states of India. The State Government of Karnataka even issued a notification on April 16, 2005 to set up human rights courts as provided under Section 30 of the Human Rights Act 1993. [29]

Despite their critical role, these National human rights institutions suffer from serious credibility crisis due to statutory limitations, operational flaws and lack of political will/support. These statutory limitations included inability to investigate abuses committed by the armed forces, visit prisons without prior permission from the executive authorities, investigate into complaints which are more than one year old, and the lack of power to implement its recommendations. Again, it is important for states to be human rights compliant at the national level by establishing national human rights institutions in accordance with the Paris Principles. [30] The Nepalese and Maldivian Human Rights Commissions have not ensured minimum compliance with the Paris Principles.

The NHRC of India often failed to respond to the victims in time, ensure transparency in its operation and follow the principle of natural justice for adjudication of the complaints and continues to suffer from credibility crisis due to statutory limitations and operational flaws. [31] On National Human Rights Institutions, the Maldives' ranking improved as the Human Rights Commission has been vested with more powers including the power to inquire into cases that occurred after the enactment of the law, and cases that occurred prior to the enactment of the law but not before January 1, 2000. The new Act was approved by the Parliament and ratified by the President on August 17, 2006. [32]

The Government of Nepal too established a Human Rights Commission as an independent autonomous statutory body. On July 9, 2006, members of the NHRC appointed by the King of Nepal resigned *en masse*. Until the Parliamentary Special Hearing Committee approved the new members of NHRC on September 12, 2007 pursuant to the recommendations of the Constitutional Council on August 30, 2007, the NHRC virtually did not exist. There was absolute protection gap in Nepal for more than a year. As of November 2007, the NHRC had about 8,700 backlog cases. Further, the recommendations of the NHRC are not implemented by the government. Since the NHRC was established in 2000, it settled 1,350 cases and issued recommendations on 149 cases as of November 2007. But the government implemented fifty three of these recommendations only. On November 4, 2007, the NHRC submitted a Letter of Memorandum to the then Prime Minister Girija Pasad Koirala urging the government, among others, to cooperate with the NHRC by implementing the Commission's recommendations and to provide the NHRC with adequate resources. [33]

The Human Rights Commission in Sri Lanka was established in March 1997 under the Human Rights Commission Act of 1996. Among South Asian countries having National Human Rights Institutions, Sri Lanka is the worst performer. In December 2007, the Sri Lankan Human Rights Commission was downgraded to observer status by the International Coordinating Committee of National Institutions citing government influence on its independence, since President Mahinda Rajapaksa appointed members of the Commission in 2006 in clear violation of the National Human Rights Commission Act that stipulates that President can only appoint them on the recommendations of the Constitutional Council which lapsed in 2005. [34]

The situation in Bhutan, Bangladesh and Pakistan are still worse, since the ruling establishments in these countries are unwilling to establish national institutions. Although a draft National Human Rights Commission Bill was presented in February 2005, the Government of Pakistan failed to adopt it in 2007. [35] The other two countries dodge on this issue.

IV

South Asian Regional Level Situation

The SAARC Charter, while elaborating the goals of the regional organization, maintains that the member countries would work together, in a spirit of friendship, trust and understanding to improve people's quality of life; accelerate economic growth, social programmes and cultural development; strengthen self-reliance and promote collaboration in economic, social and technical and scientific fields. Unfortunately, a regional human rights framework has failed to materialize under the SAARC structure as promotion of human rights has not even listed in SAARC Charter. As such, membership of SAARC does not require respect for human rights as a criterion. SAARC's failure to adopt a uniform Human Rights Code/Convention is quite phenomenal and non-availability of common forum/institution and regional level human rights enforcement mechanism is in stark contrast to innumerable and endless human rights violations that are taking place in this region.

SAARC Convention on Suppression of Terrorism

When the Member States of the SAARC recognised the seriousness of the problem of terrorism as it affected the security and stability of the region and the inevitability of taking joint action in this sphere, they adopted a Convention on Suppression of Terrorism in the Bangalore summit of 1986, to combat terrorist activities in the region. Subsequently, on November 4, 1987, the SAARC nations finally adopted the regional convention on terrorism during the third summit at Kathmandu. Accordingly, the SAARC Member States pledged to refrain from organising, instigating or participating in civil strife or terrorist acts in other Member States, which formed part of the Convention. All the Member States duly ratified the Convention and it came into force in August 1988. However, much development has not been achieved in containing the terrorist menace, due to the historically antagonistic relations between and among the Member States, notably India and Pakistan. The fact that Pakistan holds on supporting terrorists against India as an instrument of state policy to achieve its major foreign policy goal of maintaining parity with India in spite of prevailing dissimilarity, has pushed the issue to a point of no return.

However, the 1990s brought in the human rights flavour into the South Asian regional cooperation. In regard to human rights, the Heads of State or Government of SAARC observed in the Colombo Declaration of December 21, 1991, that "civil and political rights on the one hand and economic and social rights on the other are interdependent and of equal importance. Human rights issues should not therefore be viewed in narrow and exclusively political terms. In this context they (SAARC Member States) underlined the need to view the efforts of States to guarantee human rights in their full context, through the pursuit of development for all citizens in conditions of stability, which in turn guarantees the enjoyment of human rights of all persons." While reiterating their faith in democracy, human rights and rule of law, the Heads of State or

Government emphasised the need to ensure that development remains at the centre of international attention. It is interesting to note that the Office of the High Commissioner of Human Rights (OHCHR) of the UN recognises SAARC as possible "entry points for the promotion and protection of human rights, if the political will permits." [36]

In 2002, SAARC adopted the Convention on Prevention and Combating Trafficking in Women and Children for Prostitution. However, the Convention fails on many counts as there was little informed NGO input prior to the drafting. The result was a weak, inadequate and moralistic Convention. Its understanding of trafficking is confined to trafficking of women and children for the purpose of prostitution. It ignores the fact that women and children are often trafficked for use as domestic servants and other kinds of labour. Victims of trafficking also include men (and boys) who are used as domestic servants, camel jockeys and the like. Its language includes words such as "evil" and "honour of human beings", terms that reflect a moralistic approach, and which are marginal to the effective addressing of the issue.

While all the SAARC nations have signed the Convention, it has been ratified only by Bangladesh, Bhutan and the Maldives, which raises grave doubts about the effectiveness of the Convention. Though the OHCHR has endorsed this Convention as a human rights Convention, it must be emphasised that the Convention was primarily drawn up to protect the States parties' interest in clamping down on criminal activity instead of upholding the rights of the individual. Again, the drawing up of the 2002 Convention does not justify SAARC being promoted as the prospective human rights mechanism in South Asia by the OHCHR. These efforts indicate, at best, that SAARC is becoming little more human rights "conscious". [37]

SAARC has not yet adopted a specific and detailed uniform human rights charter nor the member countries have agreed to create any common regional institution to monitor adherence and implementation of various human rights instruments signed by t or to provide redress to victims of human rights abuses and to impose sanctions or punishments on the perpetrators. The idea of drafting a South Asia Human Rights Code by SAARC has been mooted informally in human rights circles but, till date, no concrete action has been taken. Introducing human rights into the agenda of SAARC is not an easy task owing to the political differences between member states and their preoccupation with other regional concerns like economic cooperation. SAARC is not independent of their members and can therefore function only in the way its members want it to.

SAARC Social Charter 2004

In the 12th SAARC meeting a Social Charter was singed on January 4, 2004 at Islamabad. This Charter spells out objectives such as poverty alleviation, promotion of the state education, human resource development, youth mobilization, population control, promotion of tolerance, pluralism, social justice, protection of the rights and interests of minorities, eradication of discrimination in all forms and so on. In spite of all these declarations and conventions, human rights violations haunt most of the South Asians and there is a dire need for regional level human rights convention and enforcement mechanism cognizant of cultural ethos/value system.

Initiatives of the Non-Governmental Organisations

Despite sustained efforts by civil society, the respective Governments of the SAARC countries have not made any serious effort to adopt a uniform Human Rights Code or Convention and to provide any common forum or institution or mechanism at the regional level, to monitor adherence and implementation of the same. Such indifference forced the regional Non-Governmental Organisations (NGOs) to take initiative and to play a significant role in the human rights front. Their activities are successful in bringing in some welcome relief in an otherwise suffocating atmosphere. Many human rights organizations in individual countries are working hard to improve the living situation of their respective peoples.

An attempt to foster cooperation between these groups organized by jurists, educators and representatives of NGOs, was made in December 1990 at the Third World Congress on Human Rights in New Delhi. This was perhaps the first occasion where non-governmental representatives of SAARC countries had a forum to discuss human rights problems in a regional context. Representatives from over fifty NGOs from the SAARC countries sat through several informal meetings which culminated in the creation of the South Asian Forum for Human Rights (SAFHR). This step is in direct response to the delinquent effort by SAARC to promote observance of and respect for international human rights. It may be noted that the preamble of the SAFHR holds that it will parallel SAARC as a regional institution.

The headquarters of the SAFHR is located in Kathmandu, Nepal and an Executive Board, comprised of two representatives from each member NGO, meets in a different location each year to determine SAFHR's agenda for the upcoming year. SAFHR intends to circulate a newsletter describing the human rights situation in the region; in times of crisis alert travellers and the world of impending human rights flashpoints; and implement a periodic training programme for human rights activists. SAFHR's long-term goal is to draft a South Asian Charter for Human Rights. The establishment of SAFHR has fulfilled the long-cherished dream of creating a focal point for discussion of transborder human rights issues. Its most notable objective is to draft South Asian Charter of Human Rights, which remains the immediate need of the hour.

V

Lessons to Learn

After elaborating the European human rights regime which has been developed under the framework of the European

Convention and after ascertaining the phenomenal successes and achievements of the system on the one hand and the problems faced by Europe and South Asia on the other, it is imperative to analyse the lessons that need to be learnt by the international community in general and the Europeans and the South Asians in particular, to make the system more foolproof in Europe and to take initiative to create such a system in South Asia.

As mentioned earlier, some scholars believe that the enforcement mechanism that has been created under the ECHR, especially the Court, has arrogated ~~of~~ its power and usurped the powers of the state and that it is overstepping in curbing the powers of the democratically elected governments, which is against the very spirit of democracy. Again, they talk about the gap between the preaching and practice of the European States in regard to their actions in containing international terrorism, which needs to be bridged.

It is well said that justice delayed is justice denied and it is noticed that in spite of the best efforts, there is inordinate delay in the ECtHR, due to its ever-mounting case load and indifference on the part of some of the Member States. As pointed out by Monjal, average duration for a case inthe strasbourg is six years and this naturally goes against the grain of effective appeal. The Europeans have to find out ways and means by which the delay can be averted. Enforcement of Protocol 14 is the right step in this direction. Practitioners like Jean-Paul Costa, who are part and parcel of the European system of judicial protection, while celebrating its undeniable success, also pin points its 'fragility', which needs to be reinforced and strengthened. Again, scholars like Ralph Beddard criticize the European Convention system for its "noticeable lack of success or enthusiasm in extending the list of rights to embrace more sophisticated rights and freedoms where, it might be thought, Europe should lead the way". [38] All these problems and shortcomings are to be addressed positively.

Likewise, the South Asians too have a few lessons to learn from the successes of the European Convention system. They should learn to appreciate the benefits of the regional level human rights regime. The merits of a regional system for human rights protection are many. It enables regions to create mechanisms whereby rights can be guaranteed in that region with particular respect given to regional customs and traditions. It has also the additional advantage that the people of that region, in keeping with the best democratic traditions and value systems, can determine issues relevant to that region.

Much of the development of the human rights regime has occurred at regional level in Western Europe, in the Americas and in Africa. Today these three regional systems sit alongside a growing international regime, often proving more effective in the guarantee of rights. In such a situation, South Asia can ill afford to remain the only region in the world where there is no regional instrument to govern human rights.

The lack of a regional system for South Asia remains a fundamental lacuna in the umbrella of protection and promotion of human rights at the regional level. This is exacerbated when put into the perspective that close to 20 percent of the world's population live in South Asia, often in circumstances of abject poverty and of rampant human rights violations. The South Asian states have developed in isolation and in competition with each other, with strong national rivalries. Again, they are sceptic about human rights as Western imposition of their standards and intervention in their internal affairs impinging on national sovereignty or as no more than western neo-colonialism. [39]

Such an outlook has reduced the scope for cooperation on this issue between South Asian states. Monjal refers to this vehement criticism of the international system as "natural discomfort with the West", which underlines the need for a regional system of rights protection in South Asia. It is precisely through a regional mechanism cognizant of the cultural ethos and value systems of the region that these difficulties can be sorted out. Instead of a blunt rejection of human rights, a venture of cooperation between the states for its interpretation in the South Asian context would be more progressive and is the need of the hour. While this might be desirable, it is hindered by fundamental differences that exist between India and Pakistan, who continues to have extremely antagonistic relationships that make it impossible to foster cross-border discussions. This unfortunate development has resulted in the failure of the creation of the system of human rights protection and promotion at the regional level. South Asia needs to fall in line with the other regional organizations in creating a mechanism to protect and promote human rights at the regional level which is in tune with its cultural ethos, value systems and traditions.

Notes

1. Joseph E. Stiglitz, "The EU's Global Mission", http://www.project-syndicate.org/print-commentry/stiglitz85/English.(18/6/2008).
2. Bruce Russett and Harvey Starr, *World Politics–The Menu for Choice*, Third Edition, Freema, 1988, p. 175.
3. http://www.nytimes.com/2007/01/03/world/europe/03iht-france.4090171.html.
4. http://www.euronews.net/2011/05/05/laurent-blanc-at-centre-of-france-football-racial-quota-scandal/
5. Dick Oosting, "Putting Human Rights into Practice", July 16, 2001, http://www.theepc.be/challenge/challenge_detail.asp?SEC=challenge&SUBSEC=issue&SUBSUBSEC=issue3&SUBSUBSUBSEC=coretopic1&REFID=261.
6. Report by the International Helsinki Federation for Human Rights Anti-terrorism Measures, Security and Human Rights, Developments in Europe, Central Asia and North America in the Aftermath of September 11, April 2003, p. 55.
7. European Court of Human Rights, *Annual Report 2010* (provisional version), Registry of the European Court of Human Rights, Strasbourg, January 2011, p. 12.
8. Philippe Boillat, "The European Convention on Human Rights

at 60: Building on the Past, Looking to the Future", http://human-rights-convention.org/Articles-interviews-2/.

9. European Court of Human Rights, *Annual Report 2009*, Registry of the European Court of Human Rights, Strasbourg, 2010, p. 32.
10. Philip Alston and J.H.H Weiler, "An "Ever Closer Union" in need of a Human Rights Policy: The European Union and Human Rights", Philip Alston et al, *The EU and Human Rights*, OUP New York, 1999, p. 30.
11. Dick Oosting, "EU Security Policy: Terrorism, Racism and Human Rights", June 7, 2002, http://www.theepc.be/challenge/challenge_detail.asp?SEC=challenge&SUBSEC=issue&SUBSUBSEC=&SUBSUBSUBSEC=&REFID=825.
12. Walter Schwimmer, "The Council of Europe: Challenges for 2001", http://www.theepc.be/documents/breakdet.asp?SEC=documents&SUBSEC=breakfast&SUBSUBSEC=&SUBSUBSUBSEC=&REFID=372
13. Viviane Reding, "The EU's accession to the European Convention on Human Rights: Towards a stronger and more coherent protection of human rights in Europe", Hearing of the European Parliament's Constitutional Affairs Committee, Brussels, March 18, 2010.
14. Asian Centre for Human Rights, *South Asia Human Rights Violators Index–2008 (SAHRVI -2008)*, New Delhi, 2008, p. 16.
15. Asian Centre for Human Rights, *South Asia Human Rights Index – 2008 (SAHRI -2008),* New Delhi, 2008. pp. 11ff.
16. *SAHRI -2008*, p. 120.
17. *SAHRI -2008,* p. 12.
18. *SAHRI -2008*, p. 119.
19. *SAHRI -2008*, pp. 12-14.
20. Dr. Vinayak Sen, a medical practitioner, who serves the tribal communities, was put behind bar as a supporter of the Maoists and recently released on bail. Governments take recourse to silence the human rights activists by branding and harassing them as sympathizers of extremist movements.
21. *SAHRI -2008*, p. 15
22. *SAHRI -2008*, p. 14
23. *SAHRI -2008*, p. 16.

24. *SAHRI -2008*, pp. 12-13.
25. *SAHRI -2008*, pp. 131-133.
26. Naxalism or the Naxalbari movement is against the landlords and bureaucracy who exploit the poor peasants and landless labourers and tribal people.
27. Suhas Chakma (ed.), *India Human Rights Report 2009,* Asian Centre for Human Rights, Preface, pp. IV-V.
28. Asian Centre for Human Rights, *South Asia Human Rights Report – 2006 (SAHRR -2006*), New Delhi, 2006, Preface, p.1.
29. *SAHRI- 2008*, p. 119.
30. http://www2.ohchr.org/english/law/parisprinciples.htm.
    The Paris Principles relating to the Status of National Institutions were adopted by General Assembly resolution 48/134 of 20 December 1993 and deal with their competence, mandate, responsibilities, composition and guarantees of independence and pluralism, infrastructure and methods of operation.
31. *SAHRR -2006*, p.119; *SAHRI -2008,* p. 127.
32. *SAHRI -2008*, p. 15.
33. *SAHRI -2008*, p. 108.
34. *SAHRI -2008*, p. 11.
35. *SAHRI -2008*, p. 14.
36. *Human Rights Features*, August-September 2005, p. 11.
37. *Ibid.*
38. Ralph Beddard, *Human Rights and Europe*, Grotius Publications Ltd., Cambridge, 1993, Third edition, p. 2.
39. In the international human rights discourse, this phenomenon is referred as universality of human rights versus cultural relativism. This distrust and discomfiture with the West is common to the developing world in general and the Asian countries, which hold on 'Asian values', in particular. In the "Bangkok Declaration" of 1993 (http://law.hku.hk/lawgovtsociety/Bangkokpercent20Declaration .htm), while reaffirming their commitment to the principles contained in the Charter of the United Nations and the Universal Declaration on Human Rights as well as the full realization of all human rights throughout the world, the Asian countries discouraged any attempt to use human rights as a conditionality for extending development assistance; emphasized the principles of respect for national sovereignty and territorial integrity as

well as non-interference in the internal affairs of States, and the non-use of human rights as an instrument of political pressure; and reiterated that all countries, large and small, have the right to determine their political systems, control and freely utilize their resources, and freely pursue their economic, social and cultural development.

Index

Index